The Orient of Style

The Orient of Style

Modernist Allegories of Conversion

BERYL SCHLOSSMAN

Duke University Press

Durham and London 1991

© 1991 Duke University Press
All rights reserved

Library of Congress Cataloging-in-Publication Data
appear on the last page of this book.

Contents

Acknowledgments vii

Preface ix

1 Introduction 1

2 The Image of Modernity 8

3 The Allegory of Conversion 17

4 Necropolis and Carnival: Monuments and Masks of Style 38

5 The Sea of Ink 71

6 Crimson and Diamonds 107

7 Passing Forms 143

8 La Charité de Giotto 178

9 La Vocation Artistique 225

Notes 261

Bibliography 281

Index 291

Acknowledgments

At every stage in the writing of this book Josué Harari has been unfailingly generous with criticism, insight, time, and support. My appreciation and my debt to him date from my first encounters with French literature and theory at Cornell University and my studies at the Université de Paris 7, before the continuation of my work for the Ph.D. under his direction at The Johns Hopkins University. It is a pleasure to express my thanks to him here.

The approach to Proust's labyrinths of modernity began with the seminars of Richard Macksey at The Johns Hopkins University. His criticism, knowledge, and generosity have been present throughout the process of writing this book. I would like to thank him and to acknowledge my debt to him in these pages.

I was privileged to have additional close readings of the manuscript from Vincent Descombes, Werner Hamacher, and Neil Hertz, of The Johns Hopkins University, as well as from Marcel Muller and Gerald Prince. For their fine readings and valuable criticism of a later stage of the manuscript, I would like to thank two anonymous readers for Duke University Press.

In its earliest stages my research was generously supported by the Department of French of The Johns Hopkins University, by a Charlotte W. Newcombe Doctoral Dissertation Fellowship from the Woodrow Wilson National Fellowship Foundation, by the Association Française des Femmes Diplômées, and by a Gilbert Chinard Scholarship from the Institut Français de Washington. I would like to express my deep appreciation to them for the support that made it possible to write this book. In Paris, Bernard Brun and the Institut des Textes et Manuscrits Modernes of the C.N.R.S. provided invaluable advice, manuscript materials, and documentation.

In the later stages of my work the University Research Committee of Emory University supported research in Europe. The Center for Advanced Studies at the University of Virginia supported my work during the final stages of writing. I would like to thank both of these institutions for their generosity.

I am very grateful to Paul R. Gross, Director of the Center for Advanced Studies at the University of Virginia, for his generous support of my research during my tenure as a Mellon Fellow. I would like to thank Mr. Gross and the Center for the financial aid that made it possible to include color illustrations.

I am deeply indebted to my editor, Reynolds Smith, for his fine reading and his outstanding support of the manuscript.

Finally, I would like to thank the members of the editorial staff at Duke University Press.

Preface

The many identities of Modernism and its sequels lead to the urgent question of origin. Who speaks in the name of the modern and its style, who signs the book? How is it possible for Flaubert to write a "book about nothing," guided by an authorial persona that has been rendered invisible?

These questions book a passage for us back to the mid-nineteenth century, when the dream of aesthetics invites us on the first voyages of Modernism. They lead to the silences and voluble excesses of Proust, and of our modernity; they turn the vocation of the writer into an artistic "open sesame" that lights up the darkness with images and colors like the ones projected by a magic lantern.

The new modernity implies the veiling of the authorial presence, its feelings and judgments. The subject disappears; its vanishing is related to the emergence of a sublime ideal of "new modern style." In Modernism there are no longer any guarantees of what the author once claimed to deliver. As analogy or metaphor, as a veil or a figure, even the image is somewhere else; it always has the alibi of the invisible. The writer filters and crystallizes; the material of art is rendered mysterious so that the oeuvre can stage its revelation.

What is left, when the novel is compared to a pane of colored glass or a fragment of layered color? The artist dissolves into the calculated artifices and striking effects of a sublime: in the place of a stable narrative frame of events, a flash of fireworks takes the reader over the threshold into the realm of allegory, the carnival and the necropolis. Allegory consecrates the ground of ruins, fragments, and mourning; the blackness of melancholy; and the petrified monuments of memory.

Like Baudelaire, Flaubert formulates literary style around the concept of time. Walter Benjamin focused on Baudelaire in order to read modernity; in *The Orient of Style*, Baudelaire plays the role of conspirator of reading. A punctual encounter with some of his writings sets the scene of an interpretation of history that is inescapably connected to modernity.

Allegory provides an understanding of the mode of representation and the temporal shape of Modernism that occurs in Flaubert and Proust. The modern city offers one of the models of impersonality and the evanescent images of fantasmagoria that illuminate Baudelairean nights of lovers, criminals, conspirators, and writers. Benjamin stages his encounter with Baudelaire in the vision of history as a constellation of historical moments rather than a linear development. *The Orient of Style* takes its cue from Benjamin and Baudelaire, the critical operators for a reading of allegory.

Proust describes beautiful representation as the "poetic dazzle of the Orient"; Bergotte, a character who plays the role of the great writer in *A la recherche du temps perdu*, sees it in the little panel of yellow wall, a detail of Vermeer's *View of Delft*. Embarked on the sea of ink, Baudelaire, Flaubert, and Proust set sail for the Orient of style.

The Orient of Style

1

Introduction

Where is the writer in his or her work? Where is "life" found in "art"? Early in the nineteenth century, the first generation of French Romantics answered these questions with a form of interiority and sentimentality that made art and life inseparable, and provoked a century and a half of reactions. Modern literary and critical convictions are rooted in the Romantic attitude and the Symbolist opposition to it: on the one hand, the identity of life and writing has opened up a full range of possibilities for autobiography and mémoire, while on the other hand, the non-identity of life and writing gave rise to the autonomy of writing, its freedom from referential obligations, and its status as a work of art. Although the identity of life and writing entails an act of faith linked to its Protestant roots, it has shaped a tradition of autobiographical writing and criticism that takes a symbiosis of art and life at face value. At the other extreme, the non-identity between life and writing that has occupied much of the modern period allows for a reading of literature (including autobiography) as fiction—beautiful dissimulations that owe no debts to referentiality.

In the late Romantic development now known as the beginnings of Modernism, the continuity of life and art was interrupted by a new element, the unprecedented and strategic emphasis on style. For Flaubert and Baudelaire in the mid-nineteenth century, the question of style dramatically altered the relationship of writer to writing. Questions of the propriety of subject matter were abruptly dismissed; the effects of horror and violence were no longer rejected; the masks of artifice that were previously categorized as antiquated or inferior to "natural" expression were suddenly revalorized. On the contrary, the masking of authorial personality became a new imperative within an idealization of style that independently formed the aesthetic of Flaubert and Baudelaire, as well as their inheritor in the twentieth century, Proust. The idiom of the French nineteenth century changed radically in the writing of Flaubert and Baudelaire: the "modern" effect of their writing makes much of the French Romanticism that preceded it appear dated. The passage of time has only intensified this impression, common to several generations of readers. In reading Proust the same effect occurs; indeed, much of the writing that followed *A la recherche du temps perdu* appears markedly less modern.

The object of inquiry that led to the writing of this book was the image of modernity that unfolds in the writings of Flaubert and Proust. What objects are captured by this image? Modernity is reflected and represented in ideology, history, painting, photography, architecture and so on; but its subjectivity is most essentially (and invisibly) implicated in a form of writing that made claims for truth and beauty beyond subject matter and codified formalism. These two "beyonds" add up to a third—style.

In the chapters that follow, the interpretation of Flaubert and Proust depends on a broad conception of style that should not be confused with stylistics. My readings trace the effects and consequences of the two writers' understanding of style as it emerges and and shapes their enterprise of writing. What is at stake is the interpretive status of certain categories of "art" and "life," rather than particular categories of linguistic or grammatical analysis. For this reason, I have chosen not to return to the well-worked categories of Flaubert's syntax or the Proustian overlap of metaphor and metonymy. Through the principles of style that operate in the aesthetic of Flaubert and Proust, it will be possible to focus on the question of style as it operates within the literary text to motivate the turns and arabesques of figural language.

For the purpose of interpreting the enterprise of Flaubert and Proust, my readings take up the question of figural language as "allegory"—the term that Dante used for the "otherness" of textual meaning in the famous Letter XIII to Can Grande. Dante insisted on the Greek etymology of "allegory" and declared allegory to be twofold: it is the second interpretive level of his four levels of scriptural meaning, and it is also his conception of the three levels considered together, set apart from the "literal" level of meaning. The non-literal levels of the text bear "other" meanings; these "other" meanings are related to the literal level as *style*. Style, the category of "artifice" ("surface," "excess," "cruelty," "impersonality"—terms that will be decoded shortly), stands *in opposition* to the view of language as "natural." In Dante's allegory, the principle for the *Commedia*, the non-literal levels of meaning are "other" precisely because they come from beyond the literal; their authority is outside the letter. As in Paul de Man's introduction to *Allegories of Reading*, rhetoric comes from an elsewhere of language to challenge grammar. But the question of medieval allegory, like the later argument about symbol versus allegory that engaged Goethe and his contemporaries, is beyond my subject: my brief evocation of the medieval and Renaissance conception of allegory is meant only to provide a backdrop for my exploration of style.

Although the nineteenth-century use of the term "allegory" brings another interpretive apparatus of meaning into view, the question of the "otherness" of allegory remains. It is displaced from the theological realm of medieval speculation to the "otherness" of figural language as the new style of modernity. In this sense, my readings of Flaubert and Proust are an attempt to come to terms with Baudelaire's "Tout pour moi devient allégorie": the depersonalization of sentiment, the representation of evanescence and loss, and the revelation of an absence that renounces (or renders impossible) the comforts of nostalgia. The declaration of loss creates a verbal monument inscribed with the permanence of mourning that concludes "Le Cygne." In response to the evanescence of life and the death of her husband, Andromaque becomes a kind of human statue, a monument of mourning, a figure within the narrator's vision of allegory and an image for that allegory. In the vision that Baudelaire attributes to the narrator of "Le Cygne," the term "allégorie" anchors a poetic voice and a figural constellation; in my readings of Flaubert and Proust, the concept of allegory operates through voice and figure to uncover the principles and effects of modern style that inscribe the artist's vocation in the work of art.

Does modernity offer something like a vocation for allegory? Proust gives an example of it in the kitchenmaid Swann calls Giotto's Charity, who overturns the easy hierarchy of art and life. The effect of allegory, the representation of the symbolic as something real, has aesthetic consequences that go far beyond figural typology or allegorical personification. The image of something real that is a representation of the symbolic—the "étrangeté saississante" (1. 82) of allegory—makes it clear that style implicates the "otherness" of meaning in figural landscape as symbolic meaning is enigmatically represented in a figure, image, or "other" painted form. Representation turns the material form into a rebus of the symbolic; "tout pour moi devient allégorie" is another name for the writer's vocation.

What I am calling the "allegory of conversion" in these readings is the representation of an investment in style. The term of allegory conceptualizes the particular framework of style associated with the writers in question; the term of conversion takes up a key word in Proust's criticism of Flaubert that indicates the transformation of language into style. At the same time conversion refers to the writer's vocation and the idealization of style. In this sense the "allegory of conversion" is another name for how "tout pour moi devient allégorie [all becomes allegory for me]"—how vision turns into writing and how language turns into style—is inscribed in the art of Flaubert and Proust.

The conception of a new style based on the absolute of style itself made the artist into a kind of priest kneeling at the altar of beauty before the masked divinity of representation (who appears as Tanit in Flaubert's *Salammbô*). As figures, hieroglyphs, and traces of black fire, the images of modernity bear the absolute Otherness of writing—allegory. Vocation marks the encounter of this "otherness" with the desire of the writer; vocation is the sublime imperative of style.

The image of modernity is created when the writer rejects a notion of writing as an organic continuity that extends naturally from life. In its place, writing emerges as a work of style that masks the author's sentiments. My specific focus is perhaps the most difficult and mysterious aspect of the Modernist enterprise—the relation between style and the experience of the writer as represented in the novel. The interpretation of this relation implies a double subversion: the secrets of subjectivity—what Proust calls the complicated and arabesqued "grimoire" of the self, i.e., the book waiting to be written—are meant to be deciphered by the artist who translates them into the figural language of the oeuvre. The work must maintain its mystery in order to preserve its status as an aesthetic object. In this sense, the retracing of the author's steps, the decoding of the secrets and their inscriptions, is the taboo imposed by a Modernist aesthetic. The second transgressive act of reading follows from the first: the reading of the text as an investment in the mysterious "otherness" of writing, the decoding of its images, bypasses the categories of Realism, Naturalism, and so on, to concentrate on allegory as the essence of certain literary texts. This subversion challenges the condemnation of allegory as "baroque," "medieval," "patristic"—all terms pronounced as insults in the modern vernacular of secularization—and the championing of literature as a natural phenomenon labeled in Goethe's time as "symbolic." With the exception of Benjamin and his contemporary exegetes, not a single critic of the French nineteenth century has considered the importance of allegory as a phenomenon that unfolds in the modern portrayal of medieval and Renaissance symbolism and aesthetics as well as a specifically Modernist poetics that brings together subjectivity, history, time, and writing. Contrary to critical opinion, when Baudelaire's narrator in "Le Cygne" says "Tout pour moi devient allégorie," he means it. His moment of vision that interiorizes everything it sees and transforms it into allegory —the signification carried by an object that is neither its author/authority nor its organic root—stands for the poetic project of Baudelaire's oeuvre, starting with *Les Fleurs du mal*.

Proust's criticism of the nineteenth century moves toward a reading of style that is not named as allegorical but that nevertheless counters a kind of anti-allegorical consensus of modern literary criticism by revalorizing the exterior "surface" of Flaubert's vision and the cruel artifices of Baudelaire's art. At the same time, Proust's critique explicitly links his aesthetic project in *A la recherche du temps perdu* with Flaubert's novels. Proust's understanding of style unravels the contemporary consensus of literary criticism that opposes Flaubert's "exteriority" to Proustian "interiority" in the name of a continuity between art and life; according to this continuity, the claim has been made that Proust's narrator ultimately writes the *Recherche*. This continuity and its supposed product, however, are pure fiction: Proustian interiority, like Baudelairean interiority, is no less artificial (or allegorical) than the exquisitely constructed "surface" of Flaubert's fiction. On this basis, my frame of reading developed from a view of Flaubert and Proust as parallel images of modernity in the nineteenth and twentieth centuries.

Although Flaubert's letters to Louise Colet offer an eloquent dossier of evidence on the importance of religious concepts of creation and language as a model for art, my reading of Flaubert, Baudelaire, and Proust shifts the question of theology and its interpretive status to its effect on representation. In these French Modernist writings, theology is assimilated in the constellation of aesthetic terms: ecstasy, revelation, and miracles of the "éternité du style" formulate style and the writer's relation to it. Theology enters the secular domain of art and shapes the vocation of the writer through the moments that inscribe a fictional text with its "beginning"; desire knotted its author to the sublime mask, the beautiful cloak, and the figures or images of art. Masked, veiled, and figured, the artist stages a carnival in the necropolis.

This book began with another image of modernity, engaged in a confrontation between theology and comedy. In *Joyce's Catholic Comedy of Language* (Madison: University of Wisconsin Press, 1985) I interpreted an aesthetic constellation of subjectivity and style—a poetics of vocation—that reflected Joyce's itinerary: his artistic beginnings were shaped by an unmediated encounter with theology. Like Gerard Manley Hopkins, Joyce moved from theology toward modern style. My method recalls the construction of a triangle that occurs in Book II of *Finnegans Wake*: the eternal, the sexual, and the scriptural, or reading the text through the filters of theology, psychoanalysis, and the beautiful inked interlaces of art. Theology keeps the stakes of Modernism high by shaping desire according to the demands of a vocation.

2

The Image of Modernity

Je suis un vieux vieux fossile du romantisme
I am an old fossil of romanticism.[1]

Vous avez trouvé le moyen de rajeunir le romantisme. Vous ne ressemblez à personne (ce qui est le premier de toutes les qualités). L'originalité du style découle de la conception. La phrase est toute bourrée par l'idée, à en craquer . . . ce qui me plaît avant tout dans votre livre, c'est que l'art y prédomine. Et puis vous chantez la chair sans l'aimer, d'une façon triste et détachée qui m'est sympathique. Vous êtes résistant comme le marbre.

[You have discovered a way of rejuvenating romanticism. You do not resemble anyone (and that is the first of all good qualities). Originality of style derives from the conception. The sentence is filled to the bursting point with the idea . . . what I like above all in your book, is that art reigns in it. And you sing the flesh without loving it, in a sad and detached manner that suits me. You are as resistant as marble.][2]

Votre article m'a fait le plus grand plaisir. Vous êtes entré dans les arcanes de l'oeuvre, comme si ma cervelle était la vôtre. Cela est compris et senti à fond.

[Your article gave me the greatest pleasure. You penetrated the secrets of the work, as if my brain were yours. The work is understood and felt completely.][3]

Flaubert and Proust occupy exceptional positions in modern French literature. Although critics often emphasize their aesthetic and stylistic differences, their common ground is immediately perceptible in terms of modernity itself. When Leo Bersani describes an essential trait of modernity in French fiction of the nineteenth and twentieth centuries as the "centrality of disruptive desire" characteristic of realism,[4] his case rests on the writings of Flaubert and Proust. In another text, however, he elaborates an opposition between the aesthetics of the two writers: "The relations that the Proustian narrator establishes between art and the rest of life seem to originate in the questions posed by Flaubert in order to be able to affirm the *separation* between art and life."[5] According to Bersani's schema, Proust's novel progresses beyond Flaubert's categories, since the narrator's clear vision of art and its correspondence with life overturns his youthful illusions and convictions.

On a different theoretical ground, another contemporary critic uncovers the roots of modernity in Flaubert's writing. In the preface to *Recherche de Proust*, Gérard Genette qualifies modernity as inseparable from "the difficulty of writing." He describes the oeuvre of Flaubert as "a first response" to this difficulty, named "la question de l'écriture" ("the question of writing").[6] The author of "Proust palimpseste" returns to the traditional opposition between Flaubert and Proust on the basis of a distinction between art and life (Flaubert) contrasted with an identification of art and life (Proust). Like Bersani, he can do so only through a certain parallelism anchored in modernity, or rather its specific manifestation in the style of Modernism:

> Proust's work alone constitutes an exemplary response to what I would call in the strongest sense *the question of writing*, which is obviously the question of the difficulty and hence the impossibility of writing, and more specifically, as Valéry emphasizes, of writing fiction—and the *Recherche du temps perdu* is certainly a work of fiction.[7]

What is the reason for this apparently ineluctable parallelism, and why is it overturned in favor of a more traditional stance by these contemporary critics? More importantly, what constitutes the "modernity" of Flaubert as opposed to that of Proust? In order to answer this question, it will be necessary to consult other interpreters of Modernist fiction.

In *Les Romanciers naturalistes* Zola evokes the author of *Madame Bovary* as the inventor of a genre, "la formule du roman moderne [the formula of the modern novel]."[8] He circumscribes Flaubert's "evolutionary" discovery as an opposition between Flaubert and Balzac: "Il a, je le répète, porté la hache et la lumière dans la forêt parfois inextricable de Balzac [I repeat, he brought the ax and the light into Balzac's hopelessly tangled forest]."[9] Zola's interpretation is taken up by Georg Lukács, who considers Flaubert as a precursor of naturalism.[10] Lukács's argument in favor of realism opposes Flaubert's invention of the style of description to Balzac's traditional style of narration. In Balzac's writing, description is merely a stage for inner human drama ("nur der Schauplatz von inneren menschlichen Dramen")[11] while the dramatic element takes the form of extraordinarily multi-faceted and complicated characters ("Die ausserordentlich vielfältigen und verwickelten Gestalten Balzacs").[12] According to this analysis, Flaubert de-emphasizes dramatic characterization in favor of a descriptive method: its effect is to reduce characterization to the level of setting. Fictional characters are mere spots of paint in an image ("Sie werden Farbenflecke in einem Bild")[13] who observe a series of images ("einer Reihe von Bildern").[14]

Flaubert's readers observe these images ("Wir beobachten diese Bilder").[15] When Lukács quotes Zola's remarks about the task of the naturalist novelist, he emphasizes Zola's terms of nonspecificity and generality: the novelist begins to build a "typecast" or "typical" plot "without possessing a single (fictional) character."[16] Lukács's terms underscore Zola's "types"; what he describes as Flaubert's "Bild," the described image that replaces dramatic characters, has meaning only through the "artifice found in formal stylization."[17] In the dramatic portrayal of characters, Flaubert sacrifices the subjective importance at the source of meaning ("dem inneren menschlichen Gewicht") to style. The types and images of Flaubert's new realism eradicate dramatic subjectivity, the so-called "human interiority" of the characters. Lukács condemns naturalist style precisely because its distance from characters treats them as if they were inanimate things, depicted by means of a "false objectivity."[18]

Although Lukács condemns Modernism, his analysis is sustained by Flaubert's aspiration to an objective representation and by his Modernist emphasis on the artifices of style. It could be argued solely on the basis of Flaubert's correspondence that the descriptive aesthetic of Modernism anchors style in the opposition between objectivity and a dramatic rendering of fictional characters. While writing *Madame Bovary*, Flaubert remarks that the internal strength of a novel's style causes its material aspect to disappear. Subject matter is indifferent, since style alone is an absolute manner of seeing things: "C'est pour cela qu'il n'y a ni beaux ni vilains sujets et qu'on pourrait presque établir comme axiome, qu'il n'y en a aucun, le style étant à lui tout seul une manière absolue de voir les choses [It is for this reason that there are neither beautiful nor ugly subjects, and that one could declare as an axiom that there is no subject at all, since style alone is an absolute way of seeing things]."[19] The indifference of the subject matter is related to what Lukács sees as a lack of interiority and a rigid distantiation associated with a coolly observing eye: "Je suis dans un tout autre monde maintenant," Flaubert writes about *Madame Bovary*,

> celui de l'observation des détails les plus plats. . . . Je veux qu'il n'y ait pas dans mon livre *un seul* mouvement, ni *une seule* réflexion de l'auteur. . . . Il faut écrire *plus froidement*. . . . Tout doit se faire à froid, posément. Quand Louvel a voulu tuer le duc de Berry, il a pris une carafe d'orgeat, et n'a pas manqué son coup. [I am in a very different world now, the observation of the flattest details. . . . I have decided that there will not be *a single* movement nor *a single* reflection of the author in my book. . . .[20] One must write more *coldly*. . . . Everything must be done coolly, deliberately. When Louvel decided to kill the duke of Berry, he drank a carafe of orgeat and did not miss his target.][21]

The importance of this remark (and dozens in the same vein) in Flaubert's aesthetic is underscored by the quasi-pedagogical dimension of his correspondence with Louise Colet.

Flaubert extends the aesthetic principles developed through

the medium of his own writing to the work of Colet and others. He invents a divorce between the artist and Art with a capital A: out of the gap between the two comes his aesthetic of Modernism. Its vocabulary includes distance, observation, authorial invisibility, and other terms that will emerge later in my reading of style.

The critical discourse of realism or naturalism, however, does not accurately reflect Flaubert's terms. They are displaced by the vocabulary taken up in the critical hindsight of Lukács and others. Although he is heralded by Zola as the founder of Realism, Flaubert mistrusted the realist banner; his contemporary identification was with Romanticism and its poetic aspect, "la poésie" or "la serre idéale" shared with his friend Alfred Le Poittevin. Flaubert writes to Colet: "Ce côté douloureux de l'homme moderne, que tu remarques, est le fruit de ma jeunesse [The painful side of modern man that you point out is the fruit of my youth]."[22]

For Lukács's purpose, the link between Zola and Flaubert is sufficient. Flaubert, however, did not reciprocate the identification made by Zola, the disciple and champion of naturalism, since he questioned the claims as well as the labels of realism and naturalism. At the end of his life, Flaubert still described himself as a "vieux romantique," an old fossil of romanticism. When *Madame Bovary* was published, many years before he used the epithet of the "old Romantic" in conversation with Turgenev, he stated to Sainte-Beuve: "Je suis un vieux romantique enragé ou encroûté, comme vous voudrez [I am an old romantic, flying into a rage or sinking in a rut, whichever you prefer]."[23]

Flaubert's often-neglected, romantic position permeates the aesthetic of "l'homme moderne," the detached creator of Art. In the letter praising *Les Fleurs du mal*, his identification with Baudelaire's "rejuvenated romanticism" is confirmed by his appreciation of the poet's critique of *Madame Bovary* (quoted in the epigraph). Flaubert praises Baudelaire's understanding of his novel in the most explicit terms: "as if my brain were yours. The work is understood and felt *completely*." On the basis of his own understanding of style, Flaubert's aesthetic of Modernism finds a counterpart in Baudelaire.[24]

Les arcanes de l'oeuvre

Les vers les plus exquis de Baudelaire, les phrases de Flaubert m'auraient paru affreux [The most exquisite lines of Baudelaire, the sentences of Flaubert would have struck me as frightful].[25]

The speaker who unites the verse and prose of Baudelaire and Flaubert at the height of "artistic Beauty" (located beyond a certain phase in his development when he would have been incapable of appreciating them) is the unnamed star of Proust's Modernist fiction. His aesthetic of Modernism as well as his specific stylistic preoccupations take up the questions of writing that locate Flaubert and Baudelaire in his critical writings as the source of Proust's Modernist inheritance. Unsurpassed in his esteem, they are accompanied only by Stendhal. In one of Proust's most explicit literary judgments, "Sainte-Beuve et Baudelaire," Proust describes Baudelaire as the greatest poet of the nineteenth century: "Et on peut dire que ce sont les meilleurs, les plus intelligents qui sont ainsi, vite redescendus de la sphère où ils écrivent *Les Fleurs du mal, Le Rouge et le noir, L'Education sentimentale* [And it can be said of the best and the most intelligent ones that they rapidly come down from the sphere where they have written *The Flowers of Evil, The Red and the Black, The Sentimental Education*]" (CSB 248).[26]

Many years later, Proust again places Flaubert and Baudelaire side by side as writers of the highest order (CSB 596). In "A Propos de Baudelaire," however, Proust describes the poet's presence in *Les Fleurs du mal* in terms antithetical to Flaubert's praise of him; these words make the artist sound very much like the Proustian character of the narrator. When Proust evokes "ce que le pauvre Baudelaire a trouvé dans l'intimité souffrante de son coeur et de son corps [that which poor Baudelaire found in the suffering intimacy of his heart and body]," he anchors the poet in a personalized world: "Monde baudelairien que vient par moments mouiller et enchanter un souffle parfumé du large, soit par réminiscences . . . soit directement, grâce à ces portiques dont il est souvent question chez Baudelaire [A Baudelairean world dampened and enchanted at intervals by a fragrant breath of the open sea, either by memories . . . or directly, thanks to the porticos that often appear in Baudelaire's writing]."²⁷

While Flaubert praised Baudelaire's aesthetic distance, the objectivity that became the axis of Flaubert's proclaimed aesthetic and the major trait of his fiction according to Lukács and others, Proust seems to read Baudelaire in terms of an aesthetic of autobiographical introspection and nostalgic subjectivity. Although the context of Modernism locates them on common ground, Flaubert's fictional exteriority seems to be antithetical to Proust's autobiographical novel of interiority.

Given the opposition between their claims for the properties of subjectivity and objectivity, can Flaubert and Proust be read together on the basis of Modernist aesthetics? The consensus of literary criticism does not justify such a reading: if the critic concedes that Proust inherited a descriptive style invented by Flaubert, he may still object that Proust used that style to quite opposite intent and effect. The descriptive style Lukács attributes to Flaubert "reduces human beings to the level of dead objects" or "lifeless fetishized objects,"²⁸ whereas the Proustian universe gives free rein to "a permanent carnival of fetishized interiority."²⁹ The opposition noted by Lukács is not limited to the framework of Marxist criticism. It can be found in criticism based on very different ideological claims — philological, New Critical, structuralist, and so on.³⁰

Closer to contemporary criticism, the opposition between the styles of Flaubert and Proust is almost taken for granted. In *The Gates of Horn* Harry Levin seems to contrast that "upstart genre" (realism), consecrated by Flaubert, to the novelists of "psychological penetration—Stendhal, Proust."³¹ This opposition is underscored by the parallel in the following sentence about Flaubert's "objectivation" and "effect of impersonality": "The inference is that the best of himself has been absorbed into the writing, which completes the life; the work perfects the man, even as *A la recherche du temps perdu* will resolve the imperfections of Marcel Proust."³² On the basis of specific elements of style, Jean Rousset opposes Flaubert's *Education sentimentale*, a model of exterior narration, to "récit autobiographique" in which the "narrative agent is located within the narration (l'agent de la narration se trouve cette fois à l'intérieur de la narration)."[33] Rousset cites *A la recherche du temps perdu* as a perfect example of "récit autobiographique" and adds that *L'Education sentimentale* and autobiographical *récit* are "at the two ends of the spectrum, the two fundamental systems of narration."[34]

According to these judgments, Flaubert's novels of descriptive exteriority create an objective scene deprived of the human dimensions of subjectivity. This mode of creation is different from the descriptive interiority of Proust's novel, in which characters never seem to appear in their own right on a subjective scene that is focused and mediated only by the narrator's consciousness. Is it possible or even desirable to read the two writers together? An answer to this question might be found in the contrasts, parallels, and "questions d'écriture" raised by Proust's "A Propos du 'style' de Flaubert."[35] This essay offers an implicit comparison of Proustian and Flaubertian views on what they saw as the heart of writing: style.

Although the essay is ostensibly a polemic in favor of Flaubert, the argument unfolds in three layers sustained by Proust's view of style. His general considerations appear to answer the unasked question of what is at stake in style itself (distinct from the writer's oeuvre and its specific actualization of style) and in what sense the effect of a work of art may be seen as the effect of its stylistic principle or virtuality. These remarks are accompanied by an analysis of some original syntactic forms, while Proust emphasizes the major principles of style in Flaubert's work, and marks them as a framework he has assimilated in his own exploration of style.

The link between general and particular considerations of style is described as *translation*, one of Proust's key terms for Baudelairean *correspondance*. The self-reflective literary spiral of "translation" is anticipated in Flaubert's focus on style as an autonomous entity. The object of "translation" is the writer's vision rendered in the singular inventions of grammatical usage; the effect of style is the renewal of the reader's vision:

Ces singularités grammaticales traduisent en effet une vision nouvelle, que d'application ne fallait-il pas pour bien fixer cette vision, pour la faire passer de l'inconscient dans le conscient, pour l'incorporer enfin aux diverses parties du discours! J'ai été stupéfait, je l'avoue, de voir traiter de peu doué pour écrire, un homme qui par l'usage entièrement nouveau et personnel qu'il a fait . . . a renouvelé . . . notre vision des choses. [These grammatical singularities indeed translate a new vision; how much application was necessary in order to anchor this vision, to provide passage for it from the unconscious to the conscious, and finally to incorporate it into the different parts of speech! I confess my astonishment at hearing that a man who renewed our vision of things through his entirely new and personal use of language has been called a writer of little talent.] (CSB 586–92)

In the following chapters I will try to trace the ways Flaubert and Proust translate their personal impressions, sensations, and passions into what Proust calls "notre vision des choses," rendered in the absolute artifice of style. Through readings of the aesthetic principles that gave rise to their works and through an interpretation of passages in the major writings that best illustrate the relation between writer and oeuvre, I will examine what is at stake in the question of style as it enters the two created worlds of Flaubert and Proust— the necropolis and the carnival—and whether it is possible to stage an encounter between the two. Modernism privileges the inscribed presence of the writer in representation; the encounter will be a double one, including two "visions" and two "translations." Style transfigures the "heart"; it resurrects the past in the instant of intoxication. The renewed "vision des choses" and the strangely desentimentalized "heart" that leaves traces of its ravishment in the text come together in the allegory of conversion.

3

The Allegory of Conversion

When we will see in person the Word of God, through whom everything has been done, and from whom the angels take their nourishment, who illuminates the angels and through whom the angels acquire knowledge, not by scrutinizing the spoken words of a tortuous tongue but by drinking the one Word whose intoxication makes them burst into praises without ever running out of praises.[1]

Windows and Magic Lanterns

In "A Propos du 'style' de Flaubert," Proust's concept of "the eternity of style"[2] indicates the common ground his fiction shares with Flaubert's domain of ecstatic revelation. Despite the absence of "le miracle d'une analogie [the miracle of an analogy]" in Flaubert's aesthetic, his fictions unfold under a sky tinted with the colors of the Proustian sublime displayed in *A la recherche du temps perdu*. When the two writers portray "extase" in fiction, the depersonalization implicit in ecstasy resonates on the level of an aesthetic principle. Flaubert wrote: "Dans l'idéal que j'ai de l'Art, je crois . . . que l'artiste ne doit pas plus apparaître dans son oeuvre que Dieu dans la nature [In my ideal of Art, I believe . . . that the artist must not appear in the oeuvre any more than God appears in nature]."[3] A Proustian parallel to this mask of invisibility worn by the authorial persona takes the shape of "involuntary memories." Proust consistently makes use of them as both primary material and a structural or compositional frame for *A la recherche du temps perdu*, described as a "Roman de l'Inconscient [Novel of the Unconscious]." These involuntary memories "ont seuls une griffe d'authenticité . . . cette vérité générale et nécessaire que la beauté du style seule traduit [alone possess a mark of authenticity . . . the general and necessary truth that is translated only by beauty of style]" (CSB 558–59). The Flaubertian withdrawal of the authorial persona finds a Freudian counterpart[4] in Proust's detachment from "la mémoire volontaire, qui est surtout une mémoire de l'intelligence et des yeux [voluntary memory, which is primarily the memory of the intelligence and the eyes]" (CSB 558). The mask worn by the artist makes him invisible; the beauty of style translates the invisibility of "la mémoire involontaire." Its ecstatic moments of distance and interiority offer both of these forms to the artist's insight.

Modernism presents the "other" vision of allegory through the eyes of the melancholic gazing at a monument of absence. This development may have had two predecessors: the Baroque deflected the path of subjectivity away from medieval theology and toward melancholy and mourning, while French Romanticism placed the image of Hamlet wearing a black-feathered hat at the center of its construct of dark exaltation and ennui. In the mid-nineteenth century, Modernist allegory rose from a new impersonal interiority of the "other" world within subjectivity, and a new allegorical temporality that clasped modernity to antiquity. The meeting between interior and exterior occurs at the crossroads of antiquity and modernity, represented in Baudelaire's image of Paris.

According to Benjamin,[5] Baudelaire's allegorical vision unveils a Paris "like glass": petrified and fragile, it surrenders meaning through its transparence. For the apostrophizing "I" in "Le Cygne," Paris is both the form of glass and the vision seen through it ("la forme et le fond"). An aesthetic barrier separates the viewer from the object; a surface of artificial transparency reveals the object at a distance. The city of glass indicates the essence of the allegorical mode of representation. The "other" is doubly estranged from the "I" through mourning of the past and the hopelessness of the future,[6] while the third level of estrangement occurs in the image itself. As Baudelaire's "oppressive image," the artifice of writing—the temporality and vision of style—indicates that what is ultimately at stake is the enterprise of allegory.

The opacity of stone turns into the sublime meaningful transparence of the pane of glass that reflects and reveals allegory. This interiorized "open sesame" is aestheticized in the writings of Flaubert and Proust, as well as in Baudelaire.[7] The aesthetic element takes the form of a visual supplement that enters the transparence of glass, subtly affecting it. Flaubert's discussions of aesthetics consistently encode this vision through style as "color."

Because style is ultimately inseparable from ordinary language, the relation between them is a matter of density rather than opposition. In Flaubert's aesthetic, however, style may be considered as an alternative to ordinary language in the same way that he describes colored glass as an alternative to ordinary daylight ("le jour ordinaire") seen through clear windows ("les verres blancs").[8] On May 15, 1852, he wrote to Colet: "Sais-tu à quoi j'ai passé tout mon après-midi avant-hier? à regarder la campagne par des verres de couleur. J'en avais besoin pour une page de ma Bovary [Do you know how I spent the whole afternoon of the day before yesterday? looking at the countryside through colored glass. I needed to do it for a page of my Bovary]."[9] Flaubert did not include the account (beginning with: "Elle regarda la campagne par les verres de couleur [She looked at the countryside through the colored glasses]") in the published version of the novel. In a formula used elsewhere to define style, he compared the perspective of someone in love to the effect of colored glass: "Quand on aime, on aime tout, tout se voit en bleu quand on porte des lunettes bleues. L'amour comme le reste n'est qu'une façon de voir et de sentir [When we love, we love everything, everything looks blue to someone who is wearing blue glasses. Like everything else, love is only a way of seeing and feeling]."[10] Flaubert's "façon de voir et de sentir" follows his observation of his own enamoured state in the same way that his comments on the "façon de voir et de sentir" of style originate in his experience. The subjective or self-reflective impact of the "verres de couleur" is confirmed in a letter written several months after the crisis at Pont-l'Evêque. Long before Flaubert had conceived of *Madame Bovary*, he compared the image of colored glass ("les verres de couleurs qui ornent les kiosks des bonnetiers retirés [the colored glass that decorates the kiosks of retired hosiers]") to his own melancholy. This "tristesse" is defined as a symptom of modernity: "Cet ennui moderne qui ronge l'homme dans les entrailles et, d'un être intelligent fait une ombre qui marche, un fantôme qui pense [The modern ennui that eats away at a man's entrails and turns an intelligent being into a walking shadow, a thinking phantom]."[11]

When the panes of colored glass reappear in the draft of *Madame Bovary* the atmosphere is marked by a specifically Flaubertian signature of the aesthetic event—a silence heavy with untranslatable meaning: "Les murs, contre un portrait, semblaient penser des choses qu'ils ne voulaient pas dire [The walls, facing a portrait, seemed to have thoughts that they did not want to speak]" (216). The untranslatable silence is anticipated by an opaque or invisible interiority, recalling Baudelaire's insistence on a past that has grown imperceptible with time: "Quand on regardait du dehors on ne voyait rien à l'intérieur [When one looked in from outside, one could see nothing]" (215). In this theater of allegorical distance, vision is presented through panes of colored glass. When Emma turns away from them and sees "le jour ordinaire" through clear glass, she dreamily returns to the realm of "la vie en beau" (Baudelaire) or "le Style" (Flaubert): "quoiqu'elle ne dormit pas, elle commençait à rêver [although she was not asleep, she was beginning to dream]" (217).

Flaubert devotes four paragraphs to what Emma sees through the glass. Both tone and affect vary enormously from one shade to another:

> A travers les bleus tout semblait triste. . . . Puis par les carrés jaunes. . . . Les nuages détachés figuraient des édredons de poudre d'or prêts à crever; . . . c'était joyeux; mais elle resta plus longtemps devant la vitre rouge . . . le ciel immense entassait des incendies. Elle eut peur [Through the blue ones everything seemed sad. . . . Then

through the yellow panes. . . . The detached clouds figured eiderdowns of golden powder ready to burst; . . . it was gay; but she lingered for a longer time before the red pane . . . the immense sky heaped up blazing fires. She became frightened (216).

These effects transform vision into style, and appear as figures.

Flaubert's palette of colored glass points toward the visionary artist's relation to the figures that enter writing. In this sense, Emma's sleepless dream is a figure of the allegorist's "other" gaze.[12] Within Flaubert's oeuvre, the "verres de couleur" function as the palette of individual tints that later will be recombined in the complex figuration of a stained-glass window. *Saint Julien l'Hospitalier*, the window in the Rouen cathedral, is used not only for Flaubert's narrative construction in *La Légende*, but also for its allegorical figuration.[13]

Proust privileges the use of glass as a medium for allegory in a similar way, but he shifts the emphasis from the untranslatable to the visible. Elements of invisibilia enter the magic lantern, his compromise between Flaubertian (and Baudelairean) colored glass and stained-glass windows. In both *Jean Santeuil* (316–17) and *A la recherche du temps perdu* (I, 9–10),[14] the "magic lantern" adds reflection ("un réflecteur" [JS 316]) and small panes or slides of colored glass to light: "La lumière . . . éclairait mystérieusement une place du mur. Et voici . . . comme si un vitrail surnaturel, non pas en verre bleu, rouge, violet, mais comme une apparition de vitrail en apparence de verre, en clarté rouge, bleu et violette, s'avançait [The light . . . mysteriously lit a place on the wall. And here . . . as if a supernatural stained glass window, not of blue, red, or violet glass, but as an apparition of a stained-glass window with the appearance of glass, in red, blue, and violet clarity, was advancing]" (JS 316). The doubled distance of these images from "material" stained-glass windows locates the effects of vision in the intimate interiority of a dream or memory detached from the visible world. For a moment, the apparitions enter the realm of the visible through "des petites planches de verre de couleurs si mystiques [small glass slides of such mystical colors]." When the light of figuration gives way to habitual lamplight, "La place mystérieuse, la trappe invisible par où les fantômes étaient apparus était confondue dans le reste du mur [The mysterious place, the invisible trap door through which the phantoms had appeared, had blended into the rest of the wall]" (JS 317).

In *A la recherche* Proust links the apparitions to stained glass in order to emphasize the transitoriness and immateriality of the visionary dimension of "verres de couleur."[15] The contrast between appearance of color and materiality of stained glass disappears from the rewritten version while the more essential contrast between the opaque wall and the "vitrail vacillant et momentané [vacillating and momentary stained-glass window]" (I, 9) is reinforced. The lamp "substituait à l'opacité des murs d'impalpables irisations, de surnaturelles apparitions multicolores [substituted for the opacity of walls' impalpable iridescences, multicolored supernatural apparitions]" (I, 9). At the same time the aesthetic focus of the "seul tableau dont se décore, et bien passagèrement [only picture that decorates, and very much in passing]" (JS 317) Jean's room—the passing form of vision through colored glass—is accentuated in the narrator's account of how the family "dissolves" the melancholy he anticipates before going to bed. He evokes the effect of the magic lantern as "cette intrusion du mystère et de la beauté dans une chambre [the intrusion of mystery and beauty into a bedroom]" (I, 10). At Balbec the narrator of the *Recherche* discovers this effect in a constellation of painterly influences associated with Elstir and his visual metaphors. Like the view of the magic lantern and the Giotto reproductions at Combray, these "tableaux" are exhibited in the narrator's bedroom; between "les plombs du vitrail [the leadwork of the stained-glass window]" (I, 809), the sea appears through the "verre glauque [glaucous glass]" of the window in the "glaces des bibliothèques [plate glass of the bookcases]." The doubled representation of the magic lantern in *Jean Santeuil* becomes the medium for the "marvelous painting" of the "figure raide, géométrique, passagère et fulgurante du soleil (pareille à la représentation de quelque signe miraculeux, de quelque apparition mystique) [the stiff, geometric, passing, and flashing figure of the sun (like the representation of some miraculous sign, some mystical apparition)]" (I, 803) reflected in the panes of the bookcases. The deferral of vocation is intertwined with the account of the "étude de nuages [cloud study]" (I, 805); it recalls the childhood melancholy associated with the lantern. Because the narrator forgets "le triste vide de la plage, parcouru par le vent inquiet [the sad emptiness of the beach, skimmed by the troubled wind]" (I, 805), he does not receive the full force of his transitory, immaterial, mystical, and beautiful impressions. Like Emma at Vaubyessard, he turns away from stained-glass images.

Emma's "rêve," the "other" vision of the allegorist, uses color to create an operative palette of style. Through an explicit unveiling of aesthetic variations in mood and tone, Flaubert's kiosk brings together melancholy, past pleasure, and figural vision at the silent site of writing, the theater of allegory. Proust takes up the "verres de couleur" associated with allegorical vision from a condensed form that is already present in Flaubert's published writings. In chapter 5 of *Bouvard et Pécuchet*, Flaubert introduces the magic lantern in a simile about fictional effects: "Alexandre Dumas les divertit à la manière d'une lanterne magique [Alexandre Dumas amused them like a magic lantern]."[16]

Blue, Varnished, and Gold

Proust's literary "lanterne magique" extends the allegorist's dream to the invisibilia of memory, the unconscious, and the site of artistry and resurrection. Through apparitions of passing figures, Proust emphasizes the mystery of the invisible and the beauty of stained glass. They emerge from an invisible panel of wall, and later from a "pan lumineux [luminous panel]" (I, 43) opened up by the revelation of the Petite Madeleine. The panel of wall that maps out the evanescent visibility of invisibilia is the object of an "open sesame" for the writer Bergotte as well as the narrator. The painter of *Jean Santeuil* has become the primary writer in the *Recherche*. This second Bergotte introduces light and color to the hieroglyphs of reading when he reaps the ultimate revelation of style from Vermeer's "little panel of yellow wall." His waking to this vision bears the entry into death: Proust's understanding of truth in art inscribed his final revisions of these pages of *A la recherche* with the subjectivity of allegory.

Bergotte's vision of mysteriously beautiful style takes Vermeer's layering of color as a model. Without this ideal the effects of style lapse into a "dryness" that lacks the dynamic fluidity and allegorical mystery necessary to reach the heights.[17] Beauty is simultaneously anchored in subjectivity and mysteriously distanced from the identification of an authorial persona. Flaubert's conception of a beauty created by art is inseparable from the ideal of Style, encoded as "le fondu," or the verb "fondre": to melt or dissolve. Again, the ideal of a style that literally puts language into solution enacts the disappearance of the individual—as well as of individual elements—into a continuously beautiful prose that reflects subjectivity without pointedly revealing an authorial origin: "J'ai imaginé, je me suis ressouvenu et j'ai combiné. Ce que tu as lu n'est le souvenir de rien du tout [I imagined, I remembered again, and I arranged. What you read is not the reminiscence of anything at all]."[18]

Like the "sad and detached" lyricism he admires in Baudelaire's poems, Flaubert's principle "de ne pas rapetisser l'Art à la satisfaction d'une personnalité isolée [not to reduce Art to the satisfaction of an isolated personality]"[19] is essential to the Modernist turn toward a new style. After the imperfection of the first *Tentation* and the first *Education sentimentale*, his gradual discovery of a new ideal of style rigorously (according to the author's "ligne droite géométrique [geometric straight line]") banishes the authorial persona. The ideal of style locates beauty in the effects of negation where an authorial imprint has vanished into thin air—"le livre sur rien [book about nothing]"[20] with the "personnalité de l'auteur absente [absence of an authorial persona]."[21] At times the negativity that sublimates the authorial personality and renders the individual invisible is presented against a background of a "double abyss." Dissolved or melted together, the two "abysses" form a third negative form—the text: "Mon livre . . . suspendu entre le double abîme du lyrisme et du vulgaire (que je veux fondre dans une analyse narrative) [My book . . . suspended between the double abyss of lyricism and vulgarity (which I want to melt together in a narrative analysis)]."[22] The melting together of the two "abysses" represents Flaubert on a tightrope between the infinite overflow of interiority ("le lyrisme") and the flat surface of the anti-heroic, anti-sentimental, and anti-dramatic portrayal of bourgeois life ("le vulgaire"). The image of the "livre suspendu" on a tightrope resonates in the context of Flaubert's love of taut, "muscular" syntax, the "virility" of the ideal sentence.

Criticism has often echoed Flaubert's endless complaining about the difficulty of writing in a new vein. Although the latent mythology of the writer as a bourgeois, quasi-psychotic crank appears in critical accounts ranging from the Goncourts to V. S. Pritchett, it may be of greater interest to look at Flaubert's distinction between "easy" and "difficult" style. While writing Emma's love scene, he comments: "Ce sera, je crois, très fort, car c'est peindre, couleur sur couleur et sans tons tranchés (ce qui est plus aisé) [It will be very fine, I believe, since it is painted color on color without distinct tones (which is easier)]."[23] Plot and reality dissolve in a layered blend of colors,[24] the ideal object of Flaubert's aspirations. The "fondu" is ultimately the ideal text itself.

Proust reinforces Flaubert's emphasis on color with the stylistic concept of "le fondu." The effects of style, its mystery and beauty, are compared to the secret of the great painters ("le vernis des maîtres"). Through Vermeer, he articulates a model for writing that reappears in the novel through Elstir's "métaphores" of colored representation on canvas:

> Ce qui fait la beauté absolue . . . des *Fables* de La Fontaine, des comédies de Molière . . . c'est une espèce de fondu, d'unité transparente où toutes les choses . . . sont venues se ranger . . . pénétrées de la même lumière . . . sans un seul mot qui reste au-dehors . . . c'est ce qu'on appelle le vernis des maîtres. [The absolute beauty . . . of La Fontaine's *Fables* and Molière's plays . . . is a kind of

melting, a transparent unity in which all things . . . have been assembled, penetrated by the same light . . . without a single word that stays outside . . . it is called the varnish of the masters.]²⁵

The "fondu" of light and color or the varnished transparence of glass unites disparate elements in absolute beauty.

Proust complements Flaubert's aesthetic vocabulary with the theological resonance of liturgical figures adapted from the framework of Baudelaire's poetics. The most Proustian of these figures is the supreme miracle of transubstantiation: "La beauté des deux ou trois plus merveilleuses phrases que je sache en français, où s'est accompli le miracle suprême, la transsubstantiation des qualités irrationnelles de la matière et de la vie dans des mots humains [The beauty of the two or three most marvelous sentences that I know in French, where the supreme miracle has been accomplished, the transubstantiation of the irrational qualities of matter and life into human words]."²⁶ This enigmatic transformation sketches the passage from the "irrational" (materiality, substance, "life") to "human words" rather than the anticipated terms of reason. The use of theological terms suggests that what is at stake is more subtle than a battle between the rational and the irrational. If a binary opposition were operative, the result of transubstantiation would be "truth," "logic," or "theory" decanted from the "falsehood" of life. Instead, Proust's remark points out that the effect of transubstantiation is the miraculous beauty of certain words in particular arrangements. It refers back to the "fondu" of "le vernis des maîtres," since he declares that the source of beauty in Daudet's sentence comes from "la liquidité bleue et vernie et dorée [the blue and varnished and golden fluidity]" of a single word.²⁷

The Proustian object that originates in invisibilia and moves through substance takes shape in a specific figural process. In fiction and outside it, the figure of "analogy" posits what is at stake in writing and even the subject of writing; without it, the melancholic view of the ruins of time would have no meaning. Proust's "analogy"—the clasping or correspondence of instants of memory that bear an inexplicable intensity of feeling, or even intoxication—confirms the importance of "fondre." An early version of the Petite Madeleine episode[28] begins with the narrator "glacé" attentive to the softening of the soaked bread in his mouth (CSB 211–12). Things begin to move within him, light and summer reappear: "Les cloisons ébranlés de ma mémoire cédèrent [the shaken screens of my memory gave way]" (CSB 212). The different forms of softening and melting are figures for the "fondu" of style.

The search for the origin of "le fondu" leads back to intoxication and anticipates the clasped and rapturous time that will be explored later. The forms of "défaillance"—swoon, faint, or lapse—evoked during the concluding (and fictionally conclusive) matinée of *A la recherche* recall Proust's earliest comments about "the very essence of my life." This essence is simultaneously more and less than a novel: "C'est l'essence . . . recueillie . . . dans ces heures de déchirure où elle découle [It is the essence . . . gathered . . . in these harrowing torn hours from which it flows]" (JS 181). Here too, rays of light melt the ice ("ces rayons qui . . . me déliaient pour un instant des glaces de la vie mondaine [the rays that loosened me for an instant from the ice of worldly life]"). Later in *Jean Santeuil*, the link to both the aesthetic term of "fondre" and the vocabulary of time and memory rendered most explicit in the final matinée is reinforced by the echo of the opening paragraph, quoted above (JS 181). This moment of silent intoxication recalls Flaubert: "Jean se sentait heureux, près de défaillir, comme dans les moments où la vie s'arrête [Jean felt happy, close to swooning, as at the moments when life stops]" (JS 300). During the matinée, the final revelation of allegory unifies the privileged moments of inexplicable intoxication lifted out of the flow of time. In a Baudelairean form of dissolving,[29] the relation between "défaillance" and "fondre" leads back to the confluence of *Correspondances*.[30]

Toward the end of *A la recherche du temps perdu* the narrator describes the act of creating a work of art as a conversion of sensation into a spiritual equivalent.[31] Beyond the grammatical margins of religious conversion, scriptural conversion extends the reflexive pronoun of subjectivity (the "se" of "se convertir") into the mystery of style, or the "other" subjectivity rendered through transubstantiation. The "convertir" of scriptural conversion emerges in the gray areas between subject and object as a transitive verb producing art.[32]

An indication that something other than the personalization associated with the French Romanticism of Lamartine and Chateaubriand is at stake in scriptural conversion may be found in the "conversion" of Jules in the first *Education sentimentale*. To become a great writer, Jules must concentrate on style: "Il entra donc de tout coeur dans cette grande étude du style [He began wholeheartedly his great study of style]."[33] In the vocabulary of Modernism, "fondre" and "confondre" are related to "convertir." Proust's conception of Flaubert's style uses the words almost interchangeably. To emphasize the luminous reflection in Flaubert's painting of reality through language, Proust uses the terms together:

> Toutes les parties de la réalité sont converties en une même substance, aux vastes surfaces, d'un miroitement monotone. Aucune impureté n'est restée. Les surfaces sont devenues réfléchissantes. Toutes les choses s'y peignent . . . Tout ce qui était différent a été converti et absorbé. [All parts of reality are converted into a single substance with vast surfaces and a monotonous mirroring. No impurity remains. The surfaces have become reflective. All things are painted on them. . . . All that was different has been converted and absorbed.] (CSB 269)

As subjectivity, the "fondu" of light and surface is ecstasy, artistically rendered and re-created.

Scriptural conversion melts and dissolves the self into art. For Jules, "Ce que la vie lui offre, il le donne à l'Art; tout vient vers lui et tout en ressort . . . panthéisme immense, qui passe par lui et réapparait dans l'Art [What life offers to him, he gives it to Art; everything comes toward him and from him . . . immense pantheism that passes through him and reappears in Art]"[34] (ES 280). "Forme" and "fond" come together in divine fusion: "Il observa . . . la forme où elle [the idea] se fond, leurs développements mystérieux . . . fusion divine où l'esprit, s'assimilant la matière, la rend éternelle comme lui-même [He observed . . . the form where it [the idea] dissolves, their mysterious expansions . . . divine fusion where the spirit, assimilating matter, renders it eternal like itself]" (236). The artist is a subject or agent of "passage" who transforms matter into sublime representation. In anticipation of Proust's term of "convertir" in *A la recherche*, the jarring material elements of reality become invisible, converted into a surface of unbroken eternal beauty.

This passage leads to the subjectivity of the allegorist: "Arrêtant l'émotion qui le troublerait, il sait faire naître en lui la sensibilité qui doit créer quelque chose [Putting an end to emotion that would be disturbing, he knows how to arouse in himself a sensibility that must create something]" (280). The image of mastery attributed to Jules prefigures the detachment and impersonality that will later become the cornerstones of Flaubert's vision of style. Even in this early text, there are many indications that allegory is rooted in melancholy, "les ruines du coeur de l'homme [the ruins of man's heart]" (223): "On s'étonne qu'un squelette ait eu la vie . . . mais on s'étonne aussi parfois que notre coeur ait possédé ce qu'il n'a plus [We are surprised that a skeleton had life . . . but we are also surprised that our heart once possessed that which it no longer has]" (224). "Emotion" gives way to "sensibility." Through mourning, the heart becomes the artist's keyboard: "Si le coeur humain est un immense clavier que d'octave en octave et d'accords en dissonances le penseur doive parcourir [If the human heart is an immense keyboard that the thinker must cover from octave to octave and from harmonious chords to dissonances]" (237). This image appears frequently in Flaubert's correspondence. Proust's "miracle" of "fondu" operates a similar distantiation of personal emotion in favor of another musical "clavier": "Ce violoniste joue très bien sa phrase de violon, mais vous voyez ses effets . . . c'est une virtuose. . . . Quand tout cela aura fini par disparaître, que la phrase de violon ne fera plus qu'un avec l'artiste entièrement fondu en elle, le miracle se sera produit [This violinist plays the violin phrase very well, but you see his effects . . . he is a virtuoso . . . When at last all that will have disappeared and the violin phrase will come to one with the artist completely dissolved in it, the miracle will have taken place]" (CSB 612).

Proust attributes the "miracle" to Flaubert. In this preface to *Tendres Stocks*, in the pastiche, and in "A Propos de Flaubert," Proust alludes to moments when the "penseur" has dissolved into the undulations and encounters of objects: "Mais chez Flaubert, par exemple, l'intelligence . . . cherche à se faire trépidation d'un bateau à vapeur . . . Alors arrive un moment où on ne trouve plus l'intelligence . . . on a devant soi le bateau qui file rencontrant des trains de bois [But in Flaubert, for example, the intelligence . . . seeks to enter the vibration of a steam boat. . . . A moment arrives when you can no longer find the intelligence . . . you have before you the moving boat that hits against timber rafts]" (CSB 612). Temporality shapes the passage through negativity of the dissolved, disappearing subject essential to Modernist aesthetics. The dimension of falling and loss is the melancholy of the allegorist, for whom the abyss includes not only death, but life itself: for Flaubert, "la Vie" and "la Mort"; for Proust, "la mort" as the conclusion to a lack of will, and to "la vie mondaine." For both, the only alternative to the abyss is the death mask of writing.

Wearing the Veil

"Débordement" or "écoulement," the overflow of interiority is the image of a sensation of loss. But this "débordement" solicits form, and through it becomes jouissance. Flaubert remarks: "Tant mieux donc qu'ils aient souffert dans leurs entrailles, si la chair du premier [the animal] est exquise, si la phrase de l'autre [the poet] est savoureuse! [So much the better that they suffered in their entrails, if the flesh of the one is exquise, if the sentence of the other is savory!]" (1ère ES, 275). Although Flaubert's forms passing through the medium of the artist, Baudelaire's *correspondance*, and Proust's image of resurrection based on involuntary memory are modes of artistic representation in secular works of literature, they portray artistic salvation through grace. The paradox of a Modernist glorification of art is not the "qui perd gagne" essential to Sartre's argument in *L'Idiot de la famille* but rather the detachment from life and death that accompanies it in the vision of allegory. The path traced from "voir, sentir [seeing, feeling]" to "faire des phrases [making sentences]" comprises the itinerary of the sublime and of style.

At the conclusion of the first *Education sentimentale*, Flaubert writes: "Jules est parti hier pour l'Orient [Jules left yesterday for the Orient]" (286). The ascetic pilgrim travels in search of his inner life, the land of style: "Sa vie est . . . obscure . . . froide au regard . . . mais elle resplendit à l'intérieur de clartés magiques et de flamboiements voluptueux; c'est l'azur d'un ciel d'Orient tout pénétré de soleil [His life is . . . obscure . . . dark to an observer's eye . . . but it shines on the inside with magic lights and voluptuous blazings; it is the azure of an oriental sky pierced through with sun]" (278). The image of style that leads the narrator "glacé [frozen]" to his illumination is echoed in the "pacte magique [magic pact]" of the Petite Madeleine episode in *A la recherche du temps perdu*.

A condensed formula for the combination of loss and overflow, emptiness and ecstasy, that shapes a theory of style leading from the first *Education sentimentale* to *A la recherche* occurs in a few lines of "Le Cygne." Baudelaire describes Andromaque "auprès d'un tombeau vide en extase courbée [curved in ecstasy near an empty tomb]." This image of her countersigns the declaration made by Baudelaire's narrator: "Tout pour moi devient allégorie." Andromaque's ecstasy and her loss reflected by the emptiness of the tomb are crystallized into a figural rendering of allegory. She becomes its hieroglyph or emblem, both enigmatic and translucently revealing the signification of her own destiny. Her curve of ecstasy is also a figure for the allegory of the speaking "I" and the unending spiral of "bien d'autres encor!"—the ongoing exile that ends the poem. Baudelaire's dazzle of allegory—"a flash then nothing!"—in the extravagant exclamation of "A Une Passante" resonates here as the overflow and emptiness of ec-stasis. Its passage into form shows that allegory and ecstasy are soldered together by Modernism. The visionary gaze of estrangement creates meaning in the future perfect of memory, exile, and death (gliding among the disparate personae of "Le Cygne" and their abrupt entrances onto the stage of Souvenir). In an early draft of Flaubert's "Dictionnaire des idées reçues," a whirlpool of petrified and ironized formulaic pronouncements, the swan "chante avant de mourir [sings before dying]."35

At the Romantic roots of Modernism, "the painful side of modern man" enters the interpretive domain through allegorical style and its concomitant intoxications rather than through a view of literary texts as natural organisms open to the assumptions and identities of psychology. In the writings of modernity, dramatic subjectivity (associated with narrative fiction) is slighted in favor of style itself. Lukács's argument against Naturalism maintains the pre-Modernist emphasis on the dramatic narrative of "erzählen"; he praises it at the expense of the descriptive style of "beschreiben," condemned as "fetishistic." Although Lukács uses this label to express his moralizing disapproval, the "fetishism" in question may be taken literally, since what is at stake in the new style(s) of Modernism (as contrasted with the more traditional prose style of "erzählen") is implicated in the relationship between literary language and its object. Is it possible to describe that relationship as a fetishistic one? In other words, is the "object" of Modernist style a fetish-object?

Early in the composition of *Madame Bovary*, Flaubert's developing new aesthetic brought him face to face with a vacuum or an abyss:

> Ce qui me semble beau, ce que je voudrais faire, c'est un livre sur rien, un livre sans attache extérieure, qui se tiendrait de lui-même par la force interne de son style . . . un livre qui n'aurait presque pas de sujet . . . C'est pour cela qu'il n'y a ni beau ni vilains sujets . . . en se posant au point de vue de l'Art pur, qu'il n'y en a aucun. [What seems to me beautiful, what I would like to write, is a book about nothing, a book without external con-

nections, that would be held together by the internal power of its style . . . a book that would have almost no subject. . . . That is why there are neither beautiful nor ugly subjects . . . from the perspective of pure Art, there are none at all.]{36}

Flaubert's "subject" (Lukács's object of description) barely exists: it is almost a negative entity. In the aesthetic of Proust's novel, the described object is uncovered as neither a "self" nor a "lived life," but rather as another non-object, a weave of memory. Fetishism seems to be directed at the ultimate partial object of "beschreiben"—the intransitive act of writing. The fetish of Flaubertian writing is not the object of "beschreiben," but "schreiben" itself: to write. According to Freud, fetishism is linked to the absence of a strategic object. A "fetishism" of modernity is intimately connected with the disappearance of a textual subject/object of writing; without it, the contemporary critic could not imagine any "questions d'écriture."

This aspect of the late Romantic-Symbolist context that links Flaubert, Baudelaire, and Proust is evident in Flaubert's correspondence, where the terms of "écrivain," "style," "faire une phrase," "travailler," "copier," and so on, resonate as elements of the intransitive mode of "to write." At the projected end of their itinerary, interrupted by Flaubert's death, Bouvard and Pécuchet take on a singular resemblance to their creator: *ils copient*. They copy, period—not "as in the past."[37] The status of "ils copient" is related to the role of the *Dictionnaire des idées reçues* within the framework of *Bouvard et Pécuchet*.[38] Without the "comme autrefois," the copying that completes their itinerary substantiates several notes in Flaubert's scenarios[39] indicating that the opinions of Bouvard and Pécuchet are meant to reflect Flaubert's opinions, and that their "copie" includes the *Dictionnaire des idées reçues* [*Dictionary of Clichés*]. In this context, the intransitive mode of Flaubert's ending of the novel seems to have been destined to include a parodic version of the "grande étude du style" pursued by the young writer in the first *Education sentimentale* (236). The absence of an object was so disturbing to the author's niece that she added the reassuring circularity of "just like old times," whereas it was Flaubert's intention that "ils copient" mark the vertiginous cliff-hanging that he himself knew as writing.

The modernist abyss of image and memory is rendered throughout Flaubert's writings. Perhaps it was Baudelaire's own sense of this allegorical aspect that led him to recognize in Emma Bovary a complex, ambivalent character, and a heroine as well, despite her bourgeois limitations. Although Flaubert's declared "object" is "le rien" rather than "the suffering of Emma," her suffering is a representation of the "côté douloureux de l'homme moderne." In addition, the ideal of the impersonal author produces Emma's bourgeois "vulgarity" as a disguise for the lyricism of the writing-speaking subject, "suspendu entre le double abîme du lyrisme et du vulgaire [suspended between the double abyss of lyricism and vulgarity]."[40] The tightrope of writing is suspended beyond the "expression" of subjectivity in the sky of the Flaubertian sublime.

Baudelaire's rendering of the authorial retreat emerges in the extravagant instant of allegory: "Un éclair . . . puis la nuit! [a flash . . . then night!]"[41] The writer fences with invisible words, the passerby dresses in mourning, and the painter or stylist grapples with the subject of modern life or its ineluctable evanescence. The impersonality of the author is the sum of the losses, disappearances, remainders, and ruins that become sublime in the reflection of an ontological absence. The presence of the past has been swallowed by the temporality of the future perfect, and the face of Baudelaire's woman in black has vanished into an echo of "Never!" All that remains is an expressionless skeleton. As in Baudelaire's "Une Charogne," past forms have drifted into memory: "La contemplation d'une femme nue me fait rêver à son squelette. C'est ce qui fait que les spectacles joyeux me rendent triste et que les spectacles tristes m'affectent peu [The contemplation of a naked woman makes me dream of her skeleton. That is why joyous sights make me sad and sad sights do not affect me very much]."[42]

The figure of antiquity inhabits the allegory of modernity. In Baudelaire's "Le Cygne," Andromaque is estranged and impersonalized. Like the swan, she has become a curved figure of emptiness and mourning, an emblem of ecstasy: "Auprès d'un tombeau vide en extase courbée." Transparently layered on the lament of the vanishing city, the account of her losses bears the double mourning of past and present. In "Une Charogne" Baudelaire writes: "Les formes s'effaçaient et n'etaient plus qu'un rêve . . . et que l'artiste achève Seulement par le souvenir [The forms were becoming obliterated and were no more than a dream . . . that the artist achieves Only through memory]."[43] "Le vieux Paris n'est plus [The old Paris is no more]": the lyricism of Baudelaire, Flaubert, and Proust revolves around a monumental absence. The "douleur" associated with it can never be assimilated to the personalized subjectivity displayed in the writings of such influential French Romantics as Chateaubriand or Lamartine.

At the same time, the Baudelairean "éclair" of fleeting and ecstatic vision is placed in a constellation of souvenir, desire, and the instant of rapture associated in the *Confessions* with the untranslatable and invisible source of Augustine's conversion. In his description the soul's vision of invisibilia occurs "in the flash of a trembling glance" ("et peruenit ad id, quod est in ictu trepidantis aspectus").[44] This "éclair" is named as the intoxication of the sublime: "I was not stable in the jouissance of my God, but I was carried toward you by your beauty, and right away violently borne away from you by my weight."[45] What remains after the momentary intoxication is souvenir: "But with me remained your memory (Sed mecum erat memoria tui)."[46]

In Modernist aesthetics, art inhabits the domain of the sacred and draws the artist toward the excesses of sin and purity. It is not by chance that the writings of Modernism so often portray the artist as virgin son, priest, and saint (or as a diabolical figure gifted with supernatural powers). Flaubert writes: "L'art comme une étoile voit la terre rouler sans s'émouvoir: scintillant dans son azur le beau ne se détache pas du ciel [Art like a star observes unmoved the turning of the earth; sparkling in its azure the beautiful does not leave the sky]."[47] He consistently speaks of Art in the same terms Augustine would apply to God. This ideal of the sublime pervades the writings of the Modernist writers in question: "Tout est là, l'amour de l'Art [Everything is in the love of Art]."[48] I am calling this vision the allegory of conversion. It forms the theoretical ground and textual background for the following reading of Flaubert and Proust.

The elements of my reading of scriptural conversion can be schematized in the following terms. Allegory, or the configurations of language that form allegorical style, may be conceived as the relationship between the domain of the speaking subject (the subject of psychoanalysis, or the subject of "the heart" for Flaubert and Proust) and the sublime creation to which he aspires as a writer—Art. The subject is not linked to Art by a mythological necessity or an automatic relation. There is no common measure between speaking subjectivity and the transubstantiations required for beautiful writing. The allegory of conversion reflects the process that transforms the materiality of ordinary language into the shining surface of art.

The early writings of Flaubert and Proust, especially the first *Education sentimentale* and *Jean Santeuil*, are evidence of the gap between the subject and Art. The fact that they abandoned them unfinished is proof of the two writers' realization that the heights of style had not yet been attained. This context may be sketched in the following terms:

1. The writer's desire for Art allows for his or her entry into vocation.

2. The gap between the speaking subject and Art is a mystery that asks the following question: How can the subject attain the sublime? The answer is found in the artist's double conversion: the "convertir" of language into style and the self-reflexive "conversion" of the author's relation to writing.

3. The answer itself is allegory as a mode of representation that inscribes fiction with an account of the writer's "intoxication" and the "otherness" of poetic language. Its aesthetic includes the principles of impersonality, memory, unsentimental interiority, and a revised rhetoric of beauty. With these new criteria, allegory throws a veil over the gap between the subject and Art; its translucence hides and declares the abyss between

them. The veil is an allegorical image for the work of art, as I will show later in the context of Salammbô and Albertine. In contrast to the early Romantic theory of the symbol and its celebration of art as an organic and natural creation, the process of Modernism makes it clear that Art cannot be assimilated to an outgrowth or extension of subjectivity's heart.

The translucent veil of allegory is the irreducible otherness of language as style. In the writings of Flaubert and Proust, figures of the veil of figuration proliferate, indicating that the "open sesame" of art requires some sleight of hand in addition to a heart full of desire. For this reason, desire is blocked at every turn; without blockage, there would be no possibility for the sublime. Without impersonality, lyricism cannot become art: without forgetting, memory cannot become revelation; without fiction, the "I" may not speak its truth. Covered with the beautiful hieroglyphs and colors of artifice, shining with the translucence of vocation, the scriptural veil articulates the writer's relation to the sublime in the allegory of conversion.

4

Necropolis and Carnival: Monuments and Masks of Style

At the heights of revelation in Proust's novel, the beautiful view of style locates the writer's investment and his fictionalized "theory of art" in the ecstatic discovery at the matinée. Ecstasy moves the narrator outside himself. The inside/outside dialectic of life and art is translated from the narrator's experience before the matinée to the "new" framework of his projected vocation. In the "oeuvre à venir," it will take the form of a new style.[1] The narrator's aesthetic includes a constellation of terms and effects that revolve around the modern allegory common to Baudelaire and Flaubert. Outside fiction and the narrator's intoxications, this aesthetic finds a counterpart in Proust's criticism. Most of the parallels to Baudelaire and Flaubert in *A la recherche* hover between the lines, but the sustained and explicit self-reflexive criticism written near the end of Proust's life reveals his investment in their nineteenth-century Modernist style. Allegorical representation masks the authorial identity and banishes personalized sentiment through the effects and voices of memory: it makes "the history of a whole life" into the story of style, or the allegory of conversion that will allow me to interpret the fiction of Flaubert and Proust through their relationship to writing.

In Proust's double inheritance, Baudelaire's aesthetics of poetry filters into the novel through Flaubert. As a work of fiction, Proust's novel of vocation draws on the lessons of *Madame Bovary*, *Salammbô*, and so on, and perhaps it draws on *L'Education sentimentale* most of all, because of its explicit translation of ecstasy into style. Proust's subtle strategy of vocation moves away from Baudelaire's predetermined "réminiscences" (III, 920); the narrator's momentous conversion toward writing translates impressions into the weave of style through an unforeseen "coup" (920) of chance. The belated workings of "involuntary memory" accompany the menacing effects of time on the "figurants" (the extras and spectators) of the most allegorical scene found in twentieth-century French fiction, the "matinée chez la Princesse de Guermantes." The "involontaire" of memory and time itself echoes Flaubert's sense of melancholic "fatality"; like Madame Arnoux at the end of *L'Education sentimentale*, the figures of allegory let down their gray hair and reveal the truth about themselves.

What is at stake in an assessment of Proust's attentive reading of Flaubert (and Baudelaire) is not so much the possibility of tracing the intertextual evidence of influences for the sake of the inevitable reductive formulae of literary history, but rather the understanding of an aesthetic of translation. Proust's essay anchors its aesthetic in Flaubert's "translation" of matter into style. Translation becomes the counterpart of Baudelaire's *correspondance*: the symbolic resonance of style and the sublime clasping of sensory/sensual elements anticipate the layers of material "reality" and symbolic meaning that add up to allegorical representation (I, 82).

This representation includes an account of ecstasy. According to medieval religious vocabulary, the subject is literally transported outside the self, "ravi en extase." In the Romantic vocabulary, ravishment includes the violent and sexual meaning of "ravir" and the interior transports of mystical "extase." The terms are definitively blurred in the interiorized flights of imagination (described as "ivresse," "emportement," "extravagance," and "félicité") constructed by Baudelaire and Flaubert. According to Proust's essay, "sensation" and "souvenir" are clasped together in a felicity or ravishment integral to the effect of beautiful style; syntax, the surface of things, and temporality are the elements that translate the ordinary imperfections of language into the "eternal." The reading of translation opens the door to another form of translation: how does reading turn into writing? In Proust's own words, how does "conclusion" become "incitement"? The answer to the question of how Flaubert's eternity of style is translated into Proust's aesthetic may be found in "A Propos du 'style' de Flaubert."

The Grammar of Translation

The term of translation anchors the reading of Flaubert's style in Proust's stylistic principles. At the heart of the Proustian aesthetic, translation is the act that turns reading into writing. Characteristic of allegory, translation is the "other" of language, the inscription of sensation as *correspondance*, and the abrupt signification of Giotto's Charity: she enters the narrator's universe as a gift from the Other whose name is Swann. Translation becomes a kind of code word for the layers of meaning and the play between inscription and image that characterize allegory: through *correspondance*, synesthesia, analogy, and metaphor, it informs the essence of Proust's style. Its self-reflexive aesthetic focus enters the reading of Flaubert and doubles it, in a new series of echoes that mark Flaubert's writing as an aesthetic and stylistic inheritance, a privileged object of translation.

A reading of Proust's essay reveals that a style characterized by continuity without gaps or intervals and by musicality of poetic effect is central to the writings of both authors.

(1) *Grammar*. Proust's initial opposition between his view of style and the view ascribed to Flaubert introduces a tacit parallelism between metaphor and syntax. Metaphor infuses style with eternity; it turns style into a continuous, endless medium for Proustian vision. Syntax translates Flaubertian vision into an endless "trottoir roulant" of writing:

> Je crois que la métaphore seule peut donner une sorte d'éternité au style, et il n'y a peut-être pas dans tout Flaubert une seule belle métaphore. . . . Mais enfin la métaphore n'est pas tout le style. Et il n'est pas possible à quiconque est un jour monté sur ce grand *Trottoir roulant* que sont les pages de Flaubert, au défilement continu, monotone, morne, indéfini, de méconnaître qu'elles sont sans précédent dans la littérature. [I believe that meta-

phor alone can give a kind of eternity to style, and in all of Flaubert, perhaps, there is not a single beautiful metaphor. . . . But after all, style is not just metaphor. And it is not possible that anyone who once stepped onto the great *moving Sidewalk* of Flaubert's pages, with their continuous, monotonous, bleak, indefinite procession, could fail to recognize that these pages are without a precedent in literature.] (CSB 586–87)

What makes style "eternal"—what allows it to survive beyond the destructive claims of fashion, period, or history? Proust's answer is metaphor. If "the temporal limits of human life" are substituted for "style," then this question and its answer point toward the fictional and aesthetic focus of *A la recherche du temps perdu*. In Proust's reading of Flaubert, however, the answer to the question is found not in a rhetorical figure, but in grammar itself: "Sans doute cette beauté pouvait tenir parfois à la manière d'appliquer certaines règles de syntaxe [No doubt this beauty sometimes came from the way in which certain rules of syntax were applied]" (CSB 587). Flaubert's syntactic inventions serve to guarantee "l'étroite, l'hermétique continuité du style [the narrow and hermetic continuity of style]" and "le rythme régulier particulier à Flaubert [the regular rhythm specific to Flaubert]" (CSB 588).

Flaubert's rigorous continuity without intervals or interruptions moves in the direction of an objectivity or impersonality of style that would seem inimical to Proust's writing. At this point, however, Proust unfolds a paradox that will ultimately overthrow the traditional opposition between the two writers. The more Flaubert eliminates resonances or traces of a personal nature from his style, the more he allows his own personality to define itself and make him into . . . Flaubert:

> Le rendu de sa vision, sans, dans l'intervalle, un mot d'esprit ou un trait de sensibilité, voilà en effet ce qui importe de plus en plus à Flaubert au fur et à mesure qu'il dégage mieux sa personnalité et devient Flaubert. [The rendering of his vision, without, in the intervals, a stroke of wit or sensibility, that is what is more and more

important to Flaubert as he gradually draws out his own personality and becomes Flaubert.] (CSB 588)

(2) *Leveling*. The artistic rendering of Flaubert's vision or the emergence of Flaubert's "personality" in his writing takes the form of an impressionist subjectivity. Proust's judgment counters the label of "objectivity" placed on Flaubert by literary criticism; at the same time, it indicates a paradox inherent in the inscriptions of indirect autobiography that occupy the stage of some prominent Modernist texts. In the intricate weave of writing, the unilateral "subject" of psychological subjectivity loses the psychologist's clear-cut forms. The "objective" and "subjective" categories of authorial and personal identity may not be valid for the particular economy of a specific writer.

The account of Flaubert's evolution toward impressionist subjectivity seems to recapitulate some of Proust's development from early fiction to *A la recherche du temps perdu*. *Les Plaisirs et les jours* and *Jean Santeuil* employ traditional devices (including a non-autobiographical presentation of fiction, use of the third person, and "objective" narration of action) that later disappear in the overflow of interiority that brings the author's early attempts to fruition in *A la recherche*. Lukács's dichotomy between narration and description is predated by Proust's contrast between action and impression:

> Ce qui jusqu'à Flaubert était action devient impression. Les choses ont autant de vie que les hommes . . . dans l'impression première que nous recevons. . . . Le subjectivisme de Flaubert s'exprime par un emploi nouveau des temps des verbes, des prépositions, des adverbes, les deux derniers n'ayant . . . qu'une valeur rythmique. [That which until Flaubert was action becomes impression. Things have as much life as people . . . in the first impression that we receive. . . . Flaubert's subjectivism is expressed through a new usage of verb tense, prepositions, adverbs, and the value of the latter two is solely rhythmic.] (CSB 588–89)

The subjective rendering of impressions produced by "cette vision continue, homogène [this continuous, homogeneous vision]" takes the form of a description or a descriptive image of an illusion (CSB 589). Proust's novel recapitulates the leveling effect that simultaneously distances the object of description and operates from inside the intimate domain of the subject's impression: the narrator is the subject of memory, not narrated events. His past impressions are the imagistic object of subjective description; at the same time, they are distanced from his persona by the course of time and the absence of narrated action.

(3) *Eternal imperfect.* In the Proustian epithet of "éternel," (1) and (2) unite to form a common stylistic ground between the two writers. What gives eternity to style? Flaubert's answer is syntax, particularly an original use of verb tense. In Proust's terms, eternity is linked to a textual continuity without intervals; it bears impression or described illusion rather than action. Away from the ravages of habitual time, the vision of eternity is a stylistic reinvention of temporality. To illustrate the "'illusion à décrire,'" Proust discloses the stylistic kernel of Flaubert's new vision, the "eternal imperfect":

> Cet éternel imparfait, composé en partie des paroles des personnages que Flaubert rapporte habituellement en style indirect pour qu'elles se confondent avec le reste . . . donc, cet imparfait, si nouveau dans la littérature, change entièrement l'aspect des choses et des êtres. [This eternal imperfect, partly composed of characters' spoken words that Flaubert habitually reports in indirect style so that they melt into the rest . . . this imperfect, so new in literature, completely changes the look of things and beings.] (CSB 590)

Proust's efforts to unfold the particular relation between style and a writer's vision bring Flaubertian stylistics into the arena of interpretation. Rendered in a new form of syntactic continuity, subjectivity contains its own secret distance from the impression revealed as "an illusion to describe." The "eternal imperfect" goes beyond the limits of human time into the visionary mode of an "indefinite past": this description of Flaubert's style could also be applied to the subjectivity of the Proustian narrator. His nostalgia, vision, and memory occupy the hundreds of pages shaped by Proust's beautiful metaphors, the stylistic eternity that allows truth to elude time.

A la recherche du temps perdu is marked by the melancholy sadness of the narrator who perceives the corrosive effects of time. According to the knot of temporality woven through the text, the ruins of time have been seen in an unspecified past; he watches his illusions crumble into dust. The startling image Proust uses to illustrate the effect of Flaubert's "éternel imparfait" may be deciphered through melancholy:

> Donc cet imparfait . . . change entièrement l'aspect des choses et des êtres, comme font une lampe qu'on a déplacée, l'arrivée dans une maison nouvelle, l'ancienne si elle est presque vide et qu'on est en plein déménagement. C'est ce genre de tristesse, fait de la rupture des habitudes et de l'irréalité du décor, que donne le style de Flaubert, ce style si nouveau quand ce ne serait que par là. [Thus this imperfect . . . completely changes the appearance of things and beings, like a lamp that you have moved to a different spot, the arrival in a new house, the old one if it is almost empty and you are in the middle of moving out. Flaubert's style, so highly original even if it were limited to this single aspect, offers this kind of sadness, caused by a break in habits and an unreal setting.] (CSB 590)

Proust's intriguing evocation of the "éternel imparfait" locates it both inside and outside time. The "passé indéfini" seems to recreate temporality from the viewpoint of eternity, beyond continuity: the eternal vision of time is an infinite series of ruins or an unending spiral of passages. Proust's image is reminiscent of the narrator's exodus through the night with Saint-Loup, guided by "la colonne lumineuse qui guida les Hébreux [the pillar of fire that guided the Hebrews]" (II, 400). This perspective was opened by the narrator's melancholic vision. Alone in the new apartment, at a textual moment layered with beginnings and endings, he weeps on a dusty roll of carpets: "pareil aux Juifs qui se couvraient la tête de cendres dans le deuil, je me mis à sangloter [like the Jews who would cover their heads with ashes in mourning, I began to sob]" (II, 392). In the essay on Flaubert, it is precisely this melancholia that is seen as the major effect of Flaubert's prose, except that the Judaic reference to passage and mourning is silenced. For Proust, the "eternal" element of literary style captures the temporality of death, ruins, ritual mourning, and melancholic sadness: style creates time and overcomes it through the eternal dimension of its consecrated form.

(4) *Life story*. Through the temporality of style, then, (1), (2), and (3) come together. Flaubert's "eternal imperfect" is taken up by Proust's eternity of metaphor in a musical continuity without intervals; action becomes impression, objective narration becomes the "subjectivisme" of an "illusion à décrire." Unlike later critics, Proust emphasizes Flaubert's use of the imperfect rather than the "style indirect libre [free indirect style]," since the latter is only one form of the "eternal imperfect." In a sentence that tacitly emphasizes the parallel between Flaubert and *A la recherche*, Proust writes: "Cet imparfait sert à rapporter non seulement les paroles mais toute la vie des gens [This imperfect is used to relate not only the words spoken by people but their whole lives]" (CSB 590). Beyond time and action, the writer's temporal focus takes him toward a descriptive image of a fictional past tense. It is consecrated as a dream, an illusion, a ruin: "*L'Education sentimentale* est un long rapport de toute une vie, sans que les personnages prennent pour ainsi dire une part active à l'action [*The Sentimental Education* is a long report of a whole lifetime, so to speak without the active participation of the characters in the action]" (CSB 590). By emphasizing "a long account of a whole lifetime" in Flaubert's novels, Proust angles Flaubert's "subjectivisme" in the direction of the *Recherche*. Proust's fictional autobiography enters the domain of the "eternal imperfect" through the rendering of a life from childhood to premature old age and the anticipation of death. Although the biographical curve is not always present in Flaubert's

fiction, the vision translated by syntax and the altered surface or appearance of things compensates for its absence in a style that is both distant and subjective.

(5) *Color*. Proust focuses on Flaubert's vision in terms of its stylistic images. His use of the imperfect tense spreads to the definite past in a constellation of lights and half-tones, the colors of the writer's palette: "Quelquefois même, dans le plan incliné et tout en demi-teinte des imparfaits, le présent de l'indicatif opère un redressement, met un furtif éclairage de plein jour qui distingue des choses qui passent d'une réalité plus durable [Sometimes, in fact, in the sloping surface all in half-tones of the imperfects, the indicative present produces a straightening effect, provides a fleeting daylight illumination that separates passing things from a reality that endures]." (CSB 591). The half-tones of the Flaubertian image recall a remark made earlier in the article: "Jacques Blanche a dit que dans l'histoire de la peinture, une invention, une nouveauté, se décèlent souvent en un simple rapport de ton, en deux couleurs juxtaposées [Jacques Blanche remarked that in the history of painting, an invention, an innovation, is often revealed in a mere tonal relation, in two colors side by side]" (CSB 589). The writer's vision appears through the paihter's image.

Although Proust's term of vision includes the painterly aspect of style, the reader of *A la recherche* senses the metaphorical translation (or *correspondance*) of sensory visual perception into the terms of a thoroughly mystical revelation of truth. Invisible elements (unknown keys to the sublime, the scandalous, the beautiful, and the true) draw vision out of the visual world and into a specifically and irreducibly written style; it sublates the painterly quality of vision within a scriptural vision of Baudelairean *correspondance*. It could be argued, however, that the "question of writing" asked and answered by "la vision" is anchored in Flaubert's use of sensory vision as the source of style. The visual element is emphasized in all of Flaubert's mature writings, including his correspondence and the *Voyages*.

During the period when he wrote *Madame Bovary* many of Flaubert's formulations of style revolved around sensory vision:

"le style étant à lui tout seul une manière absolue de voir les choses [Style alone being an absolute way of seeing things]."[2] He describes the essence of artistry in the following terms: "Mais il faut avoir la faculté de se la *faire sentir*. Cette faculté n'est autre que le génie: *voir*, avoir le modèle devant soi, qui pose [But one must have the faculty of making oneself *feel* it. This talent is none other than genius: *seeing*, having the model stand before you, posing]."[3] The artist's model is imaginary and must be seen: "avoir la faculté de travailler d'après un modèle imaginaire qui pose devant nous. Quand on le voit bien, on le rend [Having the ability to work from an imaginary model posing in front of us. When one sees it well, one can render it]."[4] Years later, in November 1866, Flaubert writes the following in a famous letter to Hippolyte Taine: "L'image intéressée est pour moi aussi vraie que la réalité objective des choses. . . . L'intuition artistique ressemble en effet aux hallucinations hypnagogiques— . . . ça vous passe devant les yeux [The image in question is as true for me as the objective reality of things. . . . Artistic intuition actually resembles hypnagogic hallucination— . . . it passes before your eyes]."[5]

The emphasis on vision in style takes a specific painterly form as layers of color. He comments on Part I of *Madame Bovary*: "Si c'est réussi, ce sera, je crois, très fort, car c'est peindre couleur sur couleur et sans tons tranchés (ce qui est plus aisé) [If it is successful, I think it will be very fine, since it is painted color on color without distinct tones (which is easier)]."[6] Flaubert's figure of painting colors that blend together imperceptibly corresponds to Proust's figures of masonry, continuity without intervals, and solidity: "Chez lui . . . on sent le besoin de la solidité, fût-elle un peu massive, par réaction contre une littérature sinon creuse, du moins très légère, dans laquelle trop d'interstices, de vides, s'insinuaient [In his writing, . . . one feels the need for solidity, even if it were a little bit massive, in reaction against a literature that is at the least very lightweight, if not empty, and mined by too many interstices and gaps]" (CSB 593). Proust analyzes the stylistic continuity achieved through syntax, the unique Flaubertian palette: "les singularités immuables d'une syntaxe déformante [the immutable singularities of a disfiguring syntax]" (CSB 593).

Where does Proust locate the result or effect of Flaubert's syntax? Grammar translates artistic vision into the subtle coloration of beauty, "la beauté de son style" (CSB 593). The beauty that sparks Bergotte's revelation of style in *A la recherche* transports him from the painted image to the written one: "il aurait fallu passer plusieurs couches de couleur, rendre ma phrase en elle-même précieuse, comme ce petit pan de mur jaune [it would have required painting several layers of color to render my sentence precious in itself, like this little panel of yellow wall]" (III, 187). I will return later to this crucial moment in the novel when Bergotte undergoes an ecstatic revelation. He enters Proust's ultimate mystery of style and dies a mystical death. The process that leads the writer from sensory vision through color to written style is rooted in the fortuitousness of *mémoire involontaire*. According to the aesthetic of *A la recherche*, this form of memory is miraculous. Neither automatic nor predetermined by exterior causes, it echoes Flaubert's description of the fortuitous or unpredictable relation between sensory and artistic vision. He criticizes the poetry of Lacaussade:

> Une réflexion esthétique m'est surgie de ce vol[ume]: combien peu l'élément extérieur sert! Ces vers-là ont été faits sous l'équateur et l'on n'y sent pas plus de chaleur ni de lumière que dans un brouillard d'Ecosse. C'est en Hollande seulement et à Venise, patrie des brumes, qu'il y a eu de grands coloristes! [Out of this volume an aesthetic reflection came to me: the exterior element is of so little use! This verse was written under the equator and one does not feel any more heat or light than in a Scottish fog. Only in Holland and Venice, homeland of haze, were there great colorists!][7]

Flaubert's vision of beauty comes from within. Beauty created by the artist cannot be equated with or compared to the "objective" realm, often referred to as "reality."

(6) *Singular vision*. Proust describes Flaubert's inner vision as

an "interior ideal." The artist's aesthetic ideal cannot be considered in the naturalist terms of historical precision or the objective "reality" championed by Zola and others. In the letter to Colet quoted above, Flaubert seems to subsume the "exterior element" to another, more obscure reality—a vision of beauty produced by the all-important faculty of the imagination. For both writers, beauty and truth are internalized. Their emergence as what Proust calls "la réalité" constitutes the writing of interiority: "je me suis toujours efforcé d'aller dans l'âme des choses [I have always forced myself to enter the heart of things]."[8] Proust's "great writers" are subject to "l'obéissance absolue à l'idéal intérieur, obscur [absolute obedience to an interior obscure ideal]" (CSB 592). The writer "doit se modeler sur une réalité tyrannique à laquelle il ne lui est pas permis de changer quoi que ce soit [must model himself on a tyrannical reality in which he is not allowed to change anything]" (CSB 592). The great artist "volontairement laisse la réalité s'épanouir dans ses livres [voluntarily allows reality to bloom in his books]" (CSB 593).

Proust's statements concerning the "interior ideal" as reality indicate the common ground of his vocabulary of aesthetic imagination with the Flaubertian vocabulary: "Y a-t-il dans leurs yeux des larmes de joie devant le Beau? . . . la Poésie, qui est *une manière de voir*, n'arrive à ses résultats extérieurs que par une conviction enthousiaste du Vrai [Do they have tears of joy in their eyes before the Beautiful? . . . Poetry, which is a *way of seeing*, only attains external results through the enthusiastic conviction of the True]."[9] The concept of "la Poésie" constructed in this quotation seems to anticipate Proust's evocation (or invocation) of "la réalité." Both terms implicate an ideal interior form of imagination within the territory of truth. This constellation gives rise to "le seul livre vrai [the only true book]," anticipated by the narrator of the *Recherche*, the exemplary writer-to-be.

Flaubert consistently identifies perfection in art with the interiority of feeling or sentiment: "*Il faut sentir* [*One must feel*]."[10] This concept of interiority is not personalized, however; it casts a shadow over the individual artist's self-consciousness:

"Tâchez donc de ne plus *vivre en vous* [Try to stop *living in yourself*]" he writes to a writer seeking advice.[11] In the same letter, the life of "l'Art" is defined as "la recherche incessante du Vrai rendu par le Beau [the unremitting search for the True rendered by the Beautiful]."[12] The artist's personality must be veiled, repressed, and silenced. Although the artist cannot create without intense sentiment, the "axiom" he attempts to inculcate in Colet is "qu'il n'y a rien de plus faible que de mettre en art ses sentiments personnels . . . L'art . . . doit rester suspendu dans l'infini, complet en lui-même, indépendant de son producteur [that there is nothing weaker than putting one's personal sentiments into art. . . . Art . . . must remain suspended in the infinite, complete in itself, independent of its maker]."[13] Proust's comments on Flaubert's rendering of reality as an impression—unburdened by the interventions of wit, sentiment, causal explanation, reasoning, and so on—gravitate to the term of "vision," an interiority that portrays reality without making itself visible. Like the mystics, the Flaubertian visionary is wholly centered in an interiority that cannot be identified as a psychological entity.

Throughout the correspondence, Flaubert indicates that the discovery of the paradoxical nature of artistic interiority separates his youthful attempts from his later achievements. The interior ideal aims at capturing reality in terms that can never be reduced to psychology's infamous "self-expression." At the same time, reality is rendered as "impression." In Proust's discussion of Flaubert's style, the terms of objectivity and subjectivity take on a new light in view of an "idéal intérieur" shared by both writers. Proust's description of the real as "effectivement subi ou matériellement manié [effectively suffered or materially handled]" (1, 82) seems to apply equally well to Flaubert's style as to the beauty of Giotto's Charity.[14] The description of the fresco and "La Charité de Giotto" occurs early in *A la recherche* as a prelude to the narrator's initiation into the world of reading, writing, and aesthetic beauty; it provides the framework for Proust's first explicit reference to allegory in the novel. It sets the fictional stage for the allegorical style that unfolds the text from the memories of *Combray* through the aesthetic principles of vocation in *Le Temps retrouvé*.

In the article on Flaubert, Proust's image of weight and materiality connected to the obscure, painful burden of "the real" comes into relief as style. Its elements include regularity of rhythm, syntactic solidity, heaviness and even vulgarity of expression: "Mais nous les aimons ces lourds matériaux que la phrase de Flaubert soulève et laisse retomber avec le bruit intermittent d'un excavateur [But we love them, these heavy materials that Flaubert's sentence picks up and drops with the intermittent noise of a digging machine]" (CSB 594). The tyranny of the interior ideal indicates the impossibility of separating "the real" from what Proust defines as style; his remarks reformulate Flaubert's well-known declarations concerning the inseparable nature of form and content.[15]

Substantiated in the writings of both authors, Proust's interpretation of style demonstrates the falseness of the psychologically based opposition between Proust's "subjectivity" and Flaubert's "objectivity." When Proust alludes to these operative categories, they appear to be as inseparable as the terms of form and content. A single vision of style takes the place of an opposition between subjective and objective. What Proust designates as "subjectivisme" would seem to be a result of Flaubert's relentless attempt to eliminate a personal and lyrical authorial presence from writing; style is articulated as a conflation of the real and the ideal. In this context, Proust's observation points toward a new conception of interiority: Flaubert offers an "impression" instead of judgment or action, and a vision rendered as an "illusion à décrire."[16]

(7) *Ecstasis*. The "idéal intérieur" gives rise to style—voiced sentences, obsessive rhythm, and "les coupes du maitre [the caesuras of the master]" (CSB 594). Proust's interpretation of Flaubert's interior vision points toward the direct and most literal effects of his mastery. In the spiral of reading and writing, the master's voice is repeated by the reader's "interior voice": "le chant que j'entendais en moi [the song that I was hearing in myself]" (CSB 594). The ultimate effect of the "idéal intérieur" seems to be "Flaubertian intoxication"—the invol-

untary reproduction of the master's original voice through style. Proust's "intoxication flaubertienne" sketches out a moment of rapturous vision that transmits style from writer to reader. In order for the reader to transcend authorial mastery (to gain access to his or her own originality of style), he must "faire un pastiche volontaire, pour pouvoir, après cela, redevenir original, ne pas faire toute sa vie du pastiche involontaire [write a voluntary pastiche, in order to become original again afterward, and not to write involuntary pastiche for life]" (CSB 594). Proust's early pastiches of Flaubert and other writers are well known; his essay on Flaubert is the only text that contains a theory of pastiche. The essay analyzes or interprets the elements of style *transcribed* ("transcrire" [CSB 595]) by pastiche—an act of "recréation vivante," a reprise of literary creation, "inconsciemment produit [unconsciously produced]" like the original vision (CSB 595, 592). In this framework, "transcrire" sounds very much like "traduire," the key term of Proust's vision of reading and writing. Through *correspondance*, synaesthesia, metaphor, allegory, and the narrator's aesthetic theory, this vision unfolds the *Recherche*.

Proust compares the master's intoxicated victims to "ces malheureux des légendes allemandes qui sont condamnés à vivre pour toujours attachés au battant d'une cloche [those unfortunates of German legends who are condemned to live forever attached to the tongue of a bell]" (CSB 594). Tied to the rhythm and song of the master's voice, they perpetuate it through involuntary pastiche. Its antidote is the writer's voluntary reproduction of the master's style. It plays out the rapture of Flaubert's stylistic effect interiorized and "transcribed" by the reader:

> Quand on vient de finir un livre, non seulement on voudrait continuer à vivre avec ses personnages, avec Mme de Beauséant, avec Frédéric Moreau, mais encore notre voix intérieure qui a été disciplinée, pendant toute la durée de la lecture à suivre le rythme d'un Balzac, d'un Flaubert, voudrait continuer à parler comme eux. [When one has just finished a book, not only would one

like to continue living with its characters, with Mme de Beauséant, with Frédéric Moreau, but also our interior voice which has been disciplined, for the entire duration of reading, to follow the rhythm of a Balzac, a Flaubert, would like to continue speaking like them.] (CSB 594)

The other form of the "intoxication flaubertienne" might be a rapture of style interiorized by Flaubert himself as an "idéal intérieur." Its effect on the reader must be cured, writes Proust, by "la vertu purgative, exorcisante, du pastiche [the purgative, exorcising virtue of pastiche]" (CSB 594). His early pastiche, the "recréation vivante" (CSB 595), exorcises Flaubertian intoxication, but it also reveals Proust's complicity with the double of "l'intoxication flaubertienne," the rapture that Flaubert captures within style. The declared negative effect of "intoxication" is treated by the act of writing pastiche; its text is haunted by the complicity of double intoxication. Pastiche points in two directions—to moments in Flaubert's texts where rapture enters fiction, and to Proust's "transcription"/ "recréation" of rapture. The spiral of reading and writing emerges as a kind of autobiography of style.

"L'Affaire Lemoine par Gustave Flaubert"[17] reflects a specific Flaubertian rapture of style, confirmed by Proust's double intoxication and its eventual incorporation in his writing. This pastiche illustrates the major aspects of style discussed in "A Propos du 'style' de Flaubert," including rhythmic innovation of syntax, musical continuity, "l'éternel imparfait," "la beauté des phrases ternaires [the beauty of ternary sentences]," and descriptive "subjectivisme." Proust renders Flaubertian interiority through an evocation of an endless "plaidoirie [address to the Court]" followed by a description of the "douceur des rêves [sweetness of dreams]" imagined and mourned by members of the audience.

The portrayal of rapture in the pastiche underscores the singularly beautiful effects of Flaubert's style that resonate in the "rythme obsesseur [obsessive rhythm]" of "le chant que j'entendais en moi [the song that I heard in myself]." Proust, the attentive reader, is temporarily "attaché au battant d'une cloche"; to detach himself from the sound of the Flaubertian bell, he will temporarily "laisser la pédale prolonger le son, c'est-à-dire faire un pastiche volontaire [allow the pedal to lengthen the sound, that is, to make a voluntary pastiche]." In other words, he must keep Flaubert's resonance within his own "interior voice" (CSB 594). The Proustian rapture that casts a shadow from the wings sets the aesthetic scene for privileged moments of voice and silence, the traces of ecstasy in Flaubert's texts.

The bell that sounds in Flaubert's novels at meditative or ecstatic moments can be heard in Proust's first sentence: "une cloche tinta [a bell rang]" (CSB 12). When Emma Bovary's funeral takes place, "La cloche tintait [The bell was ringing]."[18] In a situation reminiscent of Edgar-Lagardy's performance of "Lucia di Lammermoor,"[19] Proust takes note of a voluptuousness that often radiates from Flaubert's female characters. Emma is aroused by the singer's passionate Mediterranean expressivity, while Proust's Nathalie, listening to Lemoine's lawyer with his "accent méridional [southern French accent]," his "appel aux passions généreuses [appeal to generous passions]" (CSB 141), "ressentait ce trouble où conduit l'éloquence: une douceur l'envahit . . . [felt the agitation aroused by eloquence; a sweetness invaded her . . .]" (CSB 14). The pastiche incorporates other moments of ecstatic voice and silence. "Une cloche dont la vibration persiste [A bell with a persistent vibration]" (CSB 13) recalls the moment of Frédéric's "frissons de l'âme [shiverings of the heart]" in L'Education sentimentale: "A l'horloge d'une église, une heure sonna, lentement, pareille à une voix qui l'eût appelé [At the clock of a church one o'clock sounded, slowly, like a voice that might have been calling him]."[20] The ecstatic death of Félicité in Un Coeur simple enters Proust's parody as the parrot cum Holy Spirit adored by Flaubert's character. It lands on a Proustian hat: "une dame enleva son chapeau. Un perroquet le surmontait [A lady took off her hat. A parrot topped it]" (CSB 13). The second half of the pastiche is focused on dreams of riches laid at the feet of a woman, and dreamers "prêts à défaillir [ready to swoon]" (CSB 15). Proust's insistence on "rêve [dream]" and "défaillir [swooning]" explicitly recalls *L'Education sentimentale*.

While "rêve" and "défaillir" register key terms in Flaubert's writing, they also indicate the rapturous effect of his stylistic achievement. According to his correspondence, it plays a decisive role in shaping Flaubert's style. Moments of ecstasy blur the borderlines of consciousness and identity as they intensify perception of those boundaries through mystical images. These moments prefigure and anticipate elements of style; at times, they are reenacted as the stylistic effect that recapitulates or captures them. Flaubert's rapture of "rêve" and "défaillir" includes the following elements: a Romantic idealization, presented in the vocabulary of the fantasmatic and the sublime; a heightened consciousness that is encoded as a voluptuous swoon or vertigo; and the vision of a voice that makes itself heard through and beyond silence as a mark of vocation.

These elements are present in Proust's representation of Flaubert's style. The rapture of "rêve"/"défaillir" and its erotic focus on a woman who offers "le secret de son baiser et la douceur de son corps [the secret of her kiss and the sweetness of her body]" in exchange for the suitor's "wealth" indicate the path traced in *A la recherche du temps perdu*. In this paragraph of the pastiche, Proust inscribes his debt to *L'Education sentimentale* through an homage to what he later quotes in his essay (CSB 595) as an extraordinary rendering of temporality. It follows "la chose la plus belle de *L'Education sentimentale* [the most beautiful thing in *The Sentimental Education*]" (CSB 595)—"un blanc [a blank space]": "Ils auraient connu le cri du pétrel, la venue des brouillards, l'oscillation des navires, le développement des nuées . . . [They would have known the call of the petrel, the coming of fogs, the oscillation of ships, the development of storm clouds . . .]" (CSB 15). The two bunches of flowers ("deux grappes de fleurs violettes, descendant . . . le long d'un mur rouge qui s'effritait [two clusters of violet flowers, descending . . . the length of a crumbling red wall]") that emblematize the moment of daydreaming in Proust's pastiche will make a return appearance in a passage of *A la recherche* that echoes the rapturous element of *L'Education sentimentale*. The narrator sees "grappes de fleurs sombres [clusters of dark flowers]" while walking along the "côté des Guermantes": "Je rêvais que Mme de Guermantes m'y faisait venir . . . elle me montrait, le long des murs bas, les fleurs qui y appuient leurs quenouilles violettes et rouges et m'apprenait leurs noms [I dreamed that Mme de Guermantes was bringing me there . . . along the low walls, she was showing me the flowers that lean their violet and red distaffs against them and she was teaching me their names]" (I, 72).

The reader of Proust's version of a "sentimental education" (a title that he describes as "beau par sa solidité [beautiful for its solidity]," and equally suitable for *Madame Bovary* [CSB 588]) recognizes the fantasized female protagonist as one in a long series of love objects. She is the focus of rapture, the recipient of erotic attentions, overwhelming gifts, the narrator's fortune, his health and happiness, and so on. The comic aspects of the parody do not detract from Proust's veiled declaration of his debt to Flaubert's vision.

The pastiche uncovers the foundations of Flaubert's style and the double-edged intoxication that is its cause and effect: several moments of the pastiche transcribe the aesthetic principles of the Flaubertian sublime, formulated in Proust's letter on style. Voices represent and transcend silence; interiorized, they transform the silence of "subjectivisme" or inexpressible, rapturous impressions into a musical beautiful prose. The call of those voices enters the region of the sublime, far beyond the domain of human "bêtise [stupidity]," "idées reçues [clichés]," and social communication. In all of Flaubert's writings (including the satirical *Bouvard et Pécuchet* as well as the more romantic renderings of vocation in his novels, stories, travel journals, and correspondence) the call of the beautiful and the sublime can only be heard by the character(s) playing the writer's role. In "À Propos du 'style' de Flaubert," a remark made in another context evokes Flaubert's mysterious representation of silence through voice: "Pour exprimer d'une façon qu'il croit évidemment ravissante, dans la plus parfaite de ses oeuvres, le silence qui régnait dans le château de Julien, il dit que 'l'on entendait le frôlement d'une écharpe ou l'écho d'un soupir' [To express in a way that he obviously believes to be ravishing, in the most perfect of his works, the silence reigning in Julien's castle, he says that 'one heard the light rustle of a scarf or the echo of a sigh']" (CSB 587). The distant echo, the wind-borne resonance of bells that Proust skims from conversation between Frédéric and Mme Arnoux in the same paragraph, are more common examples in Flaubert's Romantic code of the phenomenon of eloquent silence, ripe with the fruits of the sublime—love, memory, vocation, and rapture (the "ravishing" expression). Proust pinpoints this phenomenon in the discourse of Werner's lawyer: "'Par moments, la monotonie de son discours était telle qu'il ne se distinguait plus du silence, comme une cloche dont la vibration persiste, comme un écho qui s'affaiblit [At times the monotony of his speech was such that it could not be distinguished from silence, like a bell with a vibration that persists, like an echo that grows weak]" (CSB 13).

The Flaubertian sublime and the intoxication that crowns it inhabit Proust's vision. Like the letter on style written years later, the pastiche is double-edged, since its diagnosis of Flaubertian rapture uncovers the same intoxication of style in the critics' writing. The persistent vibration of a monotonous discourse that has become indistinguishable from silence, Proust's pastiche of the "plaidoirie" aptly describes the interiorized narration of *A la recherche du temps perdu*. At the same time the parodic critique of bourgeois society is an important element of external observation in the works of both authors. It takes the form of endless speeches that doom their speakers to the condemnation of the invisible judge, the author himself: "l'élégance des formules atténuait l'âpreté du réquisitoire [the elegance of the formulations attenuated the harshness of the indictment]" (CSB 13). The pastiche invests Werner's lawyer with Flaubertian powers that return to the scene of writing in Proust's devastating trial by parody of the vices afflicting bourgeois society. The depiction of the social world surrounding the narrator is an important structural level of the novel; the vices Flaubert branded as bourgeois (as well as several that did not enter his represented world) ultimately unite the two ways in a final vision of bourgeois corruption that colors every level of Proustian society. This vision is emblematized by the "new" Princesse de Guermantes—Mme Verdurin, an incarnation of corrupt, self-serving vulgarity. The darker side of pastiche ("l'âpreté du réquisitoire") also appears to be part of Proust's Flaubertian inheritance.

The central focus of the Flaubertian sublime as well as Proust's vision of it is the intoxication of style, rendered in a sentence that prefigures the major claim made for Flaubert in "A Propos du 'style' de Flaubert." In the images of the "trottoir roulant" (CSB 587), Proust incorporates Flaubert's reinvention of the conjunction "et" and the "phrase ternaire [ternary sentence]." Both are considered revolutionary innovations, according to Proust's letter: "Et ses périodes se succédaient sans interruption, comme les eaux d'une cascade, comme un ruban qu'on déroule [And his periodic sentences followed each other without interruption, like the waters of a cascade, like a ribbon that unfolds]" (CSB 13). The eloquent resonance of silence appears to be infinite. As the emblem of Flaubertian sublimity, it can be shaped to the ends of the author(s) of intoxication: it translates dream, vertigo, and vocation into the prose of rapture. It acts as Ariadne's thread in the labyrinth of Proust's novel, leading from the opening pages of *Combray* through the conclusion: "cette sonnette qui tintait encore en moi [this doorbell that was still ringing inside me]" (III, 1046), countersigned by the role of Swann, the narrator's mentor in art and love. In a letter to Colet, Flaubert gives an account of the sublime that sounds like Proust's description of Flaubert's style:

> *Il faut sentir.*—Eh bien, est-ce que tu n'as pas, au plus profond de toi (car ce n'est ni dans le coeur, ni dans la tête, mais plus loin, plus haut), comme un grand lac où tout se reflète, où tout miroite, un murmure perpétuel qui veut s'épandre, une fluidité qui veut sortir. Ah oui! Ah oui! [*One must feel.*—Don't you have something deep

inside you (because it is not in the heart nor in the head, but farther away, higher), like a great lake where everything is reflected, where everything shimmers, a perpetual murmur that wants to spread out, a fluidity that wants to emerge. Oh yes! Oh yes!]²¹

Flaubert's perpetual murmur or mirroring lake figures the mysteries of a style that eludes both the "coeur" of personalized sentiment (the ground of his criticism of Colet's literary works) and the "tête" of conclusive judgment. This ideal is located in a suspended interiority ("au plus profond"/"plus loin"/"plus haut") that appears in an image abstracted from personality and expressivity. In the context of the chance occurrence and the secret workings of analogy, Flaubert's abstracted image could be applied to the Proustian sublime style associated with "involuntary memory" in *A la recherche du temps perdu*.

(8) *Temporality*. The common ground shared by the two authors is made explicit in Proust's conclusive remarks in the letter on Flaubert's style. Proust defends what he calls Flaubert's "merits": "L'un de ceux qui me touche le plus parce que j'y retrouve l'aboutissement de modestes recherches que j'ai faites, est qu'il sait donner avec maîtrise l'impression du Temps [One of the qualities that is most touching for me because I rediscover in it the convergence of my own modest search is that he has mastered the art of giving the impression of Time]" (CSB 595). Proust writes "Time" with the capital letter of allegory as he does in the final revelation of his novel. Beyond the usual concept of "time," it rises into the sphere of what Flaubert consecrates as "Art." Proust emphasizes the allegorical impulse behind this remark by inscribing it with the magic words of his own titles: Flaubert emerges as "Le Temps retrouvé," the endpoint of the "recherche" undertaken by Proust and attributed to the narrator of *A la recherche du temps perdu*.

Proust's argument implicates "l'impression du Temps [the impression of Time]" as the constantly determining factor of Flaubert's revolutionary vision. Inextricable from the production of style, temporality shapes rhythm, syntax, continuity, subjectivism, impressionistic rendering of a scene, dialogue, "a long account of an entire life" (CSB 590), and so on. I hope to show that the "tristesse" associated with Flaubert's reading of history and antiquity is intimately related to the question of temporality underscored by Proust. "L'impression du Temps" goes beyond technical invention and the music of the signifier; after all, Flaubert based the connection between "form" and "content" on the cohesion of beauty and truth. Proust's letter indicates his debt to Flaubert's vision of temporality, parallel to the visionary aesthetic attributed to the narrator in *Le Temps retrouvé*. Proust describes Flaubert's use of verb tenses: time creates beauty, the tone colors of "l'éternel imparfait." Within them, a subtle coloration of tense distinguishes evanescence from permanence, "distingue des choses qui passent une réalité plus durable [distinguishes a more enduring reality from passing things]" (CSB 591). Proust's remark sounds like the narrator's revelation of Time at the end of the novel. If what he terms "réalité" echoes the "réalité tyrannique [tyrannical reality]" that inhabits "l'idéal intérieur, obscur [the interior obscure ideal]" (CSB 592), then the eternity of style or the visionary impression of Time transcends the opposition of subject and object, content and form, Truth and Beauty. For Proust and his predecessor, Flaubert, "l'impression du Temps" emerges as the essential "question of writing," the vision rendered as "l'Art."

In order to illustrate the parallel of his "recherche," Proust returns to the passage from *L'Education sentimentale* quoted earlier in the context of "the eternal imperfect" that presents the course of a life (CSB 590) and parodied in the pastiche. The temporal dimension of a blank space turns a "changement de temps" into music: "A mon avis la chose la plus belle de *L'Education sentimentale*, ce n'est pas une phrase, mais un blanc [In my opinion the most beautiful thing in *The Sentimental Education* is not a sentence, but a blank space]" (CSB 595). Proust uses this provocative remark to show how the blank space takes off from the dramatic moment of Frédéric's recognition of Sénécal (at the end of Part III, chapter V); the effect of the moment of silence depends on the sentences that follow, at the beginning of chapter 6. Its abrupt expansion of temporal units of measure appears to transcend time: "Ici un 'blanc,' un énorme 'blanc,' et, sans l'ombre d'une transition, soudain la mesure du temps devenant au lieu de quarts d'heure, des années, des décades [Here a "blank," an enormous "blank," and without the shadow of a transition, the time measure becoming instead of quarters of an hour, years, decades]" (CSB 595). The sudden shift in temporal proportion following a blank space or musical rest seems to turn the "blanc" into a diminishing echo of the words that preceded it: the "blanc" becomes a vibrating Flaubertian bell, an eloquent silence. In *A la recherche* Proust modulates shifts of time and its measurement through the insertion of blank spaces that stem the flow of syntax without warning, and without the disguise of a chapter break. He integrates Flaubertian silence within the structure of the novel and the narrator's discourse, since the great revelations of "involuntary memory" are predicated on the "blank" of the forgotten.

(9) *Style*. The common ground established as "the impression of Time" is presented by Proust as the heart of writing, or the primary "question of writing." In the terms of his letter, the elements of style (a scale of notes and rhythms or a palette of colors) transform temporality into art. For both writers the shifting terms of what solicits them as an aesthetic object are ineluctably tied in the knots of time. The Romantic emphasis on modernity (modern evanescence) as historicity and antiquity (played out in the writings of Flaubert as well as Baudelaire) and Proust's Belle-Epoque vision of Romantic subjectivity filtered through a dark nostalgia associated with Symbolist aesthetics appear to meet in an interlace of evanescence and permanence. Proust pinpoints it in the stylistics of Flaubert, "qui distingue des choses qui passent une réalité plus durable [distinguishes a more enduring reality from passing things]" (191). The subject of this remark is a series of verb tenses, but it has the eschatological tone of the narrator's vocation in the last pages of *A la recherche du temps perdu*. Proust appears to enter the blank space of *L'Education sentimentale*; he parallels the acceleration of time's passage and the modulation of continuity through a poetics of time. It includes the

use of oscillating scales of temporal measurement and levels of awareness that are highlighted as the material of style.

Toward the end of the letter Proust rests his case on the preceding analysis of Flaubert's artistry of time. He underlines the stylistic parallels between *A la recherche* and Flaubert's oeuvre, by shifting rhetorical weight to "the great writers" (CSB 598). In defense of his own work against certain alleged critical judgments, he anchors his strategy of writing in an inheritance from Flaubert the novelist: the claims for autobiography are subsumed by the composition of a work of fiction. Proust's alignment of style, fiction, and time is predicated on Flaubertian temporality.

The opposition between a "mémoire" and a work of fiction (or between a work of free association and an artistic composition) resists any test of truth or authenticity that would guarantee the coincidence of authorial and fictive personae. The intervention of an artistic and artificial structure called "rigorous composition" allows Proust to shift the question of truth into the unnatural realms of temporality. This temporality is the stylistic principle of the novel that gives rise to the twice two-sided "cathedral" of symmetry. It is crowned at the top by Swann's granddaughter; its other peak is the bell of the narrator's childhood that anticipates the artistry of his future. The two sides or "ways" ("côtés") join in the creation of Mlle de Saint-Loup: *Du côté de chez Swann* encounters *Le Temps retrouvé*, in an extended doubling of lost and found that embraces youth/age, ruin/creation, forgetting/remembering, transgression/vocation. These doubles cluster together like the allegorical opposites (e.g. the couple Caritas/Invidia, evoked several times in the novel) that cover the walls of Giotto's chapel in Padua. Against all possible claims for the story of a life, the symbolic vessel of the novel is identified with a cathedral.

At the source of these symbolic oppositions, the "fortuitous laws" (CSB 599) of the unconscious impose another cathedral structure—a Freudian "monument" of past time. Proust's language operates at a double distance from the easy overlap of personae attributed to "une sorte de recueil de souvenirs, s'enchaînant selon les lois fortuites de l'association d'idées [a sort of collection of memories, connected according to the fortuitous laws of free association]" (CSB 598–99), since both the artifice of the symbolic structure and the enigmatic productions of "ressouvenirs inconscients [unconscious memories]" (CSB 599) dissolve the identification of author and narrator. Proust dismisses this identity as the precise "counter-truth" of what he calls "my novel" (CSB 598) and relegates it to a "sort of collection of memories."

After his "defense" à la Du Bellay (CSB 595) of Flaubert, he engages in a parallel and unsolicited defense of his own work. Beyond the desire to slip into the ranks of the "great writers," this passage substantiates the claim for a return to "the impression of Time." The interpretive base of "Flaubertian intoxication" enters the Modernist context of Proust's writing; it includes the labyrinth of a discourse of interiority no longer guaranteed by the promises of realism, the undecidability of an autobiographical mask and frame, and a Mallarméan emphasis on symbolicity as the delayed effect of Romanticism. The case rests on the portrayal of temporality; the strategy of Proust's version of "the impression of Time" includes a "recueil de souvenirs" (CSB 599) effect that can mislead even the most literary readers. Proust defends his work precisely on the grounds of the Flaubertian inheritance responsible for a trompe-l'œil "mémoire" effect: it is a novel. Three remarks in his defense appear to extend from the reflections on Flaubert's style.

The rigors of composition echo an absolute control exerted by the interior ideal. Flaubert's trial and error rigors of writing take place in the "gueuloir"—the yelling ring, the big-mouth laboratory of Flaubert's own invention. The tyranny that oversees Flaubert's "gueuloir" of style, the laborious transformation of vision into writing, is comparable to the discipline imposed within Proust's secluded bedroom. In the pastiche, he uses a playful allusion to the cork-lined room to draw attention to the Flaubertian consequences of artful silence: "le capitonnage de liège qui amortit le bruit des voisins [the cork lining that deadens the noise of neighbors]" (CSB 15).

In the place of the authorial persona, Proust establishes the ideal; he describes its symmetry as the effect of a compass-drawn arc. It guarantees his operation as an aesthetic structure:

> Dans *Du côté de chez Swann*, certaines personnes . . . méconnaissant la composition rigoureuse bien que voilée (et peut-être plus difficilement discernable parce qu'elle était à large ouverture de compas et que le morceau symétrique d'un premier morceau, la cause et l'effet, se trouvaient à un grand intervalle l'un de l'autre) crurent que mon roman était une sorte de recueil de souvenirs. [In *Swann's Way*, certain people . . . who do not recognize the rigorous although veiled composition (and perhaps this composition is even more difficult to discern because it was drawn with a wide opening of the compass and because the part that was symmetrical to the first part, the cause and the effect, were found at a great interval from each other) took my novel for a sort of collection of memories.] (CSB 598)

The geometrical symmetry of cause and effect is the result of "souvenir," the fictional creation of "involuntary memory."

Within the composition, it functions as an ultimate form of the Flaubertian impression, or "subjectivisme" untainted by rationalization, judgment, or intellect. Proust conceives of "mémoire involontaire" as a springboard for his version of a Flaubertian art of temporality: "Or, sans parler en ce moment de la valeur que je trouve à ces ressouvenirs inconscients sur lesquels j'assois, dans le dernier volume—non encore publié—de mon oeuvre, toute ma théorie de l'art [Without speaking at the moment, however, of the value that I have found in these unconscious memories upon which I base, in the last volume—not yet published—of my work, my entire theory of art]" (CSB 599). Proust's artistry of time emerges from the Freudian territory of "l'oubli," forgetting. Forgetting parallels the moment of silence in *L'Education sentimentale* discussed earlier; the personality of the author is literally blanked out by an aesthetic strategy of composition. Produced by an aesthetic principle of authorial impersonality, moments of Flaubertian silence—echoes, ecstasies, and intoxications—are reshaped in Proust's Modernist aesthetic according to a kind of structural depersonalization. Forgetting reflects the other side of subjectivity, the Freudian unconscious, distanced from the author's identity and the psychology of the ego. Proust points out that Flaubert's vision and the ideal that turned it into writing proceeded from the domain of the unconscious to the parts of speech through an abnegation of the author's persona. His distinction between Flaubert's letters and novels is based on the presence of Flaubert as a consistent psychological entity in his correspondence and the banishment of this entity from the realm of fiction.

Like Flaubert, Proust rejects the consistency of psychology and the guaranteed recognition of the authorial persona. The autobiographical gestures of *A la recherche du temps perdu* are the centerpiece of its fiction. The narrator is someone "qui dit 'je' et qui n'est pas toujours moi [who says 'I' and who is not always me]" (CSB 599). According to the subtle qualifier of "not always," the character cannot be identified with the author, but he cannot be totally disengaged from the author's persona. Proust takes Flaubert's impersonality a step further; the gradations of temporality and the subtle tints of Flaubert's syntax enter the domain of identity through memory, and a fiction of autobiography rises out of the stylistic lake of "l'impression du Temps." Flaubert's silences echo within inner space; the Proustian impression echoes within memory. The blank space takes effect in a context of stylistic continuity, an aesthetic structure of beauty described as "pure" and "precious."

Continuity is achieved in Flaubert's writing through a syntactic rendering of time. Proust's beautiful composition displays moments of remembered time as transitions within a continuous texture: "Pour m'en tenir au point de vue de la composition j'avais simplement pour passer d'un plan à un autre plan, usé non d'un fait, mais de ce que j'avais trouvé plus pur, plus précieux comme jointure, un phénomène de mémoire [To adhere to the point of view of the composition I used, in order to pass from one level to another, not a fact, but simply what I had found to be a more pure and more precious joint, a phenomenon of memory]" (CSB 599). The preceding sentence shows that the specific instance of "jointure" Proust takes as the battleground for his enterprise is the incident of the Petite Madeleine: "Elles citèrent à l'appui de cette contre-vérité des pages où quelques miettes de 'madeleine,' trempées dans une infusion, me rappellent (ou du moins rappellent au narrateur . . .) tout un temps de ma vie, oublié dans la première partie de l'ouvrage [In support of this countertruth, they quoted pages where several crumbs of 'madeleine,' dipped into an infusion, recall to me (or at least recall to the narrator . . .) a whole period in my life, forgotten in the first part of the work]" (CSB 599). What Proust describes here as a means of stylistic continuity is the emblem of ecstatic revelation in the novel: it is the first of a series of revelations predicated on the forgetting of "ressouvenirs inconscients," unconscious memories that become the object of repetition within the interior temporality of memory. These memory traces are also the basis for Proustian aesthetics, "my whole theory of art." Again the identity of the aesthete is suspended: it emerges from the unconscious to take shape in fiction. It is as essential to Proust's fictional style as the episode of the Petite Madeleine.

Proust's three remarks will allow me to conclude a reading of "A Propos du 'style' de Flaubert" in light of a comparative approach to the writing of the two authors. This approach is made possible by Proust's twofold interpretation of a style of temporality; his interpretation comes to light through a critique of Flaubert as well as of his own oeuvre. Beyond the claims for and against their common ground, Proust's interpretation indicates that the two authors' singularities of style are based on one underlying vision. Flaubert's focus on temporality works its way into style as syntax; Proustian temporality takes a further fictional turn by entering the domain of memory. Flaubert's rigors of construction, syntax, and silence are recalled in Proust's formulation of a new paradise of style; it uses "jointure [a joint]" to clasp or cross two elements that consistently reveal the invisibility of Time. Proust's composition or structure brings together cause and effect through binary symmetry; two textual levels are joined by the "unconscious memories" of "involuntary memory." This temporality of memory produces the fictional aesthetic associated with "the eternity of style," the doctrine of *correspondance*, and the rhetoric of metaphor or "the miracle of an analogy" (III, 871).

Flaubert

Je trône dans l'azur comme un sphinx incompris;
J'unis un coeur de neige à la blancheur des cygnes;
Je hais le mouvement qui déplace les lignes,
Et jamais je ne pleure et jamais je ne ris.

I reign over azure like an undeciphered sphinx;
I blend a heart of snow with the whiteness of swans;
I hate any movement that displaces a line,
And I never weep and I never laugh.
(Oeuvres complètes, *vol.* 1, *p.* 21; *my translation*)

5

The Sea of Ink

Amants du beau, nous sommes tous des bannis
[Lovers of the beautiful, we have all been banished].[1]

The Heart of Allegory

Like Jules in the first *Education sentimentale*, Flaubert undertakes a long journey to the Orient,[2] the land of style. The pilgrimage toward what he sees as a plurality and coexistence of holy lands initiates Flaubert the writer into excessive misery and beauty. His travels influence the form and content of an artistic vision that resonates in his aesthetic and oeuvre.[3] Through these effects, rather than on the level of a sudden discovery mythologized by Du Camp in the apocryphal "Eureka" episode, when Flaubert supposedly invented the name of Emma Bovary,[4] the voyage from November 1849 to June 1851 (as well as the trip to Carthage of 1858, made during the composition of *Salammbô*) is integral to his later writings and reminiscences.

Flaubert's vision of the Orient led to his painstaking portrayals of modern life (in Rouen, the Paris of 1848, and the provinces) and carefully documented fictional recreations of the Orient and its "antiquity" (the Middle Ages, Carthage, the Roman empire). His vision of orientalized Modernism is indirectly confirmed by Benjamin's reading of the nineteenth century. Baudelaire's Paris is the site of an interpenetration of antiquity and modernity: the evanescence of the present marks the convergence of modernity with a temporal dimension that seems to have become brittle or petrified when the quickened passage of time relegated it to the past. Perceived at a great distance from the present of modernity, the past assumes the proportions of antiquity.[5] At the origin of Flaubert's renewed gaze, its absorptions and estrangements, the "form and content" of style includes another convergence of antiquity and modernity. Their clasping enters my reading of some of his texts through the allegory of conversion.

This reading entails an implicit critique of a tendency in literary criticism that may have been promoted by some of Flaubert's judgments about his literary subjects. Critics have been tempted to split his work into two categories: the contemporary (including both *Education sentimentale* versions, *Madame Bovary, Un Coeur simple, Bouvard et Pécuchet*) and the "antique" or ancient (including the three versions of *La Tentation de Saint Antoine, Salammbô, Hérodias, La Légende de Saint Julien L'Hospitalier*). According to this split, for example, the obvious or superficial parallels between the characters of St. Anthony and St. Julian place them in the same category without consideration for the vast differences of form that seem to set *La Tentation* apart from the other prose works. Beyond the hostile reception of his final version of *La Tentation* and Flaubert's early judgment that the missing narrative thread and the personal identification of writer and protagonist seriously flawed the first version,[6] an unarticulated but essential difference between modes of speech and figure distinguishes *La Tentation* from much of Flaubert's writing.

The elements of epic inflation and hyperbole that color the *Tentation* are reinforced by its declamatory style, theatrical framework, and voices on an interior stage. In Flaubert's nondramatic writings, on the other hand, moments of epic grandeur and hyperbole are attenuated by the power of understatement inherent in Flaubert's rigorous modernity of narration: the declamatory potential of fictional characters appears to be undermined by the "eternal imperfect" of indirect free style and the unified, porphyry-like surface of his prose. Punctuated by a series of gaps, *La Tentation* is a unique mélange of fantasy, operatic drama, and interiorized meditation that cannot be assimilated into either the corpus of nineteenth-century drama intended for the stage or Flaubert's new style of fiction.

Unlike *La Tentation*, *La Légende de Saint Julien L'Hospitalier* is at the pinnacle of Flaubert's modernist fiction. It fulfills all the demands of his style, and its allegory of conversion is close to the bone of Baudelairean modernity. Proust called it "the most perfect of his works" (CSB 587).

Both works were projects that dated from the author's youth and continued to interest him throughout his life.[7] While the first *Tentation* was written several years before *Madame Bovary*, *La Légende* was written late in Flaubert's life during a difficult period colored by many losses and renunciations, including the despairing abandonment of the novel in progress, *Bouvard et Pécuchet*. Flaubert's preoccupation with style and a fiction of modernity is more central to *Saint Julien* than the mere fact of a return to the thematics of sainthood might indicate. Indeed, the text may be considered Flaubert's ultimate beautiful form, the consummation of his figural images and style, and the crowning allegory of conversion.

In addition to the split between ancient and modern subjects, the consensus in Flaubert criticism uncovers a strict demarcation between Flaubert's early writings and the mature work, beginning with *Madame Bovary*. Flaubert makes some remarks about his future literary projects in a letter to Bouilhet, sometimes quoted by critics[8] as evidence of the break between early uncompleted projects and later accomplishments. Seen through the colored glass of style, however, this letter posits the origin of Flaubert's mature conceptual framework and offers a key to reading his new style, soon to unfold in the writing of *Madame Bovary*. It resonates in the same terms through Flaubert's later years; fully documented in the letters to Colet during the early 1850s, the ideal of style may be heard again in the period of the *Trois Contes*: "Il me semble que la Prose française peut arriver à une *beauté* dont on n'a pas l'idée [I think that French Prose can attain a *beauty* that no one has ever imagined]."[9]

As they are described in Flaubert's letter to Bouilhet, the demands of this ideal are most closely met in *La Légende*. Flaubert gives an account of his new projects, and complains that the three outlines are in fact only a single one:

1 *Une nuit de Don Juan* à laquelle j'ai pensé au lazaret de Rhodes; 2 l'histoire d'*Anubis*, la femme qui veut se faire baiser par le Dieu. . . . 3 mon roman flamand de la jeune fille qui meurt vierge et mystique entre son père et sa mère . . . —Ce qui me turlupine, c'est la parenté d'idées entre ces trois plans. [1 *A Night of Don Juan* which I thought about in the Rhodes lazzaretto; 2 the story of *Anubis*, the woman who wants to be screwed by God. . . . 3 my Flemish novel about the girl who dies a virgin and a mystic surrounded by her father and mother . . . —What worries me is the kinship of ideas in these three projects.[10]

The true unity of the three projects is their focus on love, "l'amour inassouvissable sous les deux formes de l'amour terrestre et de l'amour mystique [unquenchable love in the two forms of earthly love and mystical love]."[11]

These projects contain the seeds for all of Flaubert's major fiction (except for *Bouvard et Pécuchet*). In the paragraph preceding his description of the three outlines, he indicates a foreshadowing of his final novel as a brutal, farcical, and impartial work of theatrical proportions that would react to the effects of civilization, society, newspapers, and so on. He describes this as linked to the "moral" observation made during his travels[12] while the more central projects are clearly the outgrowth of the jouissances created by Flaubert's Orient of style: "Je regrette de ne pas aller en Perse . . . Je rêve des voyages d'Asie, aller en Chine par terre, des impossibilités [I regret not having gone to Persia . . . I dream about trips to Asia, traveling by land to China, about impossibilities]."[13] He writes of traveling in the terms of regrets and dreams, enjoyment ("avoir joui") and desire ("envie mélancolique") in the same letter containing the three projects for writing.

Although the eldest of the three is the third one (the Flemish virgin), Flaubert began his description with a more recent idea for a text that was never written in its proposed form. It became the precise model for the "métaphysics" of all three projects and he also mentioned the place where the idea occurred to him. Although trivial, these details nevertheless point toward a special investment in "Une nuit de Don Juan" that Flaubert seems to have displaced to other texts.

In a letter to his mother written several weeks earlier from Rhodes, Flaubert reveals the source of memory itself—the Proustian discovery—as a momentary impression that may have been concomitant with the occurrence of this project-idea. At the instant of entering the lazzaretto where the travelers stay while in Rhodes, a moment of pre-Proustian involuntary memory links the landscape of Rhodes with Trouville, a privileged site of Souvenir for him: "Le lazaret où nous sommes maintenant est sur la pointe d'une petite presqu'île en rochers . . . La position du lazaret m'a rappelé en y mettant les pieds notre pauvre cottage de Trouville, dont tu me parles dans ta dernière lettre [The lazzaretto where we are now is at the end of a little rocky peninsula. When I stepped inside, the position of the lazzaretto reminded me of our poor cottage at Trouville, of which you speak in your last letter]."[14]

Flaubert elides his own nostalgia for the iconic figures of his youth, while he lingers over his mother's suffering, and the invisible marks of those she loved that still remain for her: "Comme ton coeur là, a dû saigner, à toutes les places [How your heart must have bled there, in all places]."[15] He erects a monument to allegory out of her mourning but then he dedicates it to his experience of loss: "Je n'oublierai jamais tous les battements de coeur que j'ai eus [I will never forget all the palpitations I had]."[16]

The Flaubertian art of involuntary memory is steeped in the blood that flows from the heart of mourning. "Modern grief" is increased by the traces of the dead left on an invisible landscape. The displacement of nostalgia to his mother's heart (a simple one, by comparison to his own) widens the frame of the Flaubertian past to include not only "the phantom of Trouville" (Flaubert's ideal love object, whom he met there) but the true phantom beloved of his youth as well, his sister Caroline. Unnamed in the letter, she is unmistakably present in Flaubert's allusion to the mourning he shared with his mother. In a sense, he silently reverses the priorities of his mother's losses; the erotic overtones of his mourning always appear to refer to Caroline as their source rather than to his father, who also died early in 1846.

It is hardly surprising, then, that love is "inassouvissable"! In this framework, allegory operates on the incommensurable and avowedly infinite scale of Baudelaire's "Le Cygne." The moment that can never be retrieved is relegated to the past that must await the miracle of allegory in order to be resurrected. Upon his second return from the Orient, a despairing Flaubert ends his journal with this plea: "résurrection du passé, à moi! à moi! [resurrection of the past, save me! save me!]"[17] Nineteen years later, he reminisces about Colet: "Où est le temps où vous lisiez ses vers chez la pauvre Muse! Ah! Comme j'y songe. Le Passé est pour moi un vice, je m'y délecte. [Where is the time when you recited her verse at the poor Muse's home! Ah! How I dream of it. For me, the Past is a vice, I revel in it]."[18]

The context of memory that Flaubert notes in his enigmatic remark about the idea for *Une Nuit de Don Juan* sets the scene of the doubled form of "unquenchable love" played out in *La Légende de Saint Julien L'Hospitalier*.

Vitraux de couleurs

At what point does the text of *La Légende* take root in Flaubert's imagination? This question cannot be answered with the date of his first references to *Saint Julien* in letters.[19] He wrote to Madame Roger des Genettes: "Je trouve que, si je continue, j'aurai ma place parmi les lumières de l'Eglise . . . je ne sors pas des saints [I think that if I continue, I will have my place among the leading lights of the Church. . . . I do not leave the company of the saints]."[20] What Flaubert translates from the stained-glass window in Rouen and the narrative sources[21] in "the most perfect of his works" (according to Proust) was waiting in the wings as a new style: Flaubert contemplated it at least as far back as the first *Education sentimentale*. Through *Madame Bovary*, he conceptualized it in an aesthetic of modern allegorical form. The key term of the new style emerges with clarity against the dark backdrop of Flaubert's autumn letters of 1875: "la Phrase." It is the precious essential element of Art, the microcosm and the minimal unit, the image and the panel of glass, the syntactic constellation and the telescope of writing. Both reflecting and reflective, the sentence is the Flaubertian adventure. Analogous to the Gothic stained-glass windows described by the Abbot Suger,[22] the symbolic elements of its material form give rise to aesthetic effects that project constantly changing light, color, and atmosphere inside the figural structure of the church.

In the most literal and textual sense, *La Légende* "begins" with several highly allegorical facets of *Madame Bovary* that were cut out of the novel. Flaubert's early sketch of the Flemish virgin suffering from the earthly and mystical forms of unquenchable love and finally dying of what Flaubert ironizes (to Bouilhet, in any case)[23] as "masturbation religieuse"—self-induced religious ecstasy?—prefigures the theme and color of the Saint Julian legend much more than *Madame Bovary*. Unlike the character of Emma, Julien suffers from the Flemish virgin's mystical love, following the diabolical effects of his fleshly desire.

Two other elisions from *Madame Bovary* form the specific allegorical context of *La Légende*, its pretext and image, as well as the aesthetic of vision that opens up the domain of the artist's allegory of conversion. In the draft episode of Emma and the "verres de couleur [colored glass panes]," Flaubert inserts a secular and elemental version of medieval stained glass. Emma looks through the glass that emblematizes her distance from a world caught in the spell of memory and artificial tone-color; alone with her illusions and dreams, she is the viewer marked by estrangement and interpretive vision. This viewer of allegory, however, lacks the ability to become impersonal, to abstract herself from sentiment.[24] It is thus the nameless "verger" in the Rouen cathedral who urges her (and Léon) to look at the Saint Julian window. He describes it while they flee to their fiacre and leave the sublime domain of art in the cathedral: "J'ai même oublié, reprit-il, de montrer à Monsieur deux vitraux fort remarquables: l'un représentant la vie de saint Julien l'Hospitalier, et l'autre des mariniers [I am even forgetting, he continued, to show Monsieur two very remarkable stained-glass windows: one representing the life of Saint Julian the Hospitator and the other some bargemen]."[25] This passage moves out of the text and back into the wings of Flaubert's manuscript, where it remains until 1875.

La Légende is indebted to a number of allegorical elements integrated in Flaubert's novels as well as to the elisions from his great work of new style. These elements form clusters in his works focused on the contemporary period, and its heritage of Romantic misreading of the medieval tradition. Despite its abundance of violent distortions, this "reading" was aesthetically fruitful in the nineteenth century. Swarming with nostalgia, the literary results refer to an already highly allegorical realm of Art, located in the context of Christian didacticism.

Flaubert's portrayal of his bourgeoise in her convent details the Romanticized literary counterparts of the medieval "gothic cage" cliché essential to her education and fate. She reads novels that seem to include every medieval "idée reçue" from Vigny to Hugo: "Ce n'étaient qu'amours, amants, amantes, dames persécutées s'évanouissant dans des pavillons solitaires, postillons . . . chevaux qu'on crève à toutes les pages, forêts sombres, troubles de coeur, serments, sanglots [It was all love affairs, lovers, beloveds, persecuted ladies fainting in lonely houses, postilions . . . horses ridden to death on every page, dark forests, confusions of the heart, oaths, sobs]" and so on (38). The medieval epic vocabulary becomes more precise and sophisticated as it moves closer to Flaubert's youthful readings and sustained interest in the relation between "the historical novel" and medieval Romanticism: "Avec Walter Scott, plus tard, elle s'éprit des choses historiques, rêva bahuts, salles des gardes et ménestrels [With Walter Scott, later on, she became enamored of historical things, she dreamed about wooden chests, guard rooms, and minstrels]" (38).

If the "gothic" mode of Emma's reading is decisive in the formation of her dreams and illusions about love—her only vocation—it is equally essential to the early Romanticism of Frédéric in *L'Education sentimentale*: "Il dessina . . . la généalogie du Christ, sculptée sur un poteau, puis le portail de la cathédrale. Après les drames moyen âge, il entama les Mémoires: Froissart, Comines, Pierre de l'Estoile, Brantôme [He drew . . . the genealogy of Christ, sculpted on a pole, then the portal of the cathedral. After medieval plays, he started on the Memoirs: Froissart, Comines, Pierre de l'Estoile, Brantôme]" (13). Not only does Frédéric's interest in the medieval recall Flaubert's own early readings but, in addition, Frédéric's vocation for writing owes as much to them as Flaubert thought that his own sensibility owed to the decisive "douleur moderne" of his Romantic youth: "Les images que ces lectures amenaient à son esprit l'obsédaient si fort qu'il éprouvait le besoin de les reproduire. Il ambitionnait d'être un jour le Walter Scott de la France [The images that his readings were bringing to mind obsessed him so much that he felt the need to reproduce them. He set his sights on becoming the Walter Scott of France one day]" (13). The integration of these references to medievalism became the textual ground of *La Légende* through a Modernist transfiguration of the medieval element in which Flaubert himself maintained a certain investment both literary and sentimental. It it perhaps because of this investment—subjected to the same ironies with which Flaubert labored most of his nostalgic attachments—that when Bouvard and Pécuchet turn to literature, they take up where Emma left off: "Ils lurent d'abord Walter Scott. Ce fut comme la surprise d'un monde nouveau [First they read Walter Scott. It was like the surprise of a new world]" (BP 395). Flaubert even goes so far as to insert a distant ironic allusion to *Madame Bovary*: "Bouvard n'en continua pas moins Walter Scott, mais finit par s'ennuyer de la répétition des mêmes effets. L'héroïne, ordinairement, vit à la campagne avec son père, et l'amoureux, un enfant volé, est rétabli dans ses droits et triomphe de ses rivaux [Bouvard continued Walter Scott nonetheless, but he finally got bored with the repetition of the same effects. The heroine ordinarily lives in the country with her father, and the suitor, a kidnapped child, is reinstated in his rights and triumphs over his rivals]" (BP 397). The transformation of this schema into a recognizable sketch of *Madame Bovary* implies a series of "malheurs" or misfortunes caused by Emma's vocation of sentiment. Like all forms of Flaubertian "fatality," the vocation of sentiment is ultimately the enemy of jouissance.[26]

Disguised as a satiric mockery of Scott in particular and the gothic-cage genre of Romantic medievalism in general, Flaubert's subtle irony at Charles's expense (and certainly at his own) recalls a similar rhetorical move in *L'Education sentimentale*. This passage does not concern the medieval epic tradition, but rather the subject of *La Légende*. It is a remarkable prefiguration of the Saint Julian story, ironically inverted. Fatality is denied once again, as the bourgeois on holiday (in flight from the demonstrations of 1848) admires the forest of Fontainebleau: "On pense aux ermites, compagnons des grands cerfs, portant une croix de feu entre leurs cornes [One thinks of hermits, companions of the great stags wearing a cross of fire between their antlers]" (324).[27] In *La Légende* (as in the window and literary sources)[28] the stag curses Julien and foretells of his parricide; he dies on the spot but makes a spectral return when Julien discovers that the "fatality" of his prophecy has been fulfilled (98, 119–20).

Through these parodic and Romantic elements, the stained glass of Gothic cathedrals lends aesthetic presence to Flaubert's medieval atmosphere. Although the Julian window is cut out of *Madame Bovary*, the visit to the cathedral sets the scene for Flaubert's subsequent return to it in 1875, when he transfigures the silent images of colored glass into writing. In this sense, it would seem that the infinite unforeseeable re-creation of the images of Saint Julian[29] and his spiral of conversion bears an essential relation to the writer's allegory of conversion, his relation to writing. Proust's own "gothic cathedral"—the four-dimensional structure of novelistic form, a stratagem deployed against accusations of free-form autobiographical memoirs—owes much to Flaubertian medievalism. I will return later to the moment in *A la recherche du temps perdu* when the graphic image of San Marco in Venice, approached at the hour of judgment, becomes the allegorical image of writing.

The thread of prefigurations for the Julien story indicates that Flaubert stages in *La Légende* what he previously kept in the wings for fear of falling back into the medieval context of his Romantic "modern grief." Nowhere is this brought more clearly into focus than during the Alhambra episode of Part I, chapter V, of *L'Education sentimentale*. The décor of the public ball on the Champs-Elysées is highly stylized, including the representation of "un cloître gothique à vitraux de couleurs [a gothic cloister with a stained-glass window]" (70). Frédéric, anxiously smothering under the effects of desire and idealization, presents his "douleur moderne" and is energetically comforted by Deslauriers. The vocabulary of this interchange bears a striking resemblance to Flaubert's self-descriptions in the less guarded (and often repeated) language of the correspondence.

In the revery preceding the Alhambra episode Frédéric imagines Madame Arnoux in the guise of Flaubert's virgin suffused with mystical love, as he imagined her in Rhodes: "Coiffée d'un hennin, elle priait à deux genoux derrière un vitrage de plomb [Wearing a hennin, she was praying on her knees behind a leadwork window]" (69). But when Deslauriers questions him after he bursts into tears (the Romantic weeping Bouvard and Pécuchet will later discover in Walter Scott), the double-edged indirect discourse of his reply recalls Flaubert's own lifelong view of his sensibility in addition to the wry irony imparted to the antihero's perception of his predicament: "Frédéric souffrait des nerfs. Deslauriers n'en crut rien [Frédéric was suffering from a case of nerves. Deslauriers didn't believe a word of it]" (70).[30] Another ironic facet of this dialogue lies in the accuracy of the cynical anti-Romantic prescription for Frédéric's ailment: "On se console des femmes vertueuses avec les autres [Solace yourself about virtuous women with the others]" (70). The suffering artist and the ruthless impassibility of the man of letters (derived from the tradition of medieval clerics) — lyricism and detachment — are united for a moment in Flaubert's diagnosis of the quintessential Flaubertian disease, the sensibility that enters the domain of art: "Le clerc reprit: '—Ah! vieux troubadour, je sais bien ce qui t'afflige! Le petit coeur? Avoue-le! Bah!' [The clerk continued: '—Ah! Old troubadour, I know what's troubling you! Your little heart? Admit it! Bah!']" (70).

The comic and ironic effects of the dialogue, multiplied by the satirical detachment characterizing Flaubert's portrayal of both the Romantic and the philistine, successfully mask the image of the author. From the heart and its sensibility through coloration and voice, "unquenchable love" is painted on the stained-glass windows of beautiful style. What begins as a "modern grief" becomes the song of the medieval artist of love. When Flaubert writes to George Sand of "votre vieux troubadour, que vous vous figurez agité et continuellement furieux [your old troubadour, whom you imagine agitated and continually raging],"[31] he refers to himself.

The connections made earlier between style and color, vision and the tinting of sensibility with aesthetic estrangement find their origin in the figure that brings them together with the Modernist suffering of the heart: the Gothic stained-glass window dazzling a viewer whose ideal of style rescues it almost intact from the clichés of Romanticism when he writes *La Légende*. Without denying the patterns and objects of signification that Flaubert undoubtedly took up from the canon of medieval Romanticism, his Modernist ideal led him to create an unprecedented work of "new" style in *La Légende*.

Like the vision through glass, the artist's vocation of style is inseparable from a nostalgic and overflowing heart. Impelled to give voice to color, the untranslatable mystery of style, the artist reflects the relation between the heart's overflow and the principles of style that depersonalize it in the stained-glass tracery of the sentence. The symbolic light of the ideal of style enters the writer, who transmutes the materiality of artistic form into a unified reflective "surface" (Proust's word) of beautiful writing. The troubadour, the Flaubertian persona of many letters, is both tender and impersonal, according to the demands of the ongoing allegory of conversion.

At a time of irreparable loss and deep depression, in late

1875 and 1876, Flaubert writes the ultimate product of his early sketch—the *Trois Contes* and most particularly *La Légende de Saint Julien l'Hospitalier*. In the early sketch of Don Juan, Anubis, and the Flemish virgin, the knot of religion and eroticism, of sublimation and the drives, that is at the base of Flaubert's entire oeuvre is already formed. On the feminine side are Emma Bovary and Salammbô, the inheritors of Saint Teresa; on the masculine side, the figure of Don Juan is the bearer of insatiable desire. The gravity of his stature finds form in Saint Anthony. The two sides enter into the creation of a single character: Julien. He alone is doubly inscribed with the twofold "unquenchable love" that drew his creator into the masked figures of excess, the images of allegory.

At a moment when the entire fabric of his art seemed to be suspended, incommensurable with life, Flaubert wrote *La Légende*. The portrait of Julien is tied to this context, as if Flaubert invested him with the finality of unquenchable suffering and sensibility after twenty-five years on the divan of style. It is a finalized image, an image of the end, an anticipated closure of "the story of an entire life." Already in 1872 (when Flaubert completed the third version of *La Tentation*) the ending of the text revealed an image of infinite finality: "Tout au milieu et dans le disque même du soleil, rayonne la face de Jésus-Christ. Antoine fait le signe de la croix et se remet en prières [At the midpoint and in the disk of the sun itself, shines the face of Jesus Christ. Anthony makes the sign of the cross and returns to his prayers]."[31] But Julien goes far beyond Saint Antoine's stated desire and vision through prayer; he is literally dissolved, "pâmé" (134) or intoxicated as the infinite enters him ("une joie surhumaine . . . comme une inondation dans l'âme [a superhuman joy . . . like an inundation in the heart]" [134]) and he is carried away as all of Flaubert's dreamers yearn to be, "emporté dans le ciel" (135).

It is worth noting that this truly successful intoxication is written while Flaubert proclaims the beginning of the end: after the deaths of Madame Flaubert and several friends, he plunged into financial ruin in an attempt to save his niece, and suddenly found himself aging, alone, uncertain of the future.

He writes repeatedly to Caroline and his closest friends: "le fond reste bien noir [the depths remain very black]."[33] A dramatic symptom of his despair is the decision to abandon *Bouvard et Pécuchet*. He writes:

> L'avenir ne m'offre rien de bon et le passé me dévore . . . Quant à la littérature, je ne crois plus en moi; *Bouvard et Pécuchet* étaient trop difficiles, j'y renonce. . . . En attendant, je vais me mettre à écrire la légende de *Saint Julien l'Hospitalier*, uniquement pour m'occuper à quelque chose, pour voir si je peux faire encore une phrase, ce dont je doute. [The future doesn't offer me anything good and the past devours me. . . . As for literature, I don't believe in myself any more; *Bouvard and Pécuchet* were too difficult, I give up. In the meantime, I'm going to write the legend of *Saint Julian the Hospitator*, solely to keep busy with something, to see if I can still make a sentence, which I doubt.][34]

The troubadour of style turns the domain of Walter Scott inside out; it is as if the heart filled with infinite love were created by the very inhumanness of desire and Flaubertian excess associated with allegorical ruins. The task of art, then, is to portray, to find the right shade of color: "J'ai la prétention de peindre Rouen." "Peignons, peignons, sans faire de théorie [I am making the claim that I will paint Rouen. Let us paint and paint, without making theories]."[35]

The empty tomb of allegory, the estrangement of the viewer from a world of ruins, and the suffering heart of the medievalized Romantic Saint Julian are all anticipated in a remarkable passage of a letter to Colet. Flaubert gives an early confirmation of the consistent relation between the "douleur moderne" of his youth and the rhetorical power of the written image of stained glass, sealed many years later by the allegory of *La Légende*:

> J'étais comme les cathédrales du XVe siècle, lancéolé, fulgurant . . . Entre le monde et moi existait je ne sais quel vitrail peint en jaune, avec des raies de feu, et des

Stained-glass windows, eight panels (13th century).
Rouen Cathedral, Notre Dame.
Permission: Art Resource, New York.

Vermeer, *View of Delft*.
The Hague, Royal Museum of Painting.
Permission: Art Resource, New York.

arabesques d'or, si bien que tout se réfléchissait sur mon
âme . . . transfiguré et mélancolique cependant. . . .
Quand je serai vieux, écrire tout cela me réchauffera. Je
ferai comme ceux qui avant de partir pour un long voyage vont dire adieu à des tombeaux chers. [I was like the
fifteenth-century cathedrals, lanceolate, blazing. . . .
Between the world and me there existed some stained-glass window painted yellow, with rays of fire, and the
golden arabesques, so that everything was reflected in
my soul . . . transfigured and melancholic, however.
. . . When I will be old, it will put new heart in me to
write it all down. I will behave like people who go to say
farewell to cherished graves before they leave on a long
voyage.]³⁶

This stained-glass estrangement figures allegory and beauty as the inseparable elements of style. It indicates that the text of *La Légende*, the explicit return both to the figuration of identity and, at the same time, to the estrangement that produces Flaubert's often reiterated "adieu au personnel [farewell to the personal]," is the writing of Flaubert's farewell to cherished tombs and the most explicit statement of allegory as the infinite reflection and transfiguration effected by his vision of style.

Because of its thoroughly allegorical status, *La Légende* may well be the Flaubertian text most resistant to interpretation. Its integration of a medieval code leaves it impermeable to psychological readings attempted by Sartre and others; its mystery remains intact. Idealization and impersonality are compounded by the Romantic estrangement of vision through Gothic glass. At the same time, Flaubertian rhetoric keeps its distance from the literature associated with Flaubert's youthful Romanticism. Flaubert's new architecture of style reshapes the Romantic continuity of personality, sentiment, and writing. A reading of the dimensions of negativity implicated in *La Légende* and their status in the Flaubertian aesthetic indicates what is at stake in this different discourse, soaring beyond the limits of narrative categories.³⁷

86 The Orient of Style

Les visions funèbres

The text of *La Légende* unfolds layers of conversions that turn a child who "ressemblait à un petit Jésus [looked like a little Jesus]" (83) into a violent, animal-like youth ("sentant l'odeur des bêtes farouches. Il devint comme elles [he smelled like wild animals. He became like them]" [92]): a wandering mercenary ("Il s'engagea dans une troupe d'aventuriers qui passaient [He joined a troupe of adventurers passing by]" [101]); an epic hero ("C'est lui, et pas un autre, qui assomma la guivre de Milan et le dragon d'Oberbirbach [It is he, and no other, who felled the viper of Milan and the dragon of Oberbirbach]" [103]); a parricide ("il bondit sur eux à coups de poignard [he attacked them with thrusts of his dagger]" [119]); a pariah ("sitôt qu'il était reconnu, on fermait les portes, on lui criait des menaces [as soon as he was recognized, the doors were closed, they would yell threats at him]" [123]); a boatman transporting passengers over a river "dont la traversée était dangereuse, à cause de sa violence [which was dangerous to cross, because of its violence]" [126]); and finally the privileged object of Christ's love ("face à face avec Notre-Seigneur Jésus [face to face with Our Lord Jesus]" [135]). Although these conversions form the thematic elements and symbolic oscillations of the text, they have not been interpreted in light of the most crucial aspect of Flaubert's sensibility—negativity. Out of negativity (the element that eludes the Sartrian analysis, caught in the wheels of psychology) emerges the subtle inscription of Flaubert's own relationship to allegory—the allegory of conversion.[38]

Although it is generally recognized that the opposition established early in the text is aligned according to the differences between Julien's father and mother, the effects of this oscillation and their subtle rendering of Flaubert's own preoccupations have slipped through the interstices of psychological and narratological approaches. Within the text, the opposition splits the medieval code into the epic and hagiographic realms of discourse: since Julien is the child of the representatives of both realms, the two-directional system of the text hinders attempts to fix his position. He is ultimately in excess of either category, as the divine signs that indicate his extraordinary fate nevertheless are surpassed by the unpredictable and extreme elements of that fate. The two currents bear Julien alternatively, in a rhythm that returns at the end of the *Trois Contes* when Iaokanann's head is borne away (203).

The opposition inaugurates the story: "Le père et la mère de Julien habitaient un château [Julien's father and mother lived in a castle]" (77). Each of the first eight paragraphs adds to the parallel series of images extending from the paradigms of father and mother. This descriptive surface includes a double allegory according to the medieval tradition that contrasts the worldly and the divine. Castle and church are idyllically interwoven: "à tous les étages, dans un pot d'argile peinte, un basilic ou un héliotrope s'épanouissait [on every floor, in a painted clay pot, a basil or a heliotrope bloomed]" (77). The emblems of wrath and divine inspiration noted by Huysmans in his discussion of medieval symbolism[39] are drawn into a knot of complicity, like the paternal drive for mastery and violent power and the maternal aspiration toward the sublime: "On vivait en paix depuis si longtemps que la herse ne s'abaissait plus [They had lived in peace for so long that the portcullis was no longer lowered]" (78). Out of this complicity come the marriage of "le bon seigneur [the good lord]" (79) and his pure, pious wife ("elle était très blanche, un peu fière et sérieuse [she was very white, a little haughty and serious]" [80]), and Julien: "A force de prier Dieu, il lui vint un fils [By force of praying to God, a son came to her]."[40]

The violence of the ruler's mastery is mitigated by his Christian character; ferocity is channeled into his social role. Like "the good Lord," "le bon seigneur" brings his vassals to justice and shuns idolatrous practices (79). His measured, moderate rule of the world is balanced by his wife's monastic measures at home: "Son domestique était réglé comme l'intérieur d'un monastère [Her housework was regulated like the inside of a monastery]" (80). The apparent symmetry of father and mother is confirmed by their two visions, each kept secret from the other, and the two kinds of signification attributed to Julien's behavior according to the divine marks they see in him: "Mais tous deux chérissaient l'enfant d'un pareil amour; et, le respectant comme marqué de Dieu [But both cherished the child with the same love; and respecting him as one marked by God]" (83). His mother's vision declaims: "Réjouis-toi, ô mère! ton fils sera un saint! [Rejoice, o mother! your son will be a saint!]" (81) The hieratic biblical style reinforces the religious message, delivered by a hermit-like figure. His father's vision, on the other hand, is exclaimed by an inspired Bohemian, who stammers a fragmentary prophecy in pure Célinian style: "Ah! ah! ton fils! . . . beaucoup de sang! . . . beaucoup de gloire! . . . toujours heureux! la famille d'un empereur [Ah! ah! your son! . . . lots of blood! . . . lots of glory! . . . always happy! the family of an emperor]" (82). Unmediated violence and desire mark this message, the worldly counterpart of the first one.[41]

The parallelism of Julien's parents figures the two forms of unquenchable love, earthly and spiritual. Since the parallels are knotted in the character of Julien himself, the lure of Flaubertian symmetry is almost irresistible.[42] At the same time, however, an asymmetrical element breaks into the story; there is nothing in the code of the text that anticipates the excessive character associated with Julien. The effraction of excessive signs (partly corroborated by the excessive desire for violence demonstrated by the child) already begins with the "grandes réjouissances [great rejoicings]" (80) that mark Julien's birth. The described signs of celebratory (and then visionary) excess are stylistically confirmed by the first true hyperbole of the text: "On y mangea les plus rares épices, avec des poules grosses comme des moutons [The rarest spices were eaten there, with chickens as big as sheep]" (80). The splendid "rejoicings" are reinforced as a trace of something that exceeds the limits of parental symmetry by the "splendeurs destinées à son fils [splendors destined for the son]" that literally dazzle both parents (81–82).

Julien's effraction answers his parents desires in spades — his desire never stops going too far. When he enters the domain of violence, his first dazzled intoxication comes from the sexually orchestrated act of killing: "Il se mit à l'étrangler; et les convulsions de l'oiseau . . . l'emplissaient d'une volupté sauvage et tumultueuse. Au dernier raidissement, il se sentait défaillir [He began to strangle it; and the convulsions of the bird . . . filled him with a wild tumult of voluptuousness. At the last stiffening, he felt himself swoon]" (87). The two worlds have created a phenomenal being whose lust conspires to destroy them both—and, through the allusions to a suicidal extension of Julien's violence, to destroy them all, in a slight displacement of the negativity essential to jouissance.

The apparent parallelism of religious and secular terms is displaced in Julien's character: moderation, reassuringly symmetrical, surrenders to the asymmetry of excess and the estrangement of its vision. If the parallel terms are shifted to the more intimate code of the correspondence, the vocabulary of Julien's excess in the parabolic dimensions of *La Légende* sheds some unexpected light on Flaubert's writing as a vast sea of negativity sustaining "the story of a whole life." Via identifications with Teresa, Antoine, Polycarpe, and others, the domain of sainthood (that is the province of femininity in *La Légende*) resonates as the "other" world of allegory. Through Art, it becomes a permanent state of excess: "J'aime mon travail d'un amour frénétique et perverti, comme un ascète le cilice qui lui gratte le ventre [I cherish my work with a frenetic and perverted love, as an ascetic loves the hair shirt that scratches his belly]."[43]

The masculine realm of mastery and violence, on the other hand, is repeatedly abjured by Flaubert. The epic sphere of *La Légende* echoes bourgeois life—marriage, business, family, and so on. Here too, the resonance of the text brings out an excessive negativity. Art is gratuitous and unpaid; bourgeois existence, however, is empty of any meaning. Seen through the vision of excess, "normal" life appears monstrous: "Tu aimes l'existence, toi; tu es une païenne . . . tu aspires au bonheur. . . . Mais moi je la déteste, la Vie. Je suis un catholique [You love existence; you're a pagan . . . you aspire to happiness. . . . But I detest Life. I am a Catholic]."[44]

The consecrated terrain of negativity and its excess is Art.

Through rage, malheur, and fatality (the cause and aftermath of rage, as well as the proof of its excess), Flaubert dissimulates the personal behind the veils of allegory: "De tous les côtés . . . je ne vois que malheur . . . Ne me maudis jamais!" "Je n'ai rien pour me soutenir qu'une espèce de rage permanente. [On all sides . . . I see only unhappiness . . . Never curse me! I have nothing to sustain me except a kind of permanent rage]."[45] Flaubert invokes the anatomy of style to convey his concern for the structure of the sentence, but his references to the scalpel, the stiletto, and the artistry of murder indicate that the slow work of the sublime includes sustained and premeditated acts of violence in a process of rewriting that consists largely of crossing out or "rature." Rage turns style into anatomy; Flaubert kills the words on the page. Style takes on the fatality of the Orient: "Quelquefois, quand je me trouve vide, quand l'expression se refuse, quand après avoir griffonné de longues pages, je découvre n'avoir pas fait une phrase, je tombe sur mon divan. . . . Je me hais [Sometimes when I find myself empty, when expression refuses to come, when after having scribbled long pages, I discover that I have not composed a sentence, I fall on my couch. . . . I hate myself]."[46] Love becomes illness: "*Je suis malade de toi* [*I am ill and you are my illness*]," Flaubert writes to Colet.[47] Out of the ruins and empty sepulchers of allegory (including an anticipation of death) comes Art, associated with the fatality that marks the single declaration of truth made by Charles Bovary, in mourning: "A quoi donc tient la majesté de leurs formes . . . ? De l'absence peut-être de toute passion . . . Le sentiment de la fatalité qui les remplit [What is the reason for the majesty of their forms . . . ? Perhaps the absence of all passion. . . . The feeling of fatality that fills them]."[48]

In *La Légende*, the appearance of bivalence or parallelism reigns until the great transformation spurred by the fulfillment of the stag's prophecy—the moment when malediction turns into fatality. Unlike his entourage, Julien knows that the evil or illness afflicting him is not "un vent funeste ou un désir d'amour [a fatal wind or a desire for love]" (98); the "funeste [fatality]" is interiorized. After the curse of his ferocious heart, he weeps in intimately Flaubertian disgust and mourning: "Une tristesse immense l'envahit . . . il pleura pendant longtemps [An immense sadness invaded him . . . he wept for a long time]" (98). This unprecedented emotion marks its bearer with the sign of allegorical suffering unto death (like Charles, who announces the workings of fate and immediately succumbs to his grief). After the parricide, Julien's negativity of mastery and violence are directed inward: "Sa propre personne lui faisait tellement horreur qu'espérant s'en délivrer il l'aventura dans des périls . . . Il résolut de mourir [His person horrified him so much that hoping to free himself of it he risked it in perilous dangers. . . . He resolved to die]" (125–26). His excess takes him beyond the demands of piety and virtue, into a Flaubertian overflow inseparable from the dissemination of style. Through suffering and solitude, the future Hospitator becomes sublime, in the Flaubertian manner: "Il contemplait avec des élancements d'amour les poulains dans les herbages . . . tous, à son approche couraient plus loin [He would contemplate with sharp stirrings of love the colts in the pasture . . . at his approach, all ran further away]" (124–25); "L'indifférence des propos glaçaient son coeur [The indifference of the comments turned his heart to ice]" (124); "Il lui fut impossible de retenir ses pleurs [It was impossible for him to hold back his tears]" (126).

Shortly before beginning *La Légende*, Flaubert described himself through the effects of Julien's banishment on his sensibility: "J'ai passé ma vie à priver mon coeur des pâtures les plus légitimes. . . . Eh bien! Je n'en peux plus! je me sens à bout. Les larmes rentrées m'étouffent et je lâche l'écluse [I spent my life depriving my heart of its most legitimate pastures. . . . I can no longer bear it! I am at the end of my rope. The held-back tears are smothering me and I open the sluice-gate]."[49] Julien's sensibility—his sad, suffering heart—reflects the boomerang effect of style: "Adieu forever to the personal."[50] In the masked figures and defigurations of allegory, Julien's excess records how style defaces the comforts of life, drawing the artist into a solitude that can receive no comfort from world or church, father or mother.

The presentation of desire moves beyond the economic reciprocity of coupled drives seen in Freud's metapsychology toward the excess of divine markings: unquenchable love may not be measured in terms of the unquenchable lust for killing. Julien's saintly love is represented as infinitely sublime, but the desire associated with it remains steeped in murderous blood, this time in the guise of suicide. It is only when Julien sees his father's face in place of his own and realizes that suicide is a variation on murder (imprinted with his own idea and form as parricide, the most sensational murder associated with antiquity) that he abandons all suicidal intentions: "il vit paraître en face de lui un vieillard . . . d'un aspect si lamentable qu'il lui fut impossible de retenir ses pleurs. L'autre, aussi, pleurait . . . Il poussa un cri; c'était son père; et il ne pensa plus à se tuer [He saw facing him the appearance of an old man . . . who looked so pathetic that it was impossible for him to hold back his tears. The other was crying too . . . he screamed; it was his father; and he did not think any more of killing himself]" (126). The reflection or vision of an unspecified "old man" inspires Julien's tears, but when it appears to respond to his melancholy with its own weeping, he screams: the apparition is the image of his father. Julien's vision turns his "real" image into the hallucinatory image of the father; the double turns the self-reflexive act of suicide into a repetition of murder. In this acting-out of Flaubert's "farewell to the personal," Julien's identity with his own image has disappeared. The allegorical power of the "other" image is sustained by this disappearance of "personal" identity between self and image. Julien's estrangement as he gazes into the fountain twists the scene of Narcissus into hallucination and allegory, the double revelation of the other. Like many of the miniaturized scenes in *La Légende*, this moment formalizes Flaubert's allegory of style and its conversion, since its affective power—both within the text and outside it, for the reader—depends on the double distance of the "farewell to the personal." This adieu is as irrevocable, for Flaubert, as Julien's funeral instructions to his wife (121).

The "object" of Julien's desire is killing: desire is negative, opening into death and the abyss of the "inassouvissable." Julien's "mal"—sin, evil, illness—is as unfathomable and unpardonable as the sin against the Holy Spirit. At the same time, the parallelism between the religious and the worldly subverted by this excess is further subverted by the uncanny collusion between saintliness and sin that impersonalizes Julien and opens him up to the heart of allegory.

Julien's desire moves into the act of evil that will become his fate: the acting-out of desire occurs in the presence of the saintly element. In the chapel (the site of eventual stained-glass representation, comparable to Emma's kiosk and the Rouen cathedral) his vocation for negativity will take hold, interrupting the easeful symmetry of church and state: "Un jour, pendant la messe, il aperçut une petite souris blanche . . . chaque dimanche il l'attendait, en était importuné, fut pris de haine contre elle, et résolut de s'en défaire [One day, during mass, he noticed a little white mouse . . . every Sunday he would await it [her], would be disturbed by it, was gripped by hatred for it, and resolved to get rid of it]" (85–86). After the curse, Julien abstains from hunting until the monk orders him to return to violence: "Enfin le vieux moine, au nom de Dieu . . . lui commanda de reprendre ses exercices de gentilhomme [At last the old monk in the name of God . . . ordered him to return to his exercises as a gentleman]" (100). The result of this order in God's name is that Julien nearly impales his mother with a javelin. He flees into the epic realm of Part II, but the scenario is nevertheless repeated when his Christian wife persuades him to return once again to the sport of negativity. Her reasoning fuels his temptation, thereby preparing the ground for parricide. At the same time, however, the decision to go hunting is made by Julien alone: "Cependant elle redoutait une aventure funeste [However she feared a fatal adventure]" (109). Julien does not heed the fears of the "funeste" [fatality] that cause her to change her mind; he had already accepted her initial judgment. God and the Devil together drive him to destruction.

Julien's fate of negativity, then, exceeds symmetry because of its inviolable fatality. Both divine and diabolical, fatality takes a further turn into the asymmetry of desire. A Freudian translation of classical antiquity indicates that the blackness afflicting Julien is due to his lack of specifically sexual desire. The intoxication of jouissance that affects him when he kills animals is portrayed as a displacement of erotic love. It is as if Julien's early resemblance to animals (confirmed by his indifference to maternal caresses [87, 92]) prevents him from becoming a subject of love. This is the ironic difference between Julien and Oedipus: Thanatos and Eros are not balanced in the metapsychology at work in *La Légende*. Even more than the Julien of the stained-glass legend and the literary tradition, Flaubert's Julien is far removed from Eros. He is satisfied with being in love for approximately two lines in the entire text: "Julien fut ébloui d'amour, d'autant plus qu'il avait mené jusqu'alors une vie très chaste [Julien was dizzy with love, especially since he had lived until then a very chaste life]" (150). Marriage immediately puts an end to this dazzle of love, and Julien yearns for his hunts and dreams of killing animals in Paradise (107).

Unlike Oedipus, he is impervious to maternal flesh: "Quand sa mère l'embrassait, il acceptait froidement son étreinte, paraissant rêver à des choses profondes [When his mother put her arms around him, he would accept her embrace coldly while appearing to dream of profound things]" (92). Flaubert emphasizes Julien's heartlessness. His "ferocious heart" connects him to the ferocious animals he hunts: "il rentrait . . . sentant l'odeur des bêtes farouches. Il devint comme elles [he would come home . . . smelling like fierce animals. He became like them]" (92).

Like Flaubert, Julien feels close to animals; he nearly dies while trying to kill them. In contrast to the view of religious communities, Julien does not see animal sacrifice as a substitute for human sacrifice; according to René Girard's theory of sacrifice, this substitution marks a major step toward nonviolence.[51] In Julien's world, animal and human sacrifice are strictly of the same order. The death drive produces an abyss of destruction out of a desire that does not distinguish between the sensitive and the heartless. The metapsychological economy of exchange unfolds in pure excess: after the crime, violence is exchanged for mourning—the other negativity that reigns in *La Légende*.

A phrase from the description of the massacre leading to the stag's curse comments on the infinite violence of fulfilled desire: "tout s'accomplissant avec la facilité que l'on éprouve dans les rêves [Everything being accomplished with the ease that one experiences in dreams]" (95). This story of a whole life is divinely marked, beyond the boundaries of realism or the *vraisemblable*, with the vision of allegory: violence, mourning, negativity, prophecy. Flaubert indicates that the desire of destruction is gratuitous; it cannot be directed toward another desire, or toward a goal. Its enigma resides in its very perversity—in the Freudian sense, constitutive of human sexuality. If the Oedipus story relates death to sexuality, Flaubert's Julien story uses its parable of the measureless excess of desire to show that sex is inseparable from death, steeped in its abyss of negativity, and equivalent to it. This enigma is translated into the text of *La Légende*; there is no possible conclusion. Represented within a form of silence that carries Julien away, the mystery of the saint never cancels out the negative, useless, inexplicable, solitary, unconquerable rage of negativity that inhabits his suffering heart. This is Flaubertian affect in its purest rendering.

Julien's crime may be construed as a blackness of vision—an act of not seeing. If vision is style, then Julien's dark act indicates an inability to see through the glass of art and allegory, the stained-glass window that plays a key role within the text. Through style and light, vision and portrayal, the stained-glass window of Flaubert's story is itself an image of rhetoric: it represents the unquenchable figuration that marks the rage of style. Perhaps more than any other character in Flaubert's writing, Julien moving through dazzling splendors and "visions funèbres [funereal visions]" allegorizes the author's voyage through the blackness that solicits writing and the intoxication of beauty emanating from the ideal of "form and content." Flaubert's ultimate form of perversion may be that he makes horror inseparable from beautiful form. The leper is Christ; the naked woman is a skeleton. Developed by both Flaubert and Baudelaire, this baroque side of Modernism captures the mystical essence of allegory.

Sur un vitrail d'église

The entire story of Julien's life is modulated by the dazzle of light and the sexual, deathly blackness of shadows. The fatal darkness of the abyss alternates with the vision of light and color; in fact, it is this blackness that makes stained glass a perfect image of art and the abysses it must confront and represent. Despite an apparent parallelism between light and dark (symbolic of virtue and vice, good and evil, sacred and profane, and so on, in the terms of medieval didacticism) a combined excess of both marks the gothic style of the story with the contrasts reminiscent of Flamboyant Gothic architecture. The curves and countercurves of Flamboyant Gothic tracery combine detailed stylization with a typically Late Gothic effect based on dramatic contrasts between light and dark, a kind of architectural version of the leaded panes of stained-glass windows.[52] Indeed, it is the term "flamboyant" that indicates the excessive asymmetry of light and dark in Flaubert's story: the eyes of the Bohemian have "les prunelles flamboyantes [blazing pupils]" (82); the stag has "les yeux flamboyants [blazing eyes]" (98); the two prophecies refer to "splendeurs éternelles [eternal splendors]" (112); Julien climbs to "la splendeur des tabernacles [the splendor of tabernacles]" (125); the animals' eyes are like sparks and stars (115); Julien sees the eye of his dead father as "une prunelle éteinte que le brûla comme du feu [an extinguished pupil that burned him like fire]" (121); the leper's eyes, "plus rouges que des charbons [redder than coals]" (130), take on "une clarté d'étoiles [a clarity of stars]" (134). The jewel-like splendor of the "flamboyant" shines with the light of excess. But Flaubert emphasizes that its combination of light and dark—the excess of its illumination—is most essentially rooted in the effects of art itself, here represented as the stained-glass window. The descriptions of the window in the bedroom Julien shares with his wife (and where he kills his parents) situate the chamber of art: "Les chambres, pleines de crépuscule, se trouvaient éclairées par les incrustations des murailles [The bedrooms, full of twilight, were illuminated by the incrustations of the walls]" (106). The shadows and jewel-lights of style reveal a Gothic interiority that is both sublime and disquieting. It is anticipated earlier by a description that precedes the arrival of the black stag who curses Julien. It is almost nightfall: "et derrière le bois, dans les intervalles des branches, le ciel était rouge comme une nappe de sang [and behind the wood, in the intervals of the branches, the sky was as red as a sheet of fire]" (96). The branches mime the lead divisions of the "vitrail," and the sky is colored like panes of glass.

Julien's crime is the result of his lack of vision in the dark; what he sees will be revealed through stained glass. For Flaubert, vision requires the stained glass of Art. The blackness of Julien's crime will bring him from "derrière le vitrail [behind the stained-glass window]" (112), closed by his wife while he is in the forest, into the realm of reflection and vision. From the abyss of his blind rage, he enters the blackness of malediction: "Les vitraux garnis de plomb obscurcissaient la pâleur de l'aube [The stained-glass windows edged with lead darkened the pallor of dawn]" (118). Following the parricide, he picks up the "flambeau [torch]" dropped by his horrified wife and enters into a vision of style determined by the stained glass that illuminates and artificially multiplies the spots of blood: "Le reflet écarlate du vitrail, alors frappé par le soleil, éclairait ces taches rouges, et en jetait de plus nombreuses dans l'appartement [The scarlet reflection of the stained glass, hit just then by the sun, cast light on these red spots, and spread more numerous ones around the apartment]" (120). This vision is echoed at the end of the story, when the sublime multiplication of spots is repeated in the horrible form of the leper's spots: "la table, l'écuelle et le manche du couteau portaient les mêmes taches que l'on voyait sur son corps [the table, bowl, and knife handle had the same spots that could be seen on his body]" (132).

Gazing at the illumination of Art from within, Julien approaches the aesthetic domain of impersonal style. Burned by the eye of his father, he turns to the feminine bearer of ineluctably personalized sentiment.[53] When personal sentiment enters the Flaubertian necropolis of allegory, he covers the face that expresses it; he hides the face of Madame Arnoux saying "farewell to the personal" in her final meeting with Frédéric in *L'Education sentimentale* (419). Julien's mother, estranged by death, is "l'autre corps, dont les cheveux blancs masquaient une partie de la figure [the other body, with its white hair masking part of the face]" (121). The world has become allegory, and Julien too covers his face and enters the impersonal realm of allegory à la Flaubert: "désormais il n'existait plus [henceforth he no longer existed]" (122). Several months after his "adieu et pour toujours au *personnel*, à l'intime, au relatif. . . . Rien de ce qui est de ma personne ne me tente [farewell and for forever to the *personal*, the intimate, the relative . . . nothing about my own person tempts me],"[54] Flaubert writes: "c'est une délicieuse chose que d'écrire! que de ne plus être soi [what a delicious thing it is to write! not to be oneself any longer]."[55]

Julien has become the silent solitary artist of impersonality: "Un moine en cagoule rabattue suivit le cortège, loin de tous les autres, sans que personne osât lui parler [A monk with a lowered cowl followed the procession, far from all the others, without anyone daring to speak to him]" (122). He disappears, like the image of the artist Flaubert advocates: "tu rouleras perdu dans l'ouragan [you will be lost, rolling in a hurricane]."[56] In a notable variant from all traditional renderings, Flaubert's Julien leaves his wife, thereby entering the total solitude from which the artist himself so fiercely suffered during the period of intense mourning of 1875–76: "Il s'en alla [He went away]" (123). Like the writer, Julien takes on a different voice before he lowers the monk's hood and disappears: "d'une voix différente de la sienne, il lui commanda de ne pas lui répondre . . . [in a voice different from his own, he ordered that she not answer him . . .]" (121). When in 1855 Flaubert recalls his efforts at masking the lyricism he felt to be his natural voice in order to find the style for *Madame Bovary*, he writes: "nous sommes seuls, *seuls*, comme le Bédouin dans le désert. Il faut nous couvrir la figure [we are alone, *alone*, like the Bedouin in the desert. We must cover our faces]."[57] He already sounds like the character he will create twenty years later, the mystical Julien.

Flaubert's allegory of conversion is further deepened in the last pages of *La Légende*. Julien covers his face and slips into a femininity of mourning, as the artist steps into the forms of his heroines; this transfiguration is confirmed when Julien plays the role of feminine flesh during the only explicit scene of sexual love in the story. In the sources Julien's wife responds to the leper's demands, but it is Julien who does so in Flaubert's version. The two forms of unquenchable love are briefly knotted together. But what is Flaubert's own investment in this moment of horror and love, the scandalously perverse sexual conclusion? In other words, why does this moment depart from the narrative of stained glass in a seemingly gratuitous brush with homosexuality, unprecedented in Flaubert's fiction?

Julien is invested with the femininity of mystical solitude, the unquenchable love of the sublime variations on sentiment and its hidden figure in art that owe their origin to the Flemish virgin of Flaubert's early projects. Flaubert loads a lifetime of writing into Julien's boat, braving the abyss of ink: "L'eau, plus noire que de l'encre . . . creusait des abîmes, elle faisait des montagnes, et la chaloupe sautait dessus, puis redescendait dans des profondeurs [The water, blacker than ink . . . hollowed out abysses, it created mountains, and the rowboat was tossing on top and then plunging down again into the depths]" (131). Julien's mystical journey through the stormy night bears the flaming eyes of the leper through the ink of Art—the Flamboyant Gothic of Modernism. The Mallarméan overtones of this interpretation are confirmed by a remark made in an early letter to Colet. Flaubert evokes "l'épouvante du pauvre artiste devant la Beauté [the poor artist's terror before Beauty]":

> La mer paraît immense vue du rivage. . . . Embarquez-vous dessus, tout disparaît: des flots, des flots. . . . Que suis-je, moi dans ma petite chaloupe! 'Préservez-moi, mon Dieu, la mer est si grande et ma barque est si petite!' c'est une chanson bretonne qui dit cela et je le dis aussi en songeant à d'autres abîmes. [The sea appears immense seen from the shore. . . . Embark upon it, everything disappears: waves and waves. . . . What am I, in my little rowboat! 'Save me, oh Lord, the sea is so wide and my boat is so small!' a Breton song says that and I say it too while dreaming of other abysses.]⁵⁸

The mystical vertigo of the writer is the effect of his disappearance into the sea of the sublime, the ideal realm of figuration, the dark night of ink. The mountains and abysses, the heights and depths of grandeur in which Flaubert navigates, are put into the writing of Julien's last trip over the river.

Through horror and feminine figuration, through rage and melancholic tears, allegory takes Julien all the way. After the long holocaust and the killings that conclude with the horrible murder of his parents, Julien disappears. Flaubert confirms this entry into style with a subtle sign of transubstantiation, presaged by the Gospel account of the wedding at Cana, when Christ turned water into wine: "Julien alla chercher sa cruche; et, comme il la prenait, il en sortit un arome qui dilata son coeur et ses narines. C'était du vin; quelle trouvaille! [Julien went to look for his jug; and, as he was picking it up, a fragrance came from it that gladdened his heart and his nostrils. It was wine; what a lucky find!]" (132). The delight of his heart is emptied: "mais le lépreux . . . d'un trait vida toute la cruche [but the leper . . . emptied the jug with a single draught]" (132). Indeed, whatever had not yet been left behind is taken away, so that Julien finds himself dispossessed for the second time, naked, possessing the emptiness of the desert (a Flaubertian image). The second disappearance transforms him into the splendors of stained glass: "Julien montait vers les espaces face à face avec N-S Jésus, qui l'emportait dans le ciel

[Julien was rising toward space face to face with Our Lord Jesus, who was bearing him away into the sky]" (135). Julien's glorious end confirms his entry into impersonality, the Oriental silence that pervades the story. Out of silence, the solitude filled with crossed-out sentences, come the splendors of writing.

For Flaubert, emptiness and art are inseparable; they bring together antiquity, the desert, and aesthetic artifice. Oriental women are both empty machines and works of art.[59] Deepening his solitude of ink and the sublime, he declared several years later that he would write *Carthage* (published as *Salammbô*) in order to "vivre dans un sujet splendide et loin du monde moderne dont j'ai plein le dos [live in a splendid subject, and far away from the modern world of which I am sick to death]."[60]

After Julien's years of silence, when the only voice heard is his own, telling his story and hearing no answer, the leper voices the most primitive demands. What Julien held back from women he gives to the leper; he gives himself over: "'—Ah! je vais mourir! . . . Rapproche-toi, réchauffe-moi! Pas avec les mains! Non! toute ta personne' ['Ah! I am dying! . . . Come closer, warm me! Not with your hands! No! your whole body']" (134). On November 14, 1850, Flaubert wrote to Bouilhet from Constantinople: "La littérature a mal à la poitrine . . . Il faudrait des Christs de l'Art pour guérir ce lépreux [Literature is consumptive . . . it would take some Christs of Art to cure this leper]."[61] Flaubert articulates the desires of the leper and gives himself over to them. The allegories of antiquity and the medieval period are transformed into the Orient of style.[62]

Flaubert plays out his affinities with saints, sages, ascetics, and the other permutations of mystical experience encountered in the Orient, in the sea of ink. Like the marks of the flamboyant in *La Légende*, combining blackness and image, the blackness of allegory is irreducibly heterogeneous. When he writes, "sans l'amour de la Forme, j'eusse été peut-être un grand mystique [without my love of Form, perhaps I might have been a great mystic],"[63] he might also be saying that without his raging love for style, he would have disappeared into suffering and horror. The vertigo of the sea of ink menaces him intimately, from within the estranged gaze of his nervous attacks. Like art, they manifest themselves through representations of ideas and images: "Ajoute à cela mes attaques de nerfs, lesquelles ne sont que des déclivités involontaires d'images [Add to that my nervous attacks, which are merely involuntary declivities of images]."[64] Imbued with deadly violence, both tragic and diabolical, the uncontrollable images unmask death: "Je suis sûr que je sais ce que c'est que mourir [I am sure that I know what dying is]."[65] From the tragic vision of "la maladie noire [the black illness]"[66] with its hallucinations and despair to the sublime sea of ink, the moving images of death must be transfigured into jouissance, the heart's delectation—"une abondance de délices, une joie surhumaine . . . dans l'âme de Julien pâmé [an abundance of delights, a superhuman joy . . . in Julien's swooning heart]" (134). The sublime ending of *La Légende* is prefigured in Flaubert's Art lesson to Colet. It might be summarized as the blackness of ink: "L'encre est mon élément naturel. Beau liquide, du reste, que ce liquide sombre! et dangereux! Comme on s'y noie! comme il attire! [Ink is my natural element. A beautiful liquid, besides, this dark liquid! and dangerous! How one drowns in it! how attractive it is!]."[67] The text of *La Légende* is confirmed by Flaubert's attempt to teach Colet the essence of Art as he had come to understand it. The lesson of Art is at the same time a lesson in the mystical heights and depths of love. In response to her bitter attacks, Flaubert defends the symbolic and emblematic dimensions of meaning against the existential and corporeal limitations of the artist. During the course of a polemic against psychology, personal sentiment, and the social and literary conventions of the Parisian community, he constructs an aesthetic of allegory.

Qui l'emportait dans le ciel

La Légende has two endings. The first closes the story with the ascension of Julien, in a fulfillment of the sublime aesthetic recorded in the correspondence. His double disappearance into figuration finally dissolves him in the splendors of heaven, the finale of jouissance. The text shifts from a medieval characterization to the timelessness of eternity; Flaubert sets the stage for a final narrative silence, a blank page.

The success of writing, its "emportement [transport]," slips the medieval into the frame of the eternal sky preceding the blank space on the page. The empty white space, however, is not final; it introduces temporality. It becomes a rhythmic interval between two sentences, or rather, between the body of Part III and the final sentence, thus marking an intrusion of textual time in the closing note of eternity. Flaubert's artifice of the blank space here is intended to guarantee that *La Légende* be read as allegory: "Et voilà l'histoire de saint Julien l'Hospitalier, telle à peu près qu'on la trouve, sur un vitrail d'église, dans mon pays [And that is the story of Saint Julian the Hospitator, almost the way you find it on the stained glass of a church, in my town]."[68]

The final sentence is a signature only in the sense of the medieval colophon—an emblematic mark or an inscription that draws attention to the origin of the text. The only identity it betrays is the deictic reference to "mon pays [my countryside, village, or place]," the site of the Julian window. Aside from Flaubert's personal celebrity, "mon pays" solicits understanding via the connection to *Madame Bovary*. Indeed, Flaubert complained during the last years of his life that the novel set in Rouen was the only one of his works that received attention. Despite this complaint, however, Flaubert clearly intended "mon pays" to be understood as an extension of the aesthetic of *Madame Bovary*—including an evocation of the window, in the manuscript passage quoted earlier: "J'ai la prétention de *peindre* Rouen [I claim to be *painting* Rouen]."[69]

It is the voice of the painter or allegorist who speaks in the last sentence, not a "Gustave Flaubert." This is confirmed by an enigmatic remark in a letter to the editor Georges Charpentier:

> Je désirais mettre à la suite de *Saint Julien* le vitrail de la cathédrale de Rouen . . . Et cette illustration me plaisait *précisément* parce que ce n'était pas une illustration, mais un *document* historique. En comparant l'image au texte on se serait dit: 'Je n'y comprends rien. Comment a-t-il tiré ceci de cela?' [I wanted to put the stained-glass window from the Rouen cathedral at the end of *Saint Julian* . . . And I liked this illustration *precisely* because it was not an illustration, but rather a historical *document*. The reader would have compared the image to the text and thought: 'I don't understand a thing. How did he derive the one from the other?'][70]

The final sentence was meant to reveal the essential allegory of Flaubert's writing, guaranteed by the break between the stained-glass representation and the story. This gap is subtly echoed in the letter (and in the second ending of the story) by the gap between author and text. Instead of an organic, natural extension of life, writing is the product of an artificial break, a detachment, a disappearance, "a blank." This constellation of excess and fatality lights up the sky of allegory.

If Flaubert's fatalism begins the story of a lifetime with the two prophecies, the double ending concludes that story with the allegorized title of "L'Excessif," his occasional signature in the correspondence of his later years. Julien's excess reflects Flaubert's attraction toward animals, along with lunatics, primitives, nomads, and so on—all the categories excluded by society—and toward excess itself. Beyond but including his avowed "pantheism," Flaubert's love of excess is specifically grounded in his aesthetics: "Les oeuvres d'art qui me plaisent par-dessus toutes les autres sont celles où *l'art excède*. J'aime dans la peinture, la Peinture; dans les vers, le Vers [The works of art that I like above all others are those that have *art in excess*. In painting, I love Painting; in poetry, Poetry]."[71]

The allegory of this excess in the characterization of Julien reflects Flaubert's lifelong excessive fantasy about animals and others excluded by bourgeois repression: animals come toward him. This formula appears in Flaubert's account of a dream he had in 1845.[72] Although this dream has been mentioned in the context of hunting in *La Légende*, it remains impenetrable unless it is considered in the context of his allegory of conversion.

Flaubert's dream begins with a walk through a forest full of monkeys that surround him. He grows fearful; one tries to caress him; and he shoots it. He awakens in a mood of tenderness and identification with the monkeys, described as "une communion toute panthéistique et tendre [a communion all pantheistic and tender]." But the most enigmatic element of the dream revolves around Flaubert's mother, who is with him in the forest. She goes against the parental grain of normalizing Flaubert and distancing him from his attraction to marginality. When her son has shot the monkey, she is the dream-speaker of this remark: "Pourquoi le blesses-tu, ton ami, qu'est-ce qu'il t'a fait? ne vois-tu pas qu'il t'aime? comme il te ressemble! [Why do you wound him, your friend, what has he done to you? don't you see that he loves you? how he resembles you!]."[73]

While expressing Flaubert's own "pantheistic" feeling, she reproaches him for his violence. This dream-reproach is confirmed ten years later, by a maternal reproach made in real life. Flaubert writes to Bouilhet: "Sais-tu que ma mère . . . m'a dit un mot sublime . . . 'La rage des phrases t'a desséché le coeur.'—Au fond, tu es de son avis [Do you know, my mother . . . made a sublime remark . . . 'The rage for sentences has dried out your heart.'—Deep down, you agree with her]."[74]

The second reproach of "rage" is another criticism of violence directed at Flaubert, the "coeur féroce [ferocious heart]" echoed by the stag's curse of Julien. Flaubert, however, describes it as "sublime" in a tone that is not exclusively ironic. The rage for sentences *is* Flaubert's rage for the sublime, and he makes that clear his whole life long. Julien's lust for killing is like Flaubert's unquenchable drive for writing—the fatality of vocation. This fatality afflicts the subject of intoxication with a curse and its fulfillment—Flaubert's version of "dépense" and "la part maudite [expenditure, the fatal gift]."

A work of fiction written by Flaubert ends irrevocably with a moment of sublime vertigo, an image of glassy ravishment. *For me, all becomes allegory*—"Tout pour moi devient allégorie." Flaubert's voice aligns with the voice of Baudelaire, and Proust's allegory has two fathers. Flaubert's predilection for multiple endings does not compromise their resemblance to Baudelaire's Andromaque, "Auprès d'un tombeau vide en extase courbée [curved in ecstasy near an empty tomb]." Intoxication reigns, and the image of glass often resonates in a sublime silence of allegory. In the ultimate conclusion, Bouvard and Pécuchet do what Flaubert spent his life doing: "they copy." The "ravishment" is his own intoxication of writing: "On s'étonne des mystiques. Mais le secret est là; leur amour, à la manière des torrents, n'avait qu'un seul lit, étroit, profond, en pente, et c'est pour cela qu'il emportait tout [People are astonished by the mystics. But that is the secret: their love, like mountain torrents, had only a single bed, narrow, deep, falling, and that is why it carried everything away]."[75]

6

Crimson and Diamonds

Ni moi ni vous ni personne, aucun ancien et aucun moderne, ne peut connaître la femme orientale, par la raison qu'il est impossible de la fréquenter.
[No one, not I nor you, no ancient and no modern, can know the oriental woman, because it is impossible to associate with her.][1]

The Flemish virgin silenced in *Madame Bovary* inhabits the sublime form of the artist riding a sea of ink. This incarnation of feminine mysticism and unquenchable love surfaces late in Flaubert's career as Julien the Hospitator. In a different form, however, Flaubert's virgin puts in a spectacular appearance soon after the completion of *Madame Bovary*, as the fictional daughter of Hamilcar. In order to decipher the estrangement and beautiful representation played out in *Salammbô*, it must be read retrospectively, from the viewpoint of its allegory of conversion, considered in the context of the stained-glass window—the crown of allegory worn by Flaubert as the legend of Saint Julian the Hospitator. The author invents her name and makes it the title of his novel: Salammbô.[2]

In *Salammbô*, Flaubert's "unquenchable love," the knot of religion and eroticism essential to his entire oeuvre, is presented in the terms of excess and hieroglyphics that rule the planetary spheres of allegory. The multiplication and expansion of allegory in this novel is so intense that it closes forever the door of easy identification that has allowed generations of readers to enter the modern world of Emma Bovary.[3] Despite this difference between the two novels, however, a reading of Flaubert's investment in the antiquity he recreates—a reading conducted through the allegory of conversion—shows that *Salammbô* derives from the outline that led to *Madame Bovary*. Like *La Légende*, *Salammbô* entwines the three early projects of Flaubert's letter to Bouilhet into a new creation: a second pilgrimage to the Orient of style. During the preparation and writing of his most scratched-out and rewritten novel,[4] Flaubert aspires to live in its "sujet splendide et loin du monde moderne [splendid subject far from the modern world]."[5] Through style, this subject maps out an interpenetration of antiquity and modernity. In this sense, its version of unquenchable suffering and sensibility places it in the framework of Flaubert's other great prose works, beginning with *Madame Bovary*.

Grounded in the art of involuntary memory, the three projects come together in the miracle of allegory, the resurrection of the past. The doubled form of unquenchable love unfolds the Flaubertian "metaphysics," or the first principle of allegory: at the site of Souvenir, the excesses characteristic of mysticism enter the domain of voluptuous love. Like Proust, Flaubert invoked a nocturnal muse; his nights of negativity drew the crimson splendor of the past out of a present melancholy. When he wrote to Bouilhet from Constantinople, the weight of memory, fatal eroticism, and death (the same elements that appear in the letter from Rhodes to Madame Flaubert) came together in the characters of his three youthful projects to prefigure the thematic material and the allegorical colors of his future writings.

Salammbô is one recombination of the three projects: the night of love and death, the mystical virgin dying young, and especially the woman who desires a god. The night associated with the *Don Juan* sketch is recalled in the uncanny nights of Salammbô, particularly her encounter with Mâtho in "Sous la Tente [Under the Tent]." This scene ends her virginity but intensifies the mysticism that sustains her pervasive identification with Tanit. Salammbô desires Moloch in the form of Mâtho, and this desire is anticipated by her yearning to possess the carnal forms of the goddess Tanit. These allegorical elements that grew out of Flaubert's original sketch entered the text of *Madame Bovary*, through moments of mystical rapture that sometimes affect Emma and that more often surface in Flaubert's descriptive narration.[6] From the first "livre sur rien [book about nothing]," these elements of allegory enter the "splendid subject" of Carthage and Salammbô, "far from the modern world."

But although these early outlines and their insistent unity may be found hovering in the wings of all of Flaubert's finished novels and stories, and although they give intriguing evidence of his allegorical enterprise (discussed earlier in the context of *La Légende*), Flaubert's discovery of style could only take place through the alembic of writing the text that would become *Madame Bovary*. The elaboration of a new allegorical form arises as a writing of modernity comparable only to the oeuvre of Baudelaire. Within this representation, the allegory of conversion gives an account of the writer's passage through the black sea of writing.

The projects about "unquenchable love" enter *Madame Bovary*, but Flaubert followed the advice of Bouilhet, influenced by Du Camp, and disguised the ideal in the grey costume of banality. The violent erasure of the narrative of the idealized figure, the Flemish virgin, may have contributed to Flaubert's displacement of beauty from the subject of prose to the fabric of prose itself; in any case, out of this experiment came the style and vision of orientalized modernism. The major elements that Flaubert disciplined out of Emma's portrayal return in the characterization of Salammbô. At the same time, however, they return from the beyond of style established in *Madame Bovary* and within the rearticulation of that style. The coupling of historical veracity and modernity in *Madame Bovary* returns full-blown in *Salammbô* as the creation of antiquity through modernity.[7] At every moment, the ideal is challenged by the claim for truth, fueled by a whirl of documentation. In turn, Flaubert's use of historical and religious materials enriches his revery of the ideal: out of this other version of unquenchable love, the love of beauty, comes the text.

In *Salammbô* a recombination of the three projects situated in the domain of splendor ushers the beautiful new style of *Madame Bovary* into the reinvented Orient of antiquity. *Madame*

Bovary is also the point of origin of *Salammbô*'s sublime negativity, many years before *La Légende*. Flaubert's reading of Saint Julian and the allegory of conversion that he wrote at the pinnacle of his writing career emerge in the text that allowed Flaubert an exodus from the blackest period of his life; it portrays the figure of the artist on the terrain of the ideal. In this sense, it resembles *Salammbô* more than it does *Madame Bovary*: *Salammbô* is at the heart of Flaubert's mature fiction, where it alone (with *Hérodias*) pursues the reveries of exotic femininity that fascinated Flaubert. The allegory of conversion takes the form of absorption and estrangement in a portrait of the artist as "orientale."

Eighteen years prior to the writing of *La Légende*, Flaubert assembled feminine identity, sainthood, Art, and excess in "the story of a whole life" to form the character of Salammbô. She succumbs to the same melancholy that possesses Julien, or rather, her holy purity is inhabited by the melancholy that haunts his sainthood. Like him she is dominated by a sacrilegious desire that is her fate. This desire will be fatal to her: in other words, sacrilegious desire will write her life story. When Salammbô begs Schahabarim to show her the visual manifestation or form of the goddess, he answers: "Jamais! Ne sais-tu pas qu'on en meurt? . . . Ton désir est un sacrilège [Never! Don't you know that one dies of it? . . . Your desire is sacrilege]" (55). In Salammbô's case, the excess of saintliness leads to her attempt to go beyond virginity and femininity to the monstrous regions of the eunuch priests. This excess prepares the complicity between purity and desire, saintliness and sin, that leads Salammbô into the paradoxical realm of Flaubert's allegory: it is both melancholic and impersonal, or depersonalized. Her melancholic desire anchors the "subjectivity" that her creator Flaubert attributes to her in the masks of religion and the mysterious, feminine Other of Tanit—the repository of Carthaginian memory and origins.

Flaubert plants the seeds of his own melancholy and impersonality in Salammbô and Julien: their negativity must be read through the author's optics of the sublime. The sadness masking the author is the "other" world of allegory, waiting to be resuscitated from the depths of Memory. This is illustrated in "Le Cygne": the visions and signs of the sphere inhabited by the narrator remove him from the context of his present tense, and turn his memory into a stage for the impossible lament of the swan and the ecstatic silences of Andromaque. In this sense, the hermeneutics of the narrator of "Le Cygne," carried away by memory, indicate the following paradox: the antiquity of Souvenir and the antiquity of history can only be brought back to life through an aesthetic of modernity. When Flaubert invokes the "splendid subject" of his novel, he always has in mind the beauty of the new style he is trying to create through the splendor of allegory. For this reason, it is aesthetically and historically unjustifiable to oppose *Madame Bovary* to *Salammbô*. Flaubert wrote to Sainte-Beuve: "Moi, j'ai voulu fixer un mirage en appliquant à l'Antiquité les procédés du roman moderne [I wanted to hold fast to a mirage by applying to Antiquity the methods of the modern novel]" (355). Out of the clouds of Souvenir comes the evanescent mirage: the allegorical image.

L'Invitation au voyage

Simultaneously antique and modern, at the source of memory and caught up in its evanescence, *Salammbô* enters the scene of Flaubert's writing with the melancholy and passion that already graphed the descent of Emma Bovary, but without the bitter ironies and the deliberately grey tones used to separate contemporary bourgeois banality from the baroque beauty of the more exotic works. Flaubert's indirect autobiography slips unrecognized through the reinvention of Carthage: like the portrayal of Julien, this hieroglyphics of the baroque distances the melancholy and passion that it represents from any threat of contemporary recognition or diagnosis, à la Du Camp, and removes them from the sentimentality of the personal, so that Flaubertian rage and ecstasy can be portrayed in an unmitigated or undiluted fashion.

Salammbô is filled with the rage evident in *La Légende*. The textual economy of negativity in the *Conte* can be seen as a scaled-down, individualized version of the elaborate panorama of suffering and jouissance that is displayed in *Salammbô*. At the same time, the unreadability of *Salammbô* (according to Sainte-Beuve's accusations) is anticipated in *Madame Bovary*. Although Flaubert attempted to defend his work against Sainte-Beuve's charges[8] on the basis of his efforts and the reality that he had attempted to render in his novel, it might have been more to the point if he had responded that whatever "unreadability" the critic found in *Salammbô* was already present in *Madame Bovary* as allegory: memory and historicity, impersonality (absorption and estrangement), and modernity.[9] Even the silhouette of Salammbô is visible in the representation of Emma, filtered through the experience of death, love, and the desert—the aesthetic elaboration that Flaubert calculated and composed during the writing of *Madame Bovary*.

The poetic, mystical virgin that he barred from this novel—the Emma he would have wanted to create—is linked to the ambivalent incarnation of saintliness and unholy rage he would later inscribe as Julien through the writing of his own form of conversion. After *Madame Bovary* and years before the *Trois Contes*, Flaubert divided their traits between Salammbô and Mâtho, masculine and feminine. At the same time, however, the allegorical dimensions of antiquity in the conception of his second novel further emphasized Flaubert's ambition as a painter of modern life: the parallel between the feminine type (both character and representative) and the cultural entity for which she stands is even more striking in the context of *Salammbô* than in the full title[10] of *Madame Bovary*. The relationship of Emma Bovary to the bourgeois provincial life indicated through her and around her is further intensified in Flaubert's conception of his novel about antiquity. While *Madame Bovary* appears consistently in his correspondence as "la Bovary"—the text conceived and titled through its central character—his attachment to the allegorical invention of Salammbô's character fantasmatically identifies her with allegory itself, through the representation of Antiquity, Style, and the Orient. On the other hand, this focus on the eroticism of style ("the Oriental woman") is an intrusion; since he frames his work according to documents about the Orient and the history of Carthage, fiction interrupts the discourse of History. Most of the characters have historical models, but Hamilcar's daughter is pure Flaubert.

After its completion, Flaubert referred to his novel through the character of Salammbô, "ma Carthaginoise."[11] The novel he called his "Carthaginian woman" is his allegory of antiquity, a text woven out of oppositions and estrangements. She emerges as a figure of antiquity throughout the work,[12] originally called *Carthage*, then *Salammbô, roman carthaginois*, and finally *Salammbô*. The "splendid subject"—Carthage and its reinvention as the figure of Salammbô—restores the gray regions of passion in *Madame Bovary* to full color, by allowing Flaubert's ideal of intoxication to occupy the scene unhindered by the stereotypes of contemporary passions. While his depiction of these stereotypes always required ironic distance, the rendering of what fascinated him in the Orient and its antiquity allowed Flaubert to enter the territory of his subject from beyond the "personal" subjectivity of sentiment, far away from love à la Walter Scott, in the horror and splendor of antiquity, the full violence of allegory.

How is the allegory of *Salammbô* different from that deployed in *Madame Bovary*? First, its passions are presented with brutal immediacy undiluted by the grayness of Flaubert's view of the contemporary bourgeoisie. Fatality, melancholy, rage, love, and so on—the horrors and splendors of passion as he conceived them—emerge in full force from negativity. What is equally important in this representation is that horror and splendor themselves, negativity and beauty, are represented as such, undisguised and in their truest Flaubertian forms. In this sense, the passions of *Salammbô* are impossible, or "unreadable": out of the excess of the ideal, out of the power of death, comes the allegorized text, Flaubert's Orient of style. His correspondence[13] was filled with his concern that the massive dose of violence in *Salammbô* would be too much for his readers: he realized he had gone beyond the limits of *Madame Bovary*. In the course of writing, the splendid subject reveals itself as the vision of the ideal, the unattainable and impossible image—or mirage—represented through an invented impossibility, the ideal of beautiful prose.

The consequences of Flaubert's choice of subject in *Salammbô* allow him to move away from what he called the "false poetry" of Emma Bovary, and the bourgeois world of "idées reçues [clichés]." When he expresses concern about the reception of the novel, he focuses on scenes of strategic military violence that may be unacceptable for his contemporaries, but in fact the representation of violence permeates the entire text. It portrays the passions as unnatural forms of excess that work against cultural or individual order and preservation; in *Salammbô* passion is fatal, a negative force that stems from the obsessional idée fixe. This fatality and the constant presence of death, grief, and memory prepare a resurrection of the monuments of antiquity through the absorptions and estrangements of the allegory of conversion. This summary of the various strands or layers of allegory could be illustrated on almost every page of the text. What is central to all these levels, however, and what ties them together as "forme et fond" (style, subject, and the exponential "form and content" of self-inscription) is the most violent element of Flaubert's allegory. The violence that continues to give *Salammbô* the reputation of being "unreadable" is its rejection of the Romantic imagination exemplified by Sainte-Beuve's *Volupté*. The Romantics used personal sentiment and the taboos of Christian religion as an alternative or a disguise for sexuality. *Salammbô* places sexuality at the center of culture; sexuality *is* religion. It is composed of an allegorical hierarchy of types, a language of hieroglyphics, and a subjectivity that is not to be confused with personal sentiment.

Distanced from the sentiment of Romantic image and ideology, this subjectivity receives its highest illustration in the strange love affair—if it can be called that—between Salammbô and Mâtho. The sublime and the sexual are inseparable in Flaubert's novel: the "barbarous" passion of the Libyan, contrasted to the refinements of Narr'Havas the Numidian, presents the seduction of Salammbô by Mâtho as a supreme act of worshiping the goddess Tanit. It also presents Salammbô's preparations for the retrieval of the most sacred of objects, the zaimph, as sexual mastery. But the terms of surrender and mastery are ambivalent here precisely because of the allegorical representation—rage, worship, melancholy, fatality—in which the object of love is impersonal as a planet, and each one wishes the other to die. For Mâtho, Salammbô *is* Tanit; for her he *is* Moloch: "'J'ai suivi la trace de tes feux, comme si je marchais derrière Moloch!' . . . 'n'es-tu pas toute-puissante, immaculée, radieuse et belle comme Tanit!' ['I followed the trace of your fires, as if I were walking behind Moloch!' . . . 'are you not all-powerful, immaculate, radiant, and beautiful like Tanit!']" (223). Each conceives of the other more as a fatal weapon than as an individual: each involuntarily dies for the other whom he or she has cursed. Their union is a brief flash, preceded by illness and rage and followed by death. Each is estranged, not only from the other, but also from himself or herself. This estrangement gives rise to Mâtho's absorption in military strategy and carnage, and to Salammbô's pursuit of the form of the goddess Tanit.

In the absence of sentimentality, Flaubert's focus on sexuality as strategy recalls Sade far more than do the scenes of military violence criticized by Sainte-Beuve as sadistic. Although Flaubert protested against Sainte-Beuve's accusation of "sadisme," it is worth noting that some of his greatest objections focused on Sainte-Beuve's misunderstanding of the characters of Salammbô and Mâtho:

> Elle ressemble selon vous à 'une Elvire sentimentale'. . . . Mais non! . . . Salammbô au contraire demeure clouée par l'idée fixe. C'est une maniaque. . . . Mâtho *rôde comme un fou* autour de Carthage. Fou est le mot juste. L'amour tel que le concevaient les anciens n'était-il pas une folie, une malédiction, une maladie envoyée par les dieux? Polybe serait bien *étonné*, dites-vous, de voir ainsi son Mâtho. Je ne le crois pas. [According to you she resembles "a sentimental Elvira". . . . Not at all! . . . On the contrary, Salammbô remains riveted to her obsession. She is maniacal. . . . Mâtho *prowls* around Car-

thage *like a madman*. Madman is the right word. Wasn't love, according to the ancients' conception of it, a form of madness, a curse, an illness sent by the gods? You say that Polybius would really be *surprised* to see his Mâtho in this light. I do not believe that he would be]" (356–57).

The author of *Volupté* cannot assimilate Flaubert's portrayal of the a-sentimental bitterness of love, allegorized as Mâtho's madness and Salammbô's obsession.

But in terms of Flaubert's text, what does it mean to say that sexuality is religion, and that in the place of sentimentality there are only the mysterious figures of allegory? It means that Flaubert creates his characters by extending a set of oppositions from the allegorical fabric of historical antiquity (the object of his studies) to the individual figures who cannot be read outside the oppositions that they incarnate. (In this sense, Flaubert's fictional allegory is perhaps even more allegorical than the historical accounts of antiquity that he used as his sources.) The following oppositions are inextricably knotted together in the fabric of fictional allegory: Mercenaries and Carthage, sun and moon, male and female, fire and water, profane and sacred, Moloch and Tanit, war and love, and so on. These categories inevitably circle back to take hold of Mâtho and Salammbô, who are absorbed and estranged in a constellation that possesses and moves them. These allegorical configurations expressed through the characters and invested in them also dominate the other narrative elements of *Salammbô*: the plot (composed of military and amorous strategies, woven together): the setting (the symbolic geography of Carthage—temples, palaces, gates, and so on); dialogue, silence, codes of communication in the novel; and, above all, Flaubert's language, forged or reinvented according to the need to "translate" the Orient by falsifying and "gallicizing" ("franciser") it.

Desire is neither natural nor organically creative: its negativity has little regard for the preservation or illusions of any so-called individual. Desire, like Dante's levels of poetic language, is alien. On its pedestal of artifice the violence of the Other establishes connections that will prove fatal.

The allegorical unfolding of *Salammbô* takes place in a city lost in the written monuments of history. Its site is covered with temples and elaborate symbolism, integrating the artifacts of a lost civilization, its accessories and refinements, the translated traces of its language, and the privileged Flaubertian space of emptiness, death, and the displaced origins of lost paradise: the desert. The place known as Carthage is the site of Salammbô's artful mystery, while the infinite desert beyond it is the site of Mâtho's desolation, burning rage, and melancholy.

In this framework Flaubert's remark to Feydeau indicates how the steps he took to distance himself from personalized sentiment moved him away from "sadness" and toward the desert, translated as the intoxication of antiquity and the artist's resurrection of the dead. The resuscitated melancholy of Carthage offers the delights of Salammbô: "Quand on lira *Salammbô* on ne pensera pas, j'espère, à l'auteur! Peu de gens devineront combien il a fallu être triste pour entreprendre de ressusciter Carthage! [When people will read *Salammbô*, I hope that no one will think about its author! Few people will suspect how much sadness was necessary in order to undertake the resuscitation of Carthage!]"[15]

Allegory, or the common ground between Flaubert, Proust, and Baudelaire, may be defined in the following terms: it is a shining veil of beauty (the Orient of style, the pane of the artist's colored glass) that reveals the identity or equivalence of sexuality and death. Writing allegory is an act of horror and splendor; it resuscitates the dead. Although this quasi-equation is valid for all of Flaubert's mature fiction, it is more clearly presented in *Salammbô* than in anything he had written up to that time.

The allegorical performance of *Salammbô* puts this equation into effect through an artistic sublation (*Aufhebung*) of history: Flaubert simultaneously recreates and interrupts history with a "love story" that represents the encounter of two civilizations in the looming shadow of Rome, soon to annihilate Carthage (98). The encounter brings the sophisticated, refined Carthage face to face with its cultural Other, the nationalities and tribes lumped together as "les Barbares" (the Mercenaries). As a "love story," however, this work is like no other; in the Romantic terms of Flaubert's period, it is not a love story at all, but rather an allegory of the power of death that exceeds any and all strategy. Through religion, war, eroticism, and ultimately art, fatality dissolves the subject. Elements from this account of dissolution become the monuments of history.

A fabric of fiction turns these monuments into the intoxication of antiquity. Its desired splendor is allegorized as the type or figure of oriental femininity; Salammbô is Flaubert's work of art. Like the goddess, she is seen veiled in a mystical cloak, "son grand manteau de pourpre sombre, taillé dans une étoffe inconnue [her great cloak of dark crimson, cut out from an unknown fabric]" (12). As a character, she incarnates a paradox of Modernist allegory. Absolutely singular and authentically poetic, for Flaubert himself (unlike Emma, who represents modern life through "fausse poésie" and bourgeois compromise), her mystery remains intact and reinforces her allegorical role as an extension of the goddess Tanit. Salammbô is the Carthaginian translation of the Flemish virgin. Because of Flaubert's interpretation of the impenetrable aura around the Oriental woman, Salammbô is even more sublime than her northern counterpart.

Swathed in crimson and diamonds and drenched in perfume, Salammbô is nevertheless the center of a scene of great sexual ambivalence. What Baudelaire diagnosed as Emma Bovary's "virility" (the key to her status as a modernist heroine according to Benjamin's principles of modern allegory)[16] occurs in the portrayal of Salammbô as the excess of her obsession with Tanit, closely associated with her "tutor," Schahabarim. One symptom of this ambivalence is the overturning of the feminine influence by a murderous rage and hatred produced by love. It appears in Salammbô's singular reaction to Mâtho. It is she, Schahabarim's pupil, who voices the curse of Moloch: "Que l'Autre . . . te brûle! [May the Other . . .

burn you!]" (91). Even after seeing her for the first time, Mâtho perceives this ambivalence. He says: "La malédiction de Moloch pèse sur moi. Je l'ai senti à ses yeux [The curse of Moloch weighs me down. I felt it in her eyes]" (20). The strangeness of this remark can only be gauged within the emblematics of the novel: the virginal Salammbô is the privileged vehicle for Tanit, the moon goddess, opposed to Moloch: "Une influence était descendue de la lune sur la vierge [An influence had descended from the moon to the virgin]" (52). In the last pages of the book Salammbô is revealed as the human form of Tanit, echoing Mâtho's adoration of her as the goddess (223): "Salammbô resplendissante se confondait avec Tanit et semblait le génie même de Carthage, son âme corporifiée [shining Salammbô melted into Tanit and seemed to be Carthage's very spirit, its soul rendered flesh]" (347).

In this context the identification of Salammbô with Moloch —the god represented by her as the Other (91) and typified in the form of Mâtho—indicates a straying of the emblematic meaning that knots these opposites together. Within this representation of antiquity, sexual ambivalence is an additional form of estrangement. It brings the portrayal of the characters closer to the knotted sexual identities of Flaubert the modern, and allows for the oblique representations that allegorize conversion.

Whereas in *La Légende* the allegory of conversion worked its way through the representation of Julien alone—the only developed character in the narrative of a solitude even more total than that of Saint Antoine—and whereas in *Madame Bovary* the ironic and satiric rendering of the modern element and its vulgar qualities limited the extent to which Flaubert's allegory of conversion could penetrate many of its characters other than Emma, the splendors of antiquity seem to have made it possible for Flaubert to extend and fully disseminate the allegory of conversion in *Salammbô* perhaps more than in any other text. This effect of the horror and splendor associated with the Orient of style is related to the sexual ambivalence that fascinated Baudelaire in the portrait of Emma.

This ambivalence seems to be a product of Flaubert's allegory of conversion in *Madame Bovary*. How does it permeate the text of *Salammbô* to a greater extent than *Madame Bovary*? Through the allegorical layers described earlier, the knot of love and violence allows for reversals and oppositions that affect not only the heroine, but other characters as well, particularly Mâtho, and beyond them a more general level of cultural conflation of religion and sexuality.

Cette tristesse étrange

Related to the original figure of Emma as the Flemish virgin, *Salammbô* differs from Emma in ways that allow Flaubert to make her sexual ambivalence more explicit. If the final version of Emma is compared to Salammbô, however, the roots of their ambivalence appear somewhat similar: neither has a mother, and the weak presence of Emma's father anticipates the fatherly element of Hamilcar's character. Although he is a strong and dramatically central character in the novel, as Salammbô's father he is distinguished mainly by his absence. It literally begins the novel: his absence sets the plot into motion with the Mercenaries' infringements during the "festin" of the first chapter, Salammbô's appearance among them, and the ensuing consequences. But the family circle of Salammbô has one important difference from the limited entourage of the still unmarried Emma—Salammbô has a tutor to initiate her in the ways of the goddess. He is literally the high priest of sexuality and Salammbô's parental authority. His first appearance explicitly defines his role: "C'était le grand-prêtre de Tanit, celui qui avait élevé Salammbô [He was Tanit's high priest, the one who had raised Salammbô]" (53). It is Schahabarim who orchestrates the encounter between Salammbô and Mâtho, and it is through this meeting that the curse she has pronounced against Mâtho becomes her own fatality. At the same time her allegorical status as the incarnation of Carthage makes her fate representative of Carthage's doom. In terms of history, the religious-sexual strand of the plot seems to have appeared more decisive to Flaubert than the military element, in spite of the display of violence, cunning, and horror. Hamilcar acts on what he thinks has occurred in his absence; he accepts the command of the Punic forces against the Mercenaries (160). But his victory will be undone by the fate of Salammbô. Betrothed to her father's ally, Narr'Havas, she dies on her wedding day, in the last lines of the novel. The metaphoric and literal levels of sexual allegory coincide: Hamilcar's victory is left unconsummated.

Unlike the unsuspecting modern men in *Madame Bovary*, Hamilcar believes the slander of the Anciens: "Il était sûr maintenant qu'elle avait failli dans l'étreinte d'un Barbare [He was certain now that she had succumbed to the embrace of a Barbarian]" (142). He is mistaken. He misinterprets her lamentation, and maintains a distance that is in fact full of rage and a desire for vengeance (154). The character who is at the sexual center of the narrative, and at the same time, is truly "impossible" or unmoveable, is Schahabarim, one of Flaubert's most spectacular creations of estrangement. This mysterious figure is central to Flaubert's strategy in the novel; he is also, and perhaps more importantly, for Flaubert, a vehicle for the allegory of conversion prefiguring the role that Julien will play many years later. As Tanit's high priest, the earlier version of an ascetic, monstrous, solitary figure filled with rage and melancholy is engaged with the same forces of negativity that will make Julien into Flaubert's final incarnation of the "principe mâle exterminateur [male principle of extermination]." This principle haunts both the modernist sensibility of the hieratic priest of Tanit (202) and the sublime sainthood that elevates Julien at the conclusion of *La Légende*. It is uncannily rehearsed in Schahabarim's final elevation and offering of Mâtho's heart to the sun at the bloody conclusion of *Salammbô* (352).

Like Julien, Schahabarim gives scriptural evidence of a Flaubertian formula indicated earlier: deprivation creates excess. It describes not only the nebulous region of "psychology," but even more, the intersection of psychoanalysis and aesthetics on the ground of the allegory of conversion. This formula may be seen as a challenge to Sartre's "qui perd gagne." In a reading of the figure of Julien, the link between the two terms of deprivation and excess emerged as the relation between the ascetic and the sublime, extended from Flaubert's self-reflection to the Modernist medievalized creation of Saint Julian. Although the priestly role and textual status of Schahabarim diverge from those of Julien (Schahabarim is not the subject of "l'histoire de toute une vie" as is his pupil, Salammbô; he occupies little space in the novel; his solitude as a eunuch, the vehicle of the "hermaphrodite Baals" [55], is irrevocable), the melancholy asceticism that makes him into a figure for the idealized realm of religion foreshadows Julien's departure from life in the world and his entrance into the sublime.

Like Julien, Schahabarim is a privileged figure of impersonality, distance, detachment. The single point of human contact in his life is Salammbô: "Mais sur l'aridité de sa vie, Salammbô faisait comme une fleur dans la fente d'un sépulcre. Cependant, il était dur pour elle [But on the arid surface of his life, Salammbô was like a flower in the crack of a sepulcher. He was harsh with her, however]" (203). His detachment is perfected, even sublime. When she weeps at his feet, he remains a model of Flaubertian impersonality: "Schahabarim, debout, restait plus insensible que les pierres de la terrasse [Schahabarim, standing straight, remained more insensitive than the stones of the terrace]" (55). This figure of sexual ambiguity is at the same time one of the most bitter, sad, and solitary characters ever created. If his lost virility leads him to the religious sublime, it also exiles him from love: "Puis, il accusait secrètement la Rabbet de l'infortune de sa vie . . . Et il suivait d'un oeil mélancholique des hommes qui se perdaient avec les prêtresses [Then he secretly accused the Rabbet of the misfortune in his life . . . And his melancholy gaze followed the men who were disappearing with the priestesses]" (54). Based on Flaubert's rejection of sentimentality à la Sainte-Beuve, this exile is clearly stated in terms that anticipate Freud: "Ce brave organe génital est le fond des tendresses humaines; . . . Jamais aucune femme n'a aimé un eunuque [This worthy organ is the source of human tenderness; . . . no woman ever loved a eunuch]."[17] Flaubert pursues this demystification with an explicit link between the detachment from sexuality and the sublime of Art: "C'est ce dégoût de la guenille qui a fait inventer les religions, les mondes idéaux de l'art [The disgust with the body's tattered rags led to the invention of religions, the ideal worlds of art]."[18]

Combined with the ideal of impersonal style, Flaubert's own melancholy ("how much sadness was necessary . . . ") enters the uncanny figure of sexual ambivalence, Schahabarim. Filled with rage, he occupies in absentia the sexual center of the novel: "il en voulait moins à la jeune fille de ne pouvoir la posséder que de la trouver si belle et surtout si pure [he held a grudge against the girl less for not being able to possess her than because he found her so beautiful and especially so pure]" (203). He writes the script for the retrieval of the zaimph, thereby condemning Salammbô to death by sexual initiation: "Le prêtre la considéra fixement, et avec un sourire qu'elle n'avait jamais vu [The priest fixed his gaze on her, and with a smile that she had never seen]" (207). Ostensibly he engages her in a battle with Mâtho, but in fact he arranges for her to counter the "ravishment" of the zaimph with her own. Her obsession with the zaimph provides a kind of complicity, while at the same time it offers an alibi—literally a cover-up—for her ambivalence toward Mâtho. Contrary to Hamilcar's belief, his virginal daughter is still completely ignorant of what the bitter priest requires from her—so Salammbô's "ravishment" will be complete. The priestly figure writes the perverse scene of her initiation into love, thereby linking the sublime representation of Art, "le manteau de Tanit [Tanit's cloak]" (207), with Salammbô's mystical "défaillance [swooning]" (207): "—Il faut que tu ailles chez les Barbares reprendre le zaimph! Elle s'affaissa sur l'escabeau . . . avec un frisson de tous ses membres. . . . Ses tempes bourdonnaient, elle voyait tourner des cercles de feu, et, dans sa stupeur, ne comprenait plus qu'une chose, c'est que certainement elle allait bientôt mourir [—You must go to the Barbarians and take back the zaimph! She collapsed . . . with a shivering in all her limbs. . . . Her temples were buzzing, she saw circles of fire turning, and in her stupor she understood only one thing, the certainty that she would soon die]" (205).

Schahabarim, then, is the agent of the novel's two forms of ravishment: by preparing the scene of "Sous la Tente," he sets up the link between the sexual and the sublime. In this sense, his role captures Flaubert's own rapture,[19] writing the love scene between Emma and Rodolphe in *Madame Bovary*. Despite his passionate "transport," the priest banishes sentiment from love, sexuality, and religious discourse. His exceptionally ambivalent identity and the funereal quality specific to his privileged role in the Orient of style make Schahabarim into an allegory of the allegorist—the site of the connection between religion and sexuality. He joins them together through "défaillance" and raging violence, the sublime and sexual forms of Flaubertian conversion. The text describes these forms of conversion as "ravishment."

Under the influence of the Orient of style, Salammbô's virginal beauty becomes the body and soul of Tanit through the ravishment of her purity. Flaubert takes this ravishment into the dark regions of corruption: the priest's strange smile of vicarious pleasure is recalled by Giscon's apparently gratuitous insult: "Je t'ai entendu râler d'amour comme une prostituée.... Ah! sacrilège! Maudite sois-tu! [I heard you gasp with love like a prostitute.... Ah! sacrilege! You are cursed!]" (230). This verbal excess, the horrified and indecent cursing of the now hideous Giscon, acts as a kind of mask for the Flaubertian delight inscribed in the scene of "Sous la Tente," presaged by the eunuch priest's strange smile. It is the jouissance of allegory consummated in the union of Salammbô and Mâtho: the unfolding of ravishment is labeled with Giscon's "râler d'amour," the death-rattle of love.

Pourpre comme le soleil

How do these forms of ravishment conflate the sexual and the sublime? How do they mark the text with the allegory of conversion? The answer to both these questions is found in a reading of the levels of allegory that unfold in the love scene following Schahabarim's seduction of Salammbô. Orchestrated by the priest, her attempt to retrieve the zaimph is prolonged and accomplished as sexual surrender to Mâtho. This brief description is in fact much more explicit than Flaubert's text. Aside from his precaution against shocking his readers,[20] his language appears to be "elsewhere," hovering beyond the scene, above it, because the allegorical enterprise of the whole novel stands or falls with this chapter.

The ravishings of love, melancholy, and desire combine with Spendius's calculations to steal the zaimph, Salammbô's involvement in Carthage's loss of it, the curse she pronounces against Mâtho when he brings Tanit's veil to her bedroom, and the fatality that affects both of them. These episodes and elements are knotted together only during "Sous la Tente": the unfolding of fatality that occupies the rest of the text takes place because of this encounter. What Giscon describes as "râler d'amour" is transcribed as a series of exclamations: only Giscon hears (or fantasizes) what he describes in his curse of Salammbô.

After the forms of "swooning" that punctuate her seduction by Schahabarim, her decision and preparation, Salammbô enters Mâtho's tent and both succumb to a series of raptures or "ravissements." Mâtho is dazzled by her beauty: "Il aurait voulu l'envelopper, l'absorber, la boire . . . il répétait: —'Comme tu es belle!' [He would have liked to envelop her, to absorb her and drink her in . . . he repeated:—'how beautiful you are!']" (221–22). Salammbô expresses her rapture as allegory. Mâtho's fires are attributed to Moloch: "'J'ai suivi la trace de tes feux, comme si je marchais derrière Moloch!' . . . il se trouvait haussé à la taille d'un Dieu. ['I followed the trace of your fires, as if I were walking behind Moloch!' . . . he felt himself raised to the stature of a God]" (223). He, in turn, declares that he took the zaimph to give it to her whom he adores as Tanit: "'n'es-tu pas toute-puissante, immaculée, radieuse et belle comme Tanit!' Et avec un regard plein d'une adoration infinie:—'A moins, peut-être, que tu ne sois Tanit?' —'Moi, Tanit!' se disait Salammbô ['are you not all-powerful, immaculate, radiant, and beautiful like Tanit!' And with a gaze full of infinite adoration:—'Unless, perhaps, you are

Tanit?'—'I, Tanit!' thought Salammbô]" (223). The forms of ravishment continue in Mâtho's account of his rage, vengeance, and violent killing as extensions of his desire for her. Stunned and stupefied, Salammbô is ravished by an awareness of irrevocable fatality (225): "elle perdait toute conscience d'elle-même... un ordre des Dieux la forçait à s'y abandonner [she was losing all her self-awareness... an order from the Gods was forcing her to surrender]" (226).

The allegorical center of the novel coincides with the moment of mutual ravishment: "'—Moloch, tu me brûles!' ['—Moloch, you burn me!']" (226). This apostrophe of the god and the evocation of his fire is a hieroglyph, an inscription, a "transport" that reveals the essence of Flaubert's modernist allegory. The "transport" or bearing away of psychological interiority is consummated in the central moment of desire and eroticism. "Farewell to the personal": Mâtho and Salammbô have disappeared into the encounter between the gods whom they represent. The zaimph is the impossible object, an allegory or unalterable "other" figure for Flaubertian ravishment: the form that embellishes and covers the goddess Tanit. The zaimph is the object of raging violence, vertiginous mystery and admiration; it is the allegory of desire, feminine beauty, and beautiful form. After the moment of sublime allegory, the meeting of rage, vertigo, desire, and beauty, Salammbô puts it on: "Elle jeta le zaimph autour de sa taille, ramassa vivement ses voiles, son manteau, son écharpe [She threw the zaimph around her waist, quickly gathered her veils, her cloak, her scarf]" (231). Its allegorical form blends in with her clothing: she is draped in veils, cloaks, scarves. In a correspondence between letter and metaphor, these articles of clothing are used as figures to describe the zaimph, "the veil" and "the cloak of the Goddess" (85).

When Salammbô accuses Mâtho of involving her in the sacrilege of stealing it, he answers: "'c'était pour te le donner! pour te le rendre! Il me semblait que la Déesse avait laissé son vêtement pour toi' ['I did it to give it to you! to return it to you! It seemed to me that the Goddess had left her garment for you']" (223). "Taillé dans une étoffe inconnue [Cut out from an unknown cloth]" like Salammbô's cloak (12), the zaimph is an allegorical object, the fabric[21] of figural language. Flaubert uses it as a pretext, the ravishing figure of ravishment, that consummates the allegory of his novel. In order to emphasize its status in this context, the fatality of allegory's ravishment—"Moloch, tu me brûles!"—is sealed in the last sentence of the text: "Ainsi mourut la fille d'Hamilcar pour avoir touché au manteau de Tanit [In this way the daughter of Hamilcar died for having touched the cloak of Tanit]" (353). The title of the final chapter is "Mâtho."

Is it possible to locate the coupling of allegory? In other words, where does Flaubert give an account of the consummation corresponding to what Giscon describes as "the death-gasp of love"? Strangely enough, there is only silence; or rather, there are two metaphors of Moloch, the figures of the god. Like him, Mâtho has disappeared into the odd impersonality of the warrior, or "the soldier": "elle était comme enlevée dans un ouragan, prise dans la force du soleil [it was as if she had been carried away in a hurricane, taken in the force of the sun]" (226). The rest of the line is literally blank with this silence. The eloquence and beauty of the "blank" separating two chapters in *L'Education sentimentale*, according to Proust, is concentrated here into a kind of elixir of time, the Before and After of allegory. Salammbô's eclipse corresponds to the narrative's silence, and the half line of blank space is Flaubert's representation of ravishment itself. In light of the explicit eroticism of "Le Serpent" (to say nothing of other texts) there can be no doubt that the "blank" here speaks for the disquieting turns of ravishment and the double abyss: estrangement and fatality, love and death.

At the center of allegory, Flaubert's layers of ravishment create the image and shining light of figuration. Beyond the claims of antiquity, they seem to allegorize Flaubert's relation to the modernity he confronts and re-creates in writing. Like Baudelaire,[22] he invents Modernism as the clasping of antique and modern elements framed in an aesthetic that says adieu to the personal. Flaubert's exploration of ravishment focuses on this crucial episode of *Salammbô* as the stage for an objectified image: located in the allegory of conversion, it gives an account of the Orient of style. This object of estrangement and enchantment is the zaimph, the cloak of the Goddess. Within a framework of Modernism attentive to the artistry of temporality in Flaubert and Baudelaire, Proust will unfold antiquity and modernity as interior time. Like the transformed "cloak of the Goddess," Albertine's Fortuny coat will become an allegorical image anchored in the major allegorical opposition structuring *A la recherche du temps perdu*. It too reflects the author's mode of representation and the ideal of style that weaves the images of beauty, love, and death into the fabric of memory, at a decisive moment in the narrator's vocation.

If the woman portrayed in the Orient of style is an "oeuvre d'art," then the zaimph is a doubly determined work of art: according to Mâtho, it is the extension of Salammbô as the figure of Tanit. Flaubert seems to have agreed with the opinion he attributes to the amorous Mâtho. Like Salammbô, the zaimph shines with colors and precious stones, in addition to the divine symbols that cover it (as well as Salammbô's clothing): "L'étoffe . . . resplendissait au soleil avec ses couleurs, ses pierreries et la figure de ses dieux [The fabric shined in the sun with its colors, its gemstones, and the figure of its gods]" (94). Early in the composition of the novel, Flaubert described his representation of Salammbô in the following words: "J'ai introduit ma petite femme au milieu des soldats. A force de lui fourrer sur le corps des pierres précieuses et de la pourpre, on ne la voit plus du tout [I have placed my little woman among soldiers. I have covered her body with so many precious stones and crimson that you can't see her at all]."[23]

The zaimph is the figure that corresponds to ravishment and its "blanc," to the feminine incarnation of the work of art, and the ideal of style. It renders the sublime sky of Flaubert's aesthetic: "on aurait dit un nuage où étincelaient des étoiles [one would have thought it was a cloud glittering with stars]." Like Salammbô's artful clothing and the temple of Tanit, like the topography and interiors of Carthage, its surface is covered with figures that emerge like writing from its folds: "des figures apparaissaient dans les profondeurs de ses plis [figures appeared in the depths of its folds]." Infinite and mysterious, it is colored like Emma's panes of glass. It illuminates the sublime expanse of night, dawn, and sun: "tout à la fois bleuâtre comme la nuit, jaune comme l'aurore, pourpre comme le soleil, nombreux, diaphane, étincelant, léger [simultaneously bluish like night, yellow like dawn, crimson like the sun, manifold, diaphanous, sparkling, weightless]" (94). The colored transparencies of Flaubert's stained-glass vision are carried along or transmitted by similes that figure what is meant to be hidden, invisible: "C'était le manteau de la Déesse, le zaimph saint que l'on ne pouvait voir [It was the cloak of the Goddess, the sacred zaimph that no one could see]" (85). The ideal of style gives rise to the sublime. Mâtho's symbolic presence is immediately heightened and he is transfigured by a thundering voice straight out of the "gueuloir" (the "yelling parlor" where the author tried out his sentences). Mâtho puts on the cloak: "'Un élan m'emporte! Salammbô! Salammbô! je suis ton maître!' Sa voix tonnait. Il semblait à Spendius de taille plus haute et transfiguré ['Salammbô! Salammbô! I am your master!' His voice was thundering. To Spendius, he appeared taller and transfigured]" (85).

Quelque chose de bleuâtre et de scintillant

Flaubert's stylistic continuity is the porphyry surface. Without a break or fissure, it is the ideal of his allegorical image, a sparkling translucent veil of artistry. He reflects himself in it, as well as Salammbô; like her, the "pen-man" ("l'homme-plume") will die of it. In this highly poetic form of Flaubertian fatality, Salammbô dies from having lifted the veil. The malediction falls upon those who go too far; they enter the excessive meanings of allegory when they go beyond the limits and break the chains of decorum. For Flaubert, excess is the Other of language, the aesthetic ideal of allegory—Art: "The works of art that I like above all others are those that have *art in excess*." What Flaubert calls "the *right* note" is also the excess of Art: "Cela s'obtient par une *condensation* excessive de l'idée [It is obtained through an excessive *condensation* of the idea]."[24]

As the means and ideal of sublime style, excess implies "la grande voix de l'Art [the great voice of Art],"[25] the feminine seductions ("cette voix de sirène [the voice of the siren]") of eternal vision. Truth is condensed and represented through illusion. In Flaubert's vocabulary the excess of art includes the metaphoric "other" resonances of "condensation"; the intense images or "painting" of the artist's subject: the figural, colorful, decorative and mysterious folds of Tanit's veil. This excess is "ma chimère de style [my chimera of style]"[26] or beauty. Up on the wuthering heights of allegory, the excessive vision of the artist sees beyond the personal, beyond passing forms, beyond the fugitive moment of the present: "Il faut toujours monter ses personnages à la hauteur d'un type, peindre ce qui ne passe pas, tâcher d'écrire pour l'éternité [It is always necessary to raise one's characters to the height of a type, to paint things that do not pass away, to try to write for eternity]."[27] The vision of the scintillating firmament moves over the borderlines that separate the sacred from the transgression that leads to malediction. Condensed out of its invisibility ("que l'on ne pouvait voir [that no one could see]" [85]), the Orient of style is seen.

Through the figure of Salammbô, Flaubert depicts the fatality of vocation: a beautiful work of art is crystallized in its erotic feminine form. The final image of *Salammbô* presents her at her throne, a fallen statue, dead in her wedding dress. This image leads her out of the inky blackness in Emma Bovary's mouth, and out of the consecrated ruins of Caroline's death, when she too is caught in a final image of beauty and death wearing a wedding dress. Flaubert wrote to Du Camp: "On lui a mis sa robe de noce. . . . Elle paraissait bien plus grande et bien plus belle que vivante avec ce long voile blanc [They dressed her in her wedding gown . . . She appeared so much taller and more beautiful with the long, white veil than when she was alive]."[28] The mixture of sublime beauty and nausea that makes the witches' brew of love and death into a sea of ink—writing—is polarized by the same allegory that rules the many layers of *Salammbô*. In a final appearance, Salammbô incarnates the Goddess in carnal and erotic form: at the height of her sublimity and loveliness, she suddenly dies. The effects of Flaubertian horror, including nausea and violence, are invested in the living corpse of Mâtho. Her death takes only an instant, while his instant is a single moment of adoration that interrupts and finalizes his endless gruesome death: "ces effroyables prunelles la contemplaient. . . . A ce moment-là, Mâtho eut un grand tressaillement [the frightful pupils were staring at her. . . . At that moment, Mâtho shuddered violently]" (349). Mâtho's shudder is certainly linked to the vertigo of Julien in the sea of black ink.

The double excess that ends the text of *Salammbô* polarizes beauty and horror as elements of its allegory, and then secretly, scandalously unites them in the final reminder of the veil, the fatal crowning point of allegory presented in "Sous la Tente." In *La Légende*, the translucent colors of antiquity crystallize style and memory in the vision of medieval stained glass. The cathedral window takes up some of the allegorical properties of Salammbô's veil, the excessive image of Art. Proust, who called the Julien story "the most perfect of his oeuvres," inserted its image of stained glass in the narrator's vision of Combray. He may also have borrowed the allegorical duality of the initial structure of *La Légende* (opposing the maternal and paternal, the masculine and feminine, in a Christian allegorical symmetry that integrates the oppositions of Flaubert's antiquity), since he expands allegorical opposition into the cathedral[29] structure that he claimed as the model for the composition of *A la recherche*.

In *La Légende* the dual structure of allegory is embedded as images within the frame of the cathedral, but it also goes beyond those limits by turning or returning to the symbolic source of the cathedral at the end. Flaubert's version of Caritas emphasizes the light of the Word, Verbum, that is the final destination of Julien's image and its transfiguration in the light of the Flaubertian word. This image is the same one that Léon and Emma rush past, in the manuscript of *Madame Bovary*. Flaubert took this scene out of the novel and reserved it for later elaboration of eroticism and religion. The Rouen window marks a Flaubertian borderline: it contains the image of "l'Excessif," the writer of excessive, enigmatic images.

The stained-glass window is the point of Flaubert's exit from the cathedral, but it is also the point of light's entry and the cathedral's "illumination." The ravishment of vision, color, and narrative resonates in a theatrical and mystical silence. In early writings, Flaubert alludes to the mystical reflection of stained glass, seen in churches. Like the images of the zaimph, allegory is untranslatable; at the same time, the impersonal rendering of the allegorical image displays it as a strategic model for painting the object and formulating images: "Il faut que l'esprit de l'artiste soit comme la mer, assez vaste pour qu'on n'en voie pas les bords, assez pur pour que les étoiles du ciel s'y mirent jusqu'au fond [The mind of the artist must be like the sea, so vast that its shores cannot be seen, so pure that the stars in the sky are mirrored down to its depths]."[30]

Flaubert's allegory of conversion and aesthetic of the image show that this point of strategy is at the greatest possible distance from personal sentiment. Through a critique of Romantic sensibility, his aesthetic elaborates a path toward Beauty and Art. It gives rise to a work of art that is obliquely inscribed with Flaubert's long voyage, spent turning a voice or a life into a work of art. Flaubert's letter to Taine in November 1866 indicates that the image is impersonal not only as an effect of literary strategy, but also as a psychoanalytic phenomenon that Flaubert explicitly linked with "l'image artistique." Hallucination is "impersonal" in the sense that its images come from beyond consciousness. The Other, as Lacan describes the elsewhere of the unconscious, is the domain of Flaubert's images as well as Proust's "clichés" of involuntary memory. The fleeting image that founds the aesthetic of Flaubert's "chimera of style"[31] is inextricable from the form and content of his nervous attacks, "lesquelles ne sont que des déclivités involontaires d'idées, d'images [which are only involuntary declivities of ideas, of images]."[32] Through the impersonal representation of horror and splendor, the heights of art and the depths of Flaubert's black illness take shape in the ravishments of allegory.

Perhaps this explains some of the pleasure Flaubert took in

writing the "legend" of the Saint Julian window; he made its images readable through the excessive Art of turning them into an allegory of conversion. The dimension of allegory answers Flaubert's rhetorical question: "Comment a-t-il tiré ceci de cela? [How did he derive the one from the other?]"

The author derived the text of La Légende from the stained-glass window by reflecting it, "translating" it, and thus turning its silent signification into Sentences. By transfiguring its images into rhetorical ones in the Sentence, Flaubert capitalized like the name of a goddess: la Phrase, or the Sentences of Art.

The figure of Julien represents what Flaubert's oeuvre sets into place and puts into form: intoxications, vocations of love and art that are woven through Madame Bovary, L'Education sentimentale, Bouvard et Pécuchet, and the other Contes. In all of these works Flaubert's oblique signature (signed indirectly, like the anagrammatic code name of the "artiste peintre, un nommé Vaufrylard [the painter, a certain Vaufrylard]"[33] can be found in the combinations of rage and ravishment that characterize his use of allegory.

Flaubert's habitual terms of negativity—infinite form, blackness, the abyss, vertigo, and "transport"—give an account of the effect of allegorical images as well as the impersonalized subjectivity that informs them. This complex and paradoxical interiority is the effect of a Modernist innovation in allegory that can be attributed to Baudelaire as well as Flaubert.

In general, allegory reduces organic harmony to membra disjecta, the suspended fragments that abandon life to memory, and ultimately symbolize violence, death, or mourning. In this context, Benjamin distinguishes Baudelaire's allegory from earlier forms.[34] The destructive impulse in Baudelairean allegory is compounded by an interior rage ("Ingrimm"), not found in Baroque allegory. Baudelaire has an interior vision ("sieht . . . von innen") of the allegorical object while the Baroque has only an exterior vision of it ("sieht . . . von aussen").[35] This exteriority is another general trait of allegory; combined with interiority or interior vision, it produces modernist allegory. In "Le Cygne," the estrangement of the inexpressive or expressionless mourner near an empty tomb creates an allegorical figure comparable to Flaubert's characters who put on the mask of impersonality. The image of Andromaque indicates how the Modernism of Baudelaire's allegory concords with Flaubert's ideal traits of style.[36]

In Benjamin's reading of Baudelaire, inner rage inhabits rhetoric as the violence of allegory. It takes analogous forms in Flaubert's work: the rage mentioned in many of his letters weaves excess into literature. Writing becomes crossing out, copying, rewriting, in an infinite and vertiginous spiral of corrections. The "gueuloir" is Flaubert's one-man theater, the invisible show of his declaimed prose. Engaged in the immensities of the grotesque or climbing to the heights of the sublime, his rage for representation, parodic as well as intensely lyrical, always exceeds the limits of his audience. It is perhaps for this reason that literary criticism allows the vertiginous suffering of the corrector to silence the delights of the "yelling parlor," as if the excess of rage had left nothing behind it but a trail of symptoms.

The effects of allegorical excess led both Flaubert and Baudelaire before the law. In both cases, the accuser voiced moral indignation against the representation of jouissance as the site of beauty and obscenity. The underlying accusation against Flaubert, however, may have had less to do with obscene beauty than with the unprecedented reaction of the author's contemporaries to the character of Emma Bovary. Exposed and suffering "in twenty French towns at the same time,"[37] Flaubert's "petite femme" became the object of readers' sentimental identification to such an extent that Flaubert was seen as violating the "pudeur [modesty]" he would later satirize in Frédéric Moreau's *Education sentimentale*. This identification is another effect of excessively skillful allegory; Flaubert may have been put on trial more for his mastery than for impropriety. The figure of Emma was (and still is) fantasmatically identified as a woman made of flesh and blood rather than ink.

The famous caricature[38] that appeared in *La Parodie* showed Flaubert dissecting a woman and removing her heart—the heart of Emma Bovary. The reaction to allegorical violence displaces both the intoxication and the work of style. Posited as a scriptural creation, the heart is disguised or displaced from its secret interiority. From beyond Emma's enigmatic grave in the text, beyond the undivined scandals of Flaubert's identification, Mlle Amélie Bosquet heard: "Madame Bovary c'est moi—d'après moi [I am Madame Bovary—she is my version of myself]." Rendered sublime through the anatomy of language, the dissected heart of love belongs to Flaubert: "Quant à l'amour, ça a été le grand sujet de réflexion de toute ma vie . . . et le coeur que j'étudiais, c'était le mien. Que de fois j'ai senti à mes meilleurs moments le froid du scalpel qui m'entrait dans la chair! [As for love, it was the one great subject of reflection for my whole life . . . and the heart that I studied was my own. At the loveliest moments of experience, how many times I felt the chill of the scalpel cutting into my flesh!]"[39] In the end, a heart can only be fantasmatically dissected through the symbolic "object" of anatomy—the language of the heart, that inexplicably shifts to the heart of vocation. Its suffering and delight subvert the sentimentality of "the language of the heart" by submitting it to reflection or the "marinade" associated with "the anatomy of style." The instrument for this "science" is a pen rather than a knife, but it is endowed with a power of symbolic dissection, conception, and analysis: "*L'anatomie du style*, savoir comment une phrase se membre et par où elle s'attache [*The anatomy of style*, knowing how a sentence is limbed and where its points of attachment are]."[40]

Rage, the violence of allegory, its arbitrary power of destruction, and a fantasmatic dissection of flesh and form mysteriously add up to an effect of rapture, the intoxication produced by and through the allegory of conversion. This locus of Flaubert's scriptural vocation spreads to the created character of Julien, the allegory of sainthood. Julien's rage is untempered by love of art: Flaubert thought that without his love of form, he might have been a great mystic.[41] Julien becomes a parricide and a saint because he does not enter Jules's school of style in the first *Education sentimentale*, the "école" of scriptural vocation. In the violent figure of the saint, Flaubert literalizes and de-sublimates his own trajectory of allegory. The killer covers his face and becomes the figure of the impersonal, the nameless penitent in a monk's robe; the parricide utters his own "It is I!" in the identity of Julien the storyteller. When Julien's rage for anatomical dismemberment turns into the grief that pierces his own heart, he may become the sublime figure of his glorious end, in the radiant permanence of stained glass.

The stained-glass image appears in the vertiginous sky of the sublime: it is an appropriate portrayal of the intoxicating beauty that was Flaubert's ideal of writing. Like one of the enigmatic plants described in *Salammbô*, however, the beauty of the author's fiction and its individual sculpted sentences seem to have become invisible in the daylight of criticism. Proust is a happy exception. Although Flaubert's "intoxication" has both positive and negative aspects, critical discussions of his creative process tend to emphasize his illnesses and suffering, as if the record of medical symptoms were what was primarily at stake in reading Flaubert. Even Barthes's thoughtful study of Flaubert's sentence emphasizes the "vertige" of corrections.[42] This vertigo is seen as symptomatic of Flaubert's suffering ("souffrance") in the process that makes of the sentence something new in literary history: a thing, "une chose." Barthes's interpretation of the new object, the Flaubertian "chose" of style, not only makes a case for the intersection of Flaubert's personality and stylistic modernity, it also offers the only critical concept produced so far that seems to take up Proust's concept of syntax as the key to Flaubert's new style. It is not by chance that Barthes's text is an homage to the linguist André Martinet, but at the same time, the substitution of linguistics for rhetoric (the code of classicism) does not do much service to Flaubert as an explanation for the anxiety associated with the new object—the sentence. For Flaubert, the sentence is not only the new "object" of writing, it is also the aesthetic object, the beautiful thing.

Another fine reading of Flaubert, by J. B. Pontalis,[43] seems to be similarly side-tracked from the question of beauty by the uncanny continuity between life and art, documented in Flaubert's correspondence. Despite his subtle readings, Pontalis echoes Pommier when he concludes that Flaubert suffered from the illness of language, "la maladie du langage." Why is it, however, that these critics filter the artist's incomparable works through the fascinating suffering that is only one side of the "evidence," half the message of the correspondence?

It is obvious that the major culprit in this domain is Sartre himself, obsessed with everything about Flaubert except the beauty of his writing. Sartre elevates knowledge—the imaginary, described as everything that can be known about a man—at the expense of aesthetics, rendered invisible. Sartre's voluminous work on Flaubert is an attempt to write about everything but *reading* Flaubert. Proust's conclusions and incitations, his *Journées de lecture*, are not on the Sartrean (or post-Sartrean) agenda.

Of course, the critical alibis for not reading Flaubert are "true" in the sense that the suffering and anxiety that accompanied the sacrifice of "life" to "art" are eloquently documented in Flaubert's letters. The theoretician of allegory is in no position to deny the presence of melancholy, the planet that is the mover of allegory: *delectatio morosa*, Flaubert's "marinade."

His delights of melancholy create unimaginably beautiful sentences, anticipated by what he writes of the delicious "method of feeling" or way of life that stretches every book out for him and through him. Sentences are adventures: the voluptuousness of writing could only be matched by "le voyage," another Baudelairean center of figural language, encoded as correspondence. Writing novels spreads out identification and sensibility and moves them beyond the limits of the self, into "Illusion," the infinite textual place of allegorical images. This is the site of authorial dissemination, the enjoyment described earlier as jouissance. Without it, Flaubert's suffering would have neither context nor meaning: "c'est une délicieuse chose que d'écrire! que de ne plus être *soi*, mais de circuler dans toute la création dont on parle [writing is a delicious thing! no longer to be *oneself*, but to circulate within the entire creation of which one speaks]."[44]

The absence of a representation of personal identity frees Flaubert to become the anatomist of style. His views on beauty, style, and the enterprise of writing prose are often cited as evidence of obsession, perversion, and illness, as if to demonstrate that the uncanny effects of Flaubert's prose that incited the contemporaries of *Madame Bovary* to drag him before the silencing agency of the law are still active. Flaubert's aesthetic strategy may be read quite differently, however. In a certain sense his correspondence elaborates the tenets of a theory of allegory, the approach to the Other world of beauty that enabled him to become—through a particular study of "anatomy"—the allegorist.

In the first *Education sentimentale*, Flaubert learned that the representational powers of style depend on the mask worn by the authorial persona, the interdiction to speak directly through heroic or parodic forms. The depth of personal sentiment has disappeared: the chest has been dissected and the removed heart has been dissolved in ink. Flaubert, the "heartless" writer, has subjected his heart to an intoxication of absence or estrangement. In "Le Cygne," Baudelaire's heroine, another victim of morose delectation, lingers near an empty tomb, forever curved in ecstasy. Only sublimation or the delights of allegory can mark a return from exile—a resurrection of the past—in a new style. Proust too has underlined the felicity of that return; reading concludes with incitations, it spirals into writing. The beautiful sentence of Frédéric's belated "invitation au voyage" prepares the alternation of departures and renunciations that string the Proustian necklace of memory with ecstasies during a long account of a lifetime, heading for ruin and waylaid by vocation.

Proust depicts those ecstasies with the unmistakable markers of the transformation of deathly exile into resurrection. Flaubert's portrayal of the writer's vocation anticipates the Proustian pearl—resurrection as style—even as it silences the sublime delights of writing by declaring them to be the product of "grief," like the pearl, "the oyster's illness."[45] While this declaration and the hundreds of others found in his correspondence are interesting, they cannot legitimately be used to silence the voice that speaks throughout Flaubert's fiction, and most unmistakably in the story of Julien. Critical emphasis on pain and illness appears to silence the indisputable obscenity of jouissance that indicates the connection between sexuality (including fetischism, masturbation, voyeurism, syphilitic epilepsy, and so on) and the writing of beautiful prose.

One of the first agents of repression acting against Flaubert may have been his niece when she indicated that Bouvard and Pécuchet are copying, at the end of the novel, "comme autrefois." Writing was Flaubert's infinite end, however, in the sense that Proust makes it the end and vocation of the narrator in *A la recherche du temps perdu*. The enormity of that vocation—its fatality, as Flaubert would call it—cannot be assimilated to rote repetition; it is the writing and rewriting of style, infinitely new, and infinitely more beautiful. Flaubert knew that as well as any writer has ever known it, and he intended it to be the "end" of *Bouvard et Pécuchet*. Proust's critique of Flaubert indicated that Flaubert was his source for this discovery: in the following chapters, I will indicate the particular turns of allegory in Proust's novel, its writing and "end." In Flaubert's last book, the desired ending was going to leave the reader with an indelible image of the two characters at work: "they copy." The last word would have Bouvard and Pécuchet writing, after all other conversions. After all: writing, period.

Proust

"Sache qui'il faut aimer, sans faire la grimace,
Le pauvre, le méchant, le tortu, l'hébété,
Pour que tu puisses faire à Jésus, quand il passe,
Un tapis triomphal avec ta charité.

"Hear this: you must love, without a grimace,
The poor, the heartless, the dumb, the tortuous,
So that when Jesus will pass through, you may lie
Down, a victor's carpet made of charity.
(Oeuvres complètes [vol. 1, p. 139; my translation]

7
Passing Forms

Le détour de bien des années inutiles par lesquelles j'allais encore passer avant que se déclarât la vocation invisible dont cet ouvrage est l'histoire.
[*The detour of many useless years that I still had to pass through before the invisible vocation that is the story of this work was announced.*]
(II, 397)

In the preceding chapters the enterprise that founds Flaubert's style and the forms it is given in specific texts are filtered through the enigmatic interruption of French Romanticism—Modernism. Style emerges in the writings of Flaubert and Baudelaire as both cause and effect, ideal and textual materiality. It includes a rigorous conception, a new form of impersonality, the inscription of a certain violence, and a rendering of allegory. In my reading of Flaubert, I showed how this question of style takes effect in the writer's aesthetic and oeuvre, and I briefly indicated the connection between Flaubert and Baudelaire.[1]

Their affinities can be read between the lines of Flaubert's letter to the author of *Les Fleurs du mal,* quoted earlier.[2] His unusual literary identification with Baudelaire may be read as an aesthetic complicity that links the two inventors of Modernism. Flaubert's absolute of style, his modern allegory filled with ravishment and rage, his emphasis on temporality, and the new "farewell to the personal" find a unique contemporary parallel in Baudelaire's artistry. Flaubert's aesthetic categories and forms produce the terms for the commentary in his letter on the *Fleurs du mal* and hint at the possibility of interpreting Baudelaire's oeuvre through Flaubertian optics. After an interpretation of Proust's shift from nineteenth-century Modernism to the twentieth-century contexts and concerns that dominate *A la recherche du temps perdu*, I will return to the Baudelairean resonances of the allegory of conversion à la Flaubert.

The parallel between Flaubert and Baudelaire is neither a happy coincidence nor a strategem of literary history. If Baudelaire's oeuvre may be interpreted in the light of Flaubert's writings, and if my reading of Flaubert moves in the same direction as Flaubert's interpretation of Baudelairean modernity, then perhaps the allegory of conversion that unfolds in Flaubert's oeuvre can give an account of what is at stake in Baudelaire's writing as well. These parallel inventions of Modernism were conceived both as essentially Romantic and irreducibly distanced from Romanticism. The innovation that Flaubert considered as the heart of *Les Fleurs du mal* was also at the center of Flaubert's new creation.

Two aspects of the new relation to writing link Baudelaire to Flaubert: the economy of writing as the absolute and infinite, whose flowers (Art, or "les fleurs du mal") will open in the eternity projected in Baudelaire's poem "La Mort des Artistes," and the allegory of modernity, including a representation of the writer's anchoring or investment in this absolute vision (the vision that anchors the writer in language). Imbued with Romanticism, they construct their oeuvres as a transgression of its parameters, an excess of its limits. In Baudelaire's terms, Night has fallen on "Le Coucher de Soleil Romantique [The Romantic Sunset]." In this context, the historical label of "L'Art pour l'Art" is a point of entry: it is impossible to conceive of the absolute and mysterious enterprise of Flaubert and Baudelaire without it, but on the other hand, the platform of "Art for Art's Sake" cannot account for the banishment of sensibility, the focus of a new interiority of memory and image, and a new basis for representation in the relation between sensation and style or life and art. Inscribed in the work as the allegory of conversion, this relation is marked with a vocabulary of ecstasy, ravishment and sublime vocation. Attentive to the nuances of this aesthetic vocabulary in Baudelaire and Flaubert, Proust claims it as his inheritance from them. The working through of Romanticism, or trans-romanticism, unfolds in Proust's attempt to infuse narrative with a new poetic prose style.³

It is hardly a coincidence that the two authors whose presence is most strongly perceived in *A la recherche* and whose roles as "first class writers" overshadowing almost all other French authors receive the greatest emphasis in Proust's critical writings. From the point of view of this new relation to writing—Modernism, or the economy and allegory of the trans-romantic—the parallel developments of Flaubert and Baudelaire form a double influence on the constellation of stylistic principles and leitmotifs discussed in Proust's criticism, recorded in pastiche and other texts, and developed as artistic representations in *A la recherche*. Although the points of convergence of Flaubert's and Baudelaire's aesthetics had already been made visible in their oeuvre and their conceptions of style, particularly concerning the new poetics of prose, *A la recherche du temps perdu* demonstrates the complicity linking the two halves of this inheritance.

Especially in his analyses of Flaubert and Baudelaire, Proust's remarks on style provide an echo chamber or field of resonance for the effects he adapts from their writings. This literary criticism is partly confirmed in the theoretical frame of the narrator, but it is primarily Proust's style throughout *A la recherche* that reflects a translation of the critical criteria and aesthetics derived from his interpretive readings of Flaubert and Baudelaire into the textures of fiction.

Le violon frémit

Where does Proust locate what is at the heart of style? On the surface, this question receives two very different answers in Baudelaire and Flaubert, but if Proust's essays on Flaubert's "génie grammatical [grammatical genius]" (CSB 299) and Baudelaire, the "imagier d'une cathédrale [cathedral imagemaker]" (CSB 628), are considered in light of the modes of representation Proust attributes to each of the two writers rather than the biographical aspects of sensibility, the poet and the novelist suddenly appear as creators of a single aesthetic: Modernist allegory.

"A Propos du 'style' de Flaubert"[4] reveals how Proust 'translates' Flaubert into his own idiom, whereas "A Propos de Baudelaire" remains more elusive. In spite of this disparity, it is possible to retrace Proust's doubled itinerary through the two Modernists. If the reader begins with what Proust considers as the end point of art, Baudelaire and Flaubert are united in the promised land of eternity: Proust's retrospective arrangement unfolds the development of their styles that leads them to the allegorical site of the "eternal."

A central element of Proust's aesthetic is the power of the allegorical enterprise to transcend the limits of the visible. In the episode of the death of the writer Bergotte, the narrator places the demands of art in the mystical context of the laws emanating from a mysterious elsewhere, "une vie antérieure [an anterior life]": "Ces lois inconnues auxquelles nous avons obéi . . . sans savoir qui les y avait tracés—ces lois . . . qui sont invisibles seulement—et encore!—pour les sots [These unknown laws that we have obeyed . . . without knowing who traced them—these laws . . . that are invisible only for idiots—and even for them!]" (III, 188). These provocative declarations are staged in order to surreptitiously allow entry to the following sentence: "De sorte que l'idée que Bergotte n'était pas mort à jamais est sans invraisemblance [So that the idea that Bergotte was not dead forever is not implausible]." This image of the artist's transcendence of death appears in a passage from *A la recherche* that Proust reworked until his own death: its focus on an artistic eternity, the eternity of style, is portrayed through the encounter between Bergotte and Vermeer's panel of yellow wall. I will return later to the figure of Bergotte as the writer who anticipates and shapes the narrator's vocation. What is important for understanding the role of Baudelaire and Flaubert in Proust's aesthetic figures, however, is the narrator's enigmatic indication that the suspension of the writer's death is not as unrealistic as it seems.

According to a notebook entry, the narrator's remark preceded an affirmation of Bergotte's resurrection through art: "Toujours est-il que ce fut à une résurrection que je pensai quand je vis (ici mettre le passage placé je ne sais où de ces oeuvres faisant la veillée devant sa tombe . . .) [In any case the thought of a resurrection came to me when I saw (insert here the passage from some place or other about his works holding a watch before his grave . . .)]" (III, 1080). The ultimate form of eternal resonance is encoded in the scene of the carafes in the Vivonne as "allitération perpétuelle [perpetual alliteration]" (I, 168), the counterpart of the narrator's promise to return with lines; this eternal survival of the work of art is consistently and less allusively expressed in Proust's criticism. As early as "Sainte-Beuve et Baudelaire," Baudelaire's "perpetual alliteration" is evoked through the term of eternity: "Il semble qu'il [Baudelaire] éternise par la force extraordinaire, inouie du verbe . . . un sentiment qu'il s'efforce de ne pas ressentir au moment où il le nomme, où il le peint plutôt qu'il ne l'exprime [It seems that with the extraordinary, unheard-of power of the verb, . . . he [Baudelaire] eternalizes a feeling that he strives to resist at the moment when he names it, when he paints it rather than expressing it]" (CSB 252). The painted image that replaces expression and the banishment of sentiment are aspects of allegorical representation that create what Proust calls the unprecedented (and perhaps unheard) power of the word. This oblique approach to sentiment paradoxically renders it eternal as poetic language. The image represented as a form of both painting and naming turns sentiment into representation; its unparalleled artistry makes it eternal. The terms of Proust's "eternalizing" are allegorical, focused on the evanescence conquered only by the artist's mastery, the miracle of beautiful style. But what is most important is that the allegorical aesthetic corresponds to the allegory of the poetic image: represented, painted, and named.

Many years later Proust will describe Flaubert's style as the invention of an "eternal imperfect"; he declares that this imperfect "change entièrement l'aspect des choses et des êtres [completely changes the appearance of things and beings]"

(CSB 590). This transformation or conversion of appearance is a major element of Flaubert's temporal music. It reflects an aesthetic permeated with the allegorical representation (the image as painted, named, and not felt) of an allegorical vision illustrated in *L'Education sentimentale*—melancholy evanescence, oriental excess, and a Romantic sense of loss heightened by memory following "a blank" (595). At the beginning of this article, however, Proust's famous declaration of what constitutes eternity in style makes a strategic opposition to Flaubert's style. Proust argues that Flaubert's stylistic eternity derives from syntax and the temporality of allegory. Flaubert's use of the "blank" substitutes for metaphor, the touchstone of the Proustian sublime and the subject of his claim for style: "je crois que la métaphore seule peut donner une sorte d'éternité au style [I think that metaphor alone can give a kind of eternity to style]" (586). But the "imagier" par excellence, "le plus grand et le plus artiste des écrivains [the greatest and the most artistic of writers]" (629), "le poète qui aurait pu être imagier d'une cathédrale [the poet who could have been a cathedral image-maker]" (628), is Flaubert's literary counterpart, Baudelaire.

The colored image, and even more the Christian didactic image of cathedrals, is a key term in the aesthetics of allegory.[6] Proust's insistence on the image is one of the most important links between his critiques of Flaubert and Baudelaire. Although it is not named in Proust's letters, allegory is the central issue of his reading of Flaubert as a supreme stylist: an aesthetic distantiation of personal sentiment permeates the new "vision of things" (586). Proust expresses it as a transformation, the author's disappearance into an art that reveals not him but things themselves, through style: "Cette transformation de l'énergie où le penseur a disparu et qui traîne devant nous les choses [This transformation of energy in which the thinker has disappeared drags before us the things themselves]" (CSB 612). In his "Préface aux 'Tendres Stocks,'" Proust describes the "fondu" through a tacit allusion to the famous stylistic dissolving effect, the blank space in *L'Education sentimentale*, modulated by the passage that follows it. At the point of supreme artistry, the artist becomes invisible: "Mais chez Flaubert par exemple, l'intelligence cherche à se faire trépidation d'un bateau à vapeur, couleur de mousses, îlots dans une baie [But in Flaubert, for example, the intelligence seeks to become the vibration of a steamboat, the color of seafoam, islets in a bay]" (CSB 612). The author is mystically dissolved into "things" (elsewhere called "reality") and the result is the miracle of style, or virtuosity. The beautiful sentence is described through a synaesthetic metaphor prominent in *A la recherche*, where the composer's sentences are one of the decisive links between Swann's love and the narrator's turn toward writing. Vocations of art and love are allegorically rendered as Vinteuil's musical "phrases": "Ce violoniste joue très bien sa phrase de violon, mais vous voyez ses effets, vous y applaudissez, c'est un virtuose. Quand tout cela aura fini par disparaître, que la phrase de violon ne fera plus qu'un avec l'artiste entièrement fondu en elle, le miracle se sera produit [This violinist plays his violin phrase very well, but you see his effects, you applaud them, he is a virtuoso. When at last all of that will have disappeared, and the violin phrase will come to one with the artist completely dissolved in it, the miracle will have taken place]" (612).

The singular and fundamentally Proustian image of the "violin phrase" echoes a remark made by Flaubert: "Ils [mes nerfs] sont sonores et vibrants, je ne suis peut-être qu'un violon. Un violon quelquefois ressemble tant à une voix, qu'on dit qu'il a une âme [They [my nerves] are resonant and vibrating, perhaps I am merely a violin. Sometimes a violin sounds so much like a voice that it is said to have a soul]."[7] The letter continues with an evocation of his mourning for his sister several months earlier: as I indicated in the preceding chapters, his permanent mourning is intimately linked to the "maladie noire" or nervous illness that afflicts him. According to Flaubert's judgment, this illness is inseparable from melancholy and a vision filled with streams of unnatural ("estranged") images. The figure of the violin string emblematizes the subject of allegory: resonance and excess, interiority and distance from sentimentality, evanescence and the monuments of mourning.

In "Sainte-Beuve et Baudelaire," Proust derives the figure

of the violin phrase from "Harmonie du Soir": "Le violon frémit comme un coeur qu'on afflige [The violin quivers like a tortured heart]"[8] (CSB 251). The remarkable continuity between Proust's early view of Baudelaire (in "Sainte-Beuve et Baudelaire") and the letter on Baudelaire written after the war is based on the constellation of "sensibility" (including "douleur," "souffrance," and "frémissement"), "cruelty" (including "dureté" and "méchanceté"), and representation that attains truth through "impassibility" associated with beauty. When he quotes the line from "Harmonie du soir," Proust remarks "combien est cruel le vers délicieux [how cruel is this delectable line of verse]" (251). In 1921 as in 1909, the constellation of allegorical terms in his reading of Baudelaire is elaborated through "Les Petites Vieilles." Its accomplishment of allegorical delights leads Proust to praise the mastery and sublime beauty of the poem.

Proust's later reading emphasizes an aspect of Baudelairean sensibility that is essential to Flaubert's allegory: the interiority of death. In the presence of the blackness of allegory ("Peut-être hélas! faut-il contenir la mort en soi. . . . [Alas! perhaps one must contain death inside oneself . . .]" [621]), the "impassibility" of the allegorical mode of representation creates an effect of "mystery" or invisibility through art and its "transformations." Mixing cruelty and exquisite beauty, the figure of the violin string exemplifies allegory. Proust extends it in the form of "accent" to *Les Fleurs du mal*: "A côté d'un livre comme *Les Fleurs du mal*, comme l'oeuvre immense d'Hugo paraît molle, vague, sans accent! [Compared to a book like *Les Fleurs du mal*, how flaccid, vague, and unaccentuated appears Hugo's immense oeuvre!]" (621): "la corde chez Baudelaire est tellement plus serrée et vibrante [Baudelaire's strings are so much tighter and more resonant]" (628). Cruel and delicious, the accomplishments of allegorical art pervade the unfolding of vocation in *A la recherche* through the love of Swann's Odette, the narrator's Gilberte and especially Albertine, whose delights and cruelty dominate the narrator even beyond her disappearance: through art, most directly in the effects of Vinteuil's music (on both Swann and the narrator), in writing, painting, and even Françoise's cooking. A side effect of her exquisite cuisine is strangely decisive for the narrator's vocation—Françoise's martyrdom of the kitchenmaid.

Out of this unnatural, strange interiority stripped of human sentiment come the hieroglyphics of allegory, the figures and images that must be deciphered according to the "grimoire compliquée et fleurie [complicated and florid book of spells]" (III, 879) of the narrator's vocation in *A la recherche*. Another view of the enigmatic images of allegory is encoded as the presence of mystery—"une impression de mystère" (621)—considered in the context of the fabrication of an effect. Proust uses Hugo, "gros mangeur [big eater]" and "grand jouisseur [coarse sensualist]" (621), as a foil for Baudelaire. If the creator's weaving is visible (à la Hugo) it cannot attain the heights of invisibilia, the "impalpable," or the mystery of Baudelaire's cruel delights. Here and in other writings on Baudelaire, Proust's use of the term "mystery" has a religious resonance inseparable from the "accent" or voice of style. Double-edged like the images of Flaubert, Baudelaire's images include a further mystery, a specifically Baudelairean twist to allegory. Proust describes it as "ces accents religieux dans les pièces sataniques [the religious tones in his satanic poems]" (621).

These mysterious resonances or "accents" are essential to what brought Baudelaire before the law—allegory. At the same time, they are responsible for the portrayal of an "impression" beyond the heights of "sublime verse." Proust underscores the sublimity of Baudelaire's achievement as mystical meaning: "Il semble pourtant impossible d'aller au-delà [And yet it seems impossible to go beyond it]" (623). Baudelaire's mystical sonority is illustrated in the final stanza of the religious-satanic poem, "L'Imprévu": "Et pourtant cette impression, Baudelaire a su la faire monter encore d'un ton, lui donner une signification mystique [And yet Baudelaire was able to raise the pitch of this impression, to give it a mystical meaning]" (623). For Proust, the image of these lines is exquisite because it emerges as a hieroglyph of allegorical mystery, the "fondu" [dissolving] of ecstasy, synaesthesia, correspondence, and the fusion of delight and cruelty. The transfiguration of "frémissement [quivering]"—suffering, horror, and negativity—into an art that shines with a mysterious, mystical light and cannot be pinned down to a single source links Proust's evocation of Baudelaire to my reading of Flaubert.

The uncanny mixture of evanescence, eternity, and fatal damnation recalls some of the contexts of Flaubert's allegory of conversion elaborated in the preceding chapters. This temporality is mirrored in Proust's description of the "étrange bonheur [strange happiness]" (623) of those who hear the trumpet. Proust takes up the "mystery" in *A la recherche du temps perdu*: in one sense, it is the object elaborated through the "signification mystique [mystical meaning]" of the quest or "recherche." Proust's "hors-temps [outside-time]," time's purest essence, is mystically decanted out of the swept ruins of time, lost and resurrected as "le Temps." Aesthetics and fiction are linked in Proust's novel of vocation through the invisibilia of a religious vocabulary: the unperceived, the spiritual, the moral, and the allegorical emerge as a vision of both the apocalyptical horrors of time and the shining glories of resurrection in the vocation of the artist. The terms of the miracle of beautiful style, transubstantiation, and "le fondu [dissolving]" that are discussed in Proust's other writings stem from Flaubert's view of style: structure, syntax, and temporality. This conception is based on the invisible transformations of fate and time, and the "étrange bonheur" of the allegorist who brings beautiful sentences out of the abyss.

Flaubert's art of temporality, the combination of memory and image in allegory, is Proust's model for a paradoxical interiority that originates in exterior vision. In "Réponses à une enquête des annales," Proust protests against the label of "roman d'analyse [analytic novel]" by declaring a preference for the telescope as his "favorite implement" rather than a microscope (CSB 640). He indicates the shift of telescopic vision from the exterior to the mysteries of the "inconnu [unknown]" in a remark that describes the trajectory of vocation: "Ce qui semble extérieur, c'est en nous que nous le découvrons [We discover inside ourselves the things that seem to be external]" (640). Painting, the allegorical figure of the art of writing derived from Flaubert and Baudelaire, is further allegorized by Leonardo, who subordinates the visible to the invisible: "*Cosa mentale*, dit par Léonard de Vinci de la peinture, peut s'appliquer à toute oeuvre d'art [*A thing in the mind*, Leonardo da Vinci's epithet for painting, can be applied to all works of art]" (540). Proustian interiority is predicated on invisibilia, the mysteries that are represented through a code of emblems, hieroglyphs, or figures. The revelation of the meaning or truth hidden in these images points toward the interiority that shaped them.

In *A la recherche* Proust adds another term to this allusive grounding of allegory. Permeated with aestheticized "miracles" and "mystères" (I, 500–502) the narrator echoes Swann's "étrange bonheur [strange happiness]" in the cruel delights of love: "Le bonheur, le bonheur par Gilberte, c'était . . . une chose toute en pensées, c'était, comme disait Léonard de la peinture, *cosa mentale* [Happiness, happiness caused by Gilberte, was a thing made entirely out of thoughts, it was, as Leonardo said of painting, *cosa mentale*]" (I, 500). Proust's "cosa mentale" of love expands the definition of interiority to the invisibilia inherent in the object of vocation. They paint the trajectory through the entire novel of a feminine unknown, most explicitly marked in the narrator's vision of Vinteuil's music. The twofold "cosa mentale"—the allegorical interiority of art and love—summarizes the path taken in *A la recherche du temps perdu*. Emblematized as Leonardo's "chose toute en pensées [thing made entirely out of thoughts]," it leads to beautiful style based on interiority without sentimentality: allegory. One of Proust's formulations of the interlace of art and love as the mysterious feminine figure of art and artistry derives not only from Flaubert's variations on the Flemish virgin, but also from a reading of Baudelaire's "Charité."

Proust singles out an allegorical rendering of Charity in "Le Rebelle."[10] In "Sainte-Beuve et Baudelaire," he relates it to the portrayal of "Les Petites Vieilles" and the eternity of the painterly image: he further develops this constellation in "A Propos de Baudelaire" where he rests his case for Baudelaire's unparalleled artistry on the mysterious encounter between the "cruel" and the "delicious." The earlier argument begins with a distinction between what is felt ("ressenti") by the poet and his representation of it: "Et cruel, il l'est dans sa poésie, cruel avec infiniment de sensibilité. . . . Il a donné de ces visions qui, au fond, lui avaient fait mal, j'en suis sûr, un tableau si puissant, mais d'où toute expression de sensibilité est si absente [And cruel he is in his poetry, cruel with an infinite amount of sensibility. . . . He turned the visions that, I am sure, had deeply hurt him, into painting of great power, but in which any expression of sensibility is overwhelmingly absent]" (CSB 250, 251). In the name of the sublime beauty of Baudelaire's verse, Proust opens an abyss between the "souffrances . . . ressenties jusqu'au fond de ses nerfs [sufferings . . . felt to the depths of his nerves]" (250) and the cruel distance of the Baudelairean sublime, the "impassibility" of representation. Although Proust does not mention it, his remarks on Baudelaire draw a parallel to Flaubert's epistolary descriptions of his nervous illness and the abyss separating it from the aesthetics of the Modernist sublime.

Proust restates his formula as the mark of Baudelaire's genius ("la force extraordinaire, inouïe du verbe [the extraordinary, unheard-of power of the verb]"): "cette subordination de la beauté à la vérité, à l'expression [this subordination of beauty to truth, to expression]" (252). If this view of representation ("une peinture extérieure [an exterior painting]" [252]) is taken as an essential statement of the Modernist aesthetic, its tacit definition of allegory overturns the Romantic doctrine of the symbol as a natural, organic extension of art from life. At the center of Proust's strategy is an illustration of sublime expression bereft of sympathy. He quotes a verse about charity, "un de ces vers immenses et déroulés de Baudelaire [one of Baudelaire's immense and unrolled lines of verse]" (252), to illustrate the contradiction between the subject (charity) and its representation ("Mais y a-t-il rien de moins charitable . . . que le sentiment où cela est dit [But is there anything less charitable . . . than the sentiment with which it is uttered]"): "Pour que tu puisses faire à Jésus, quand il passe, / Un tapis triomphal avec ta charité" (252).

The most succinct indication of what is at stake in such

verses can be found in "A Propos de Baudelaire": "Il ne voulait pas laisser voir sa pitié, il se contentait d'extraire le *caractère* d'un tel spectacle [He did not want to reveal his pity, he contented himself with extracting the *character* of such a scene]" (625). The unnamed definition of allegory allows Proust to locate the sublime result of an aesthetic of excess in the cruel beauty of Baudelaire's poetry (625–26). Flaubert conceptualizes Excess as the aesthetic quality of an art that is completely devoted to representation and untainted by sentiment. Proust echoes Flaubert's economy of Excess: the "extraordinary power of the word" in Baudelaire's writing hides pity under a mask of cruelty, in order to focus on representation. Free of sentiment, Baudelaire's verse impassibly reveals the essence of its object.

The conversion into words of an impression and the silenced sentiment elicited by it is at the heart of Proust's concept of personal disappearance. The evidence of virtuosity, this concept also appears as "le miracle," "le fondu," and "le vernis des maîtres." These epithets give another account of what Proust describes as "cosa mentale" and its consequences in art: greatness without pity, suffering silenced by cruelty, and the encounter between love and rage discussed earlier as allegory à la Flaubert. Although Baudelaire's satanism puzzled Flaubert (despite the ongoing project of *La Tentation de Saint Antoine*), his Charity, classified with "Les Petites Vieilles" as the eternity of allegory, combines cruelty, sensibility, and beauty in a manner exemplary of Flaubert's allegorical portrayals leading from the Flemish virgin through the characters of Emma, Salammbô, Julien, and others.

The inward constellation or the "cosa mentale" of art turns the delights of love and the suffering of cruelty and violence into Modernist allegory. Rooted by modernity in the fateful link between art and life, the writer's vocation for (and through) the sublime, this allegory is also a reflection of the artist's delicious sufferings of style, or the allegory of conversion.

The vocabulary of the Bible and theology locates the sources for the allegorical image and its aesthetic elaboration; the Modernist vocabulary of art revolves around ineffable transfiguration, mystery, and invisibilia. In Proust's writing, this vocabulary leads from Flaubert's allegorical surfaces of "novels of introspection" and his portraits of mystical excess to another expert in Baudelairean Charity. This other "imagier d'une cathédrale" is Swann, who lives out a Ruskinian "religion of Beauty" (as well as its ambivalent excess, idolatry) by moving through life as if it were an expanse of painted canvas illuminated by the chiaroscuro effect of love and suffering—the Modernist interiority of the "cosa mentale." Swann shapes and countersigns the narrator's vocation for allegory by introducing him to the greatest cathedral imagemaker, the innovator of the Renaissance in art: Giotto.

Through the presentation of Giotto's painting of Caritas, described in the novel as "La Charité de Giotto," Proust's mode of representation in *A la recherche* is named and evoked for the first time as allegorical (I, 82). For this reason, the integration of Giotto's Charity within fiction, as a character's nickname, is a particularly strategic element of the allegorical frame of art and its mysteries. Proust develops the correspondence between the symbolic layers of Renaissance (and medieval) art and modernity, doubled by the other interpretation of Time as an original lost paradise retrieved only in modern allegory. The frame for this aesthetic allegory in the *Recherche* is interlaced with the architecture of didactic allegory: "'Les Vices et les Vertus' de Padoue et de Combray ['The Vices and the Virtues' of Padua and Combray]." The voices of the narrator that unfold and mediate the images of allegory are also the object of a complex layering through different temporal cross sections.[11] Within this elaborate fictional framework, based on the allegorical effects of Time, the constellation of Proust's key terms of creation (art and love) and destruction (failed vocations, lack of will, suffering and death) are fully set into motion and guaranteed as allegory through the mystery associated with an apparently insignificant fictional character.

Corpus Mysticum

Proust's kitchenmaid, named "La Charité de Giotto," is strangely set apart from the rest of the world at Combray; little is known of her, including her "other" name. The enigma of her identity is interrupted only by her association with Giotto, her "état [condition]," and her additional suffering at the hands of Françoise, who makes the beautiful and delicious asparagus into an exquisite torture. Proust's figure is another version of Baudelaire's "Charité." The uncanny atmosphere of cruelty and eloquent tenderness that surrounds her recalls the explosive line from *Les Fleurs du mal*: "La servante au grand coeur dont vous étiez jalouse [The good-hearted maid of whom you were jealous]."[12] The mute, suffering (and, through allegory, sublime) heart of the kitchenmaid also echoes the ardor of "Un Coeur simple"; Flaubert's character of Félicité is very visible in *Jean Santeuil* as an early avatar of Françoise. I will return later to the question of the "grand coeur" and "Giotto's Charity"; first, however, the intimate relation between the identity of the kitchenmaid as Giotto's fresco and the mystery of her "other" identity will allow for the unraveling of her role in Proust's allegory.

The initial enigma of the "fille de cuisine" may be expressed in Proustian terms as the mystery of the invisible. The metaphorical spirals of saturation, emergence, crystallization, renaissance, and resurrection indicate that this sense of mystery is both religious and sexual, emblematic of art and love. Mystery is the ineffable, borrowed from Flaubert's "untranslatable" silences through the "blank" of *L'Education sentimentale*, and turned into a Proustian name for the object of dream and revelation. The narrator is caught between beauty and horror, the loveliness that cannot be put into words and the scandal of sexuality that condemns him to guilty silence; his inability to express an aesthetic sensibility (e.g., "Zut!" [I, 155]) is paralleled by the enduring silence of the voyeur at Montjouvain (I, 159). The ineffably beautiful produces a failed artistic rendering while the ineffably abject gives rise to unvoiced horror.

The ineffable is both the sublime of religion and art, and the unnameably abject; Proustian mystery shapes both versions at the ambiguous borderline between Judaism and Christianity. Proust's beloved mother was Jewish, and his Judaic roots, fantasmatic formulations, and acts of naming hover in the margins of the novel. Like the narrator, however, he held to the markers of Catholic identity, perhaps in order to distance himself from the Bloch who secretly inhabited him. This context might explain how Proust, an ardent supporter of Dreyfus,[13] could listen in silence to the anti-Semitic tirade of his friend Robert de Montesquiou, and confirm this peculiar silence in a letter written to Montesquiou on the following day: "si je suis catholique comme mon père et mon frère, par contre ma mère est juive [While I am Catholic like my father and brother, my mother however is Jewish]."[14] In retrospect, the sufferer of the Passion emerges from the blank margin of separation as the new Moses revered by Christians and the false Messiah dismissed by Jews. For Christians, Moses the prophet is reduced to a prefiguration, while for Jews, the figure of Christ blends into a series of false Messiahs, projecting the true Messiah into some as yet unidentified womb. True or false, on Proust's line separating the Christian *après-coup* from the Judaic anticipation, the Jewish "virgin" is waiting in delight and suffering for the allegorical figure of a Word or a figure.

The knot of mystery is emblematized by a thinly disguised *Juive* on the point of giving birth to the author who creates his work of symbol and mystery, of love (*caritas*) and filiation, of fecundation through a voice that miraculously transcends time. At another remove, or on another level of the edifice of metaphor, she is that *Juive* whose libidinal attachment, via "Maman" and the narrator's "maman," was consecrated by the autobiographically displaced homosexuality of the author and not the narrator—Giotto's *Charity*. She makes a brief reappearance when the narrator discovers that Charlus is a homosexual: "Jusqu'ici je m'étais trouvé, en face de M. de Charlus, de la même façon qu'un homme distrait, lequel, devant une femme enceinte dont il n'a pas remarqué la taille alourdie, s'obstine, . . . à lui demander indiscrètement: 'Qu'avez-vous donc?' Mais que quelqu'un lui dise: 'Elle est grosse,' soudain il aperçoit le ventre et ne verra plus que lui [Until now I had found myself, when facing M. de Charlus, in the same situation as a distracted man who, facing a pregnant woman whose swollen waistline he has not noticed, stubbornly insists . . . on asking her indiscreetly, 'What is the matter with you?' But if someone says to him: 'She is pregnant,' suddenly he notices her belly and sees nothing else]" (II, 613). And of course, the only other question in the *Recherche* that could be considered appropriate as a possible substitute for "What is the matter with you?" is habitually asked by a privileged paternal figure of love, artistic sensibility à la Ruskin, and Jewish identity—Swann: "Comment va la Charité de Giotto? [How is Giotto's Charity?]" (I, 80) to which one would have to answer: "Still pregnant."

The ongoing status of this allegorical pregnancy seems to indicate the fantasmatic dimension linking the image of the virginal Jewish mother, Madame Proust, to her faithfully fixated son. But more importantly, the dimension of allegory focuses on Giotto, the medieval portrait painter of invisible faces. His symbolic and aesthetic authority rearticulates theology: the trajectory of the Virgin through her fifteen Joyful, Sorrowful, and Glorious Mysteries; her maternal relation to the incarnation of the Word, within the Catholic mystery of the configuration of the Trinity; the mystery of Transubstantiation; and the Church as the Mystical Body of Christ. Christian theology introduces the question of the desiring flesh into the domain previously reserved for the Judaic God the Father, and his Spirit: this question forms the background for the knot of Christian allegory. The inscription of Giotto in the *Recherche* mediates Proust's vision of the artist bringing forth or giving birth to the work of art. That labor of love is possible only as a transmutation of the evil and unhappiness, the *mal(heur)*, of human love. For human, read impure: except for motherly (and grandmotherly) love, depicted as immaculate, all responses of a passionate nature fit into this category. In the Proustian rendering of *mal(heur)*, the seeds of evil are mysteriously left intact.

The dimension of mystery (and mysteries plural) gives rise to the rhetorical relation of the Virgin to the Trinity in the

Magnificat, the praise she sings to God upon learning that she will bear the Word made flesh. Her exaltation, or praise *magnifying the Lord*, is echoed by the assiduous reader of the Bible[15] who puts the following description of anticipated creation in the narrator's mouth: "mon livre n'étant qu'une sorte de ces verres grossissants comme ceux que tendait à un acheteur l'opticien de Combray: mon livre, grâce auquel je leur fournirais le moyen de lire en eux-mêmes [my book merely being a kind of magnifying glass like the ones that the optician of Combray would hold out to a client; my book, thanks to which I would provide them with the means of reading inside themselves]" (III, 1033). Proust registers this turn from letter to metaphor (or the spiral of letter and metaphor) in a typically subtle and yet unmistakable fashion: in a long and often-quoted passage on reading,[16] he founds the rhetoric of the Virgin on the question of the symbol. Although the rhetorical dimensions of this passage have been the object of critical commentary, the vehicle of the Virgin has remained unvoiced.

Proust's presentation of the Virgin in his text bears the relation between sinful flesh and praise of God, between maternal love and scriptural creation. The kitchen maid is described "à travers la succession des formes passagères en lesquelles elle s'incarnait," "dans un état de grossesse déjà assez avancé quand nous arrivâmes à Pâques [through the succession of passing forms in which she was incarnated, already in a condition of rather advanced pregnancy when we arrived at Easter]" (I, 80). Mystery is explicit: "elle commençait à porter difficilement devant elle la mystérieuse corbeille, chaque jour plus remplie, dont on devinait sous ses amples sarraux la forme magnifique [she was beginning to have difficulties carrying before her the mysterious basket, filling out more with each day, whose magnificent form could be divined beneath her ample smocks]" (I, 80). "Elle ressemblait en effet à ces vierges . . . [In effect she resembled those virgins . . .]." Later in life, in convents, says the narrator, he will meet "les incarnations vraiment saintes de la charité active [the truly saintly incarnations of active charity]" (I, 82). Proust inserts several inscriptions of the "figure" itself: "Certaines des figures symboliques de Giotto" (I, 80); "Malgré toute l'admiration que M. Swann professait pour ces figures de Giotto"; "l'image de cette fille était accrue par le symbole [certain symbolic figures by Giotto; Despite all the admiration that M. Swann professed for the Giotto figures; the image of this maid was augmented by the symbol]" (I, 81); "la beauté spéciale de ces fresques tenait à la grande place que le symbole y occupait, et que le fait qu'il fut représenté, non comme un symbole . . . mais comme réel, . . . donnait à la signification de l'oeuvre quelque chose de plus littéral [the particular beauty of these frescoes depended on the large space that the symbol occupied in them, and the fact that it was represented, not as a symbol . . . but as something real, . . . gave to the meaning of the work something more literal]" (I, 82).

With this comment on Giotto, Proust dissolves the easy identification of allegory as personification or figural typology based on a straightforward one-to-one parallelism. He alludes to three facets of allegory that maintain separate functions within a single allegorical image, and he presents the three as formulations of "otherness" or the negativity that affects representation: the symbol is not represented as a symbol, but as something real; the image of the real (the woman portrayed as Caritas) is not represented as real, but as a symbolic figure; the "signification" of the work is not represented as naming, but as something "literal." "Fond" shifts back to "forme," meaning comes face to face with the letter. Negation intervenes in a supplementary term that leads from Proust's reading of Giotto's Caritas to his own writing of "La Charité de Giotto": the letter, the letters forming the image of the name, "Caritas," challenge the vocabulary of "incarnation," "creation," and "truth" with the evanescence of "passing forms," the kitchenmaids. Allegory sets up the following double paradox: through passing forms, the letter (and its ladder of "other" meanings) of fiction will approach the permanence of art and a revelation of truth. The literal portrait, the image of the name ("Caritas" [I, 81]), and the realistic portrait of the image and the symbol gave the meaning of the work something more literal, or more literary. The question of figuration adumbrated by Proust slips from the painted portrait to something like a description of a fictional rendering of meaning. He writes: The symbol is not represented as a symbol. This enigmatic declaration of the mode of allegory spreads from the "fille de cuisine" to the entire cast of characters in the *Recherche*, when Proust says that all of them (except for the Larivière family) are fictional (III, 846).

Autobiographical figuration is perhaps less straightforward and more problematic than is generally assumed. The autobiographical figure is not represented as an autobiographical figure, but as a "real" character—a fictional character. In the fictional context of this passage, *la Charité de Giotto* is described: "elle tend à Dieu son coeur enflammé, disons mieux, elle le lui 'passe' [she holds out to God her heart in flames, or rather, let us say that she 'passes' it to him]" (I, 81). Twenty-five pages earlier, when the "Petite Madeleine" dramatically operates like love ("de la même façon qu'opère l'amour" [I, 45]) on the "past" of Combray, the narrator's "lost paradise," he qualifies the search for truth with the following statement: "Chercher? pas seulement: créer. Il [his 'esprit'] est en face de quelque chose qui n'est pas encore et que seul il peut réaliser, puis faire entrer dans sa lumière [To seek out? not only that: to create. It [his spirit] is facing something that has not yet come into being and that he alone can create, then bring into the light]" (I, 45). Giotto's Charity echoes this act of giving birth, and she repeats the miraculous version of the operation of love. Figuration, the Word made real, and the creation focus on passage: the heart enflamed with love is passed to God, time is perceived in its passage, and, according to the fate of every human apparition recorded in its pages, everyone and everything in *A la recherche* could be characterized in terms of "formes passagères." At the other end of the novel, Proust explicitly insists on the hollowing-out of passage in the turn toward the revelation of his Petite Madeleine. During the matinée, the narrator evokes "des êtres issus de cet air aigre et ventueux de cette sombre ville de Combray où s'était passée mon enfance, et du passé qu'on y percevait dans la petite rue, à la hauteur du vitrail [beings born of the sharp and windswept air in the dark town of Combray where my childhood had passed, and from the past that was perceptible there in the little street, at the height of the stained-glass window]" (III, 856). This sentence marks a turning point toward death and away from the failure and hopelessness of the narrator's lost vocation.

Passage may lead through death, and back to the revelation figured as the open sesame of the *Recherche*; Easter (Pâques) in Combray is the fictional locus of paradise. *Pascha* is the leap of the Exterminating Angel, over the Israelites. According to the orders given by Moses, their marks on the door would save them at the instant of Passover. Then the Exodus took place, out of death or what Albertine's letter called "complete night." Within *A la recherche*, Exodus leads out of "la nuit presque complète [the nearly complete night]" when, many years prior to the "vocation invisible dont cet ouvrage est l'histoire [invisible vocation of which this work is the story]," the fog "montrait l'entrée comme la colonne lumineuse qui guida les Hébreux [showed the entrance like the pillar of fire that guided the Hebrews]" (II, 397, 400). Here and elsewhere in the text, Proust's version of the Exodus of the Jews indicates certain difficulties of identification that leave traces in fiction.[17] For those who would prefer to close the "porte réservée aux Hébreux [door reserved for the Hebrews]," as the narrator does (II, 401), Passover will be absorbed in a symbolic mode, as a figuration, in Easter: the leap of the Angel is countered by Christ's passage through the negative regions of crucifixion and death, toward the "happy night" of Holy Saturday and the resurrection. In the Revelation of the stones of Venice, in the Baptistery of Saint Mark (another "Bible historiée [illuminated Bible]," like the Cathedral) the narrator is provided with the following thought: "de nouveau la vision éblouissante et indistincte me frôlait comme si elle m'avait dit: 'Saisis-moi au passage . . . ' [once again the dazzling indistinct vision had grazed me lightly, as if to say: 'Take me as I pass by . . . ']" (III, 867). The narrator anticipates the declaration of artistic resurrection, and he spells out the parallels of the original opening of the "recherche": "Mais pourquoi les images de Combray et de Venise m'avaient-elles, à l'un et à l'autre moment, donné une joie pareille à une certitude, et suffisante, sans autres preuves, à rendre la mort indifférente? [But why had the images of Combray and Venice, at one moment and at the other, given me a joy that was like a certainty, and that sufficed, with no other evidence, to render death indifferent?]" (III, 867). Take hold of me in (my) passing, says that vision. Through a jubilatory victory over death, it leads back to the initiation of Easter, "le mois de Marie" at Combray, and the lost paradise that will become fiction's *paradise lost*.

Love and letters, paradise and passage, are created and played out under the tutelage of Swann; the Judaic father in the wings gives the gift of *la Charité*. Under his influence, Combray will be retrospectively marked as the site of the narrator's literal initiation into love. The discussion of *la Charité* immediately precedes an evocation of *the Lady in pink*, Odette: the far-ranging object of desire, Swann's love, Gilberte's mother, Elstir's Miss Sacripant, and so on. Immediately following the offering to God of Charity's enflamed heart, Marcel enters the world of fiction and reading. His literary initiation also takes place in Combray, with Swann playing the paternal role. Because of Swann (and Bloch), the narrator reads Bergotte; as the Jewish alter ego whose identification with the narrator will fascinate and plague him to the end, Bloch also plays an important role in the narrator's literary apprenticeship (I, 90). The intertwining of Judaic symbolic paternity and Marian (i.e. Catholic) filiation, figuration, and love gives rise to the eroticized intelligence and the artistic sensibility that are dramatized and in certain ways incarnated in the *Recherche*. If the negative counter-sign is what Proust and the narrator call idolatry (the worship of false gods, without spirit and without voice) the positive or successful sign of this configuration is the creation of creation itself.[18] The famous dichotomy of life and art, dear to fin de siècle judgment, is less clear-cut in Proust's text than it might appear.

It is no coincidence that in one account of the narrator's vocation, the mysterious call ("le mystérieux appel") of

Vinteuil's Septuor, the herald of art, is described in the terms of a feminine seduction, "cette créature invisible dont je ne connaissais le langage et que je comprenais si bien—la seule Inconnue qu'il m'ait jamais été donné de rencontrer [this invisible creature whose language I did not know but understood so well—the only Unknown that I ever have had the gift of meeting]" (III, 260). The musical motif inscribes this event with the ineffable joy of paradise: "Enfin le motif joyeux resta triomphant; . . . c'était une joie ineffable qui semblait venir du paradis [At last the joyous motif remained triomphant; . . . an ineffable joy seemed to come from paradise]" (III, 260). Proust links the narrator's impressions of Vinteuil's music with the moments of revelation telescoping the images of the spires of Martinville, the trees near Balbec, and eventually the cobblestones of Venice. These impressions are cut off from the rest of life and from the visible world. The deciphered hieroglyphics of Vinteuil's Septuor offer "cette joie inconnue, l'espérance mystique de l'Ange écarlate du Matin [this unknown joy, the mystical hope of the scarlet Angel of Morning]" (III, 263). At the end of *A la recherche du temps perdu*, the narrator returns to the description of his moments of "felicity." He links it to the words of artistic transmission spoken by the writer Bergotte ("vous avez les joies de l'esprit [you have the spiritual joys]"), the role played by Vinteuil's representation of artistic jubilation, and the original vision opening his "recherche" out of the banal silence of the forgotten (III, 866).

In this context, art functions as an alembic that purifies sensations. Primary and inviolable, they cannot be assimilated within the reflective structure of what Proust calls "intelligence." The sensory materials of "La saveur d'une madeleine trempée dans une infusion, tant d'autres sensations [The savor of a madeleine dipped into an infusion, so many other sensations]" (III, 866), are accidentally repeated or made real again at certain moments of equally accidental recall or presentification. Although the effect on the individual viewer cannot be predicted, the symbolic role of the work of art serves to separate the pure sensation from the dross of habit, rationalization, lack of concentration, and so on, and "synthesize" it in artistic creation. Synthesis is twofold: a unity of disparate elements and an artificial or artful rendering. The narrator locates felicity in Vinteuil's music, representing the miracle of visionary (artistic) jubilation: "tant d'autres sensations dont j'ai parlé et que les dernières oeuvres de Vinteuil m'avaient paru synthétiser [so many other sensations that I have mentioned and that Vinteuil's last works had appeared to me to synthesize]" (III, 866).

The invisibilia of Proustian Time indicate that the jubilation in question is related to the revelation of truth: the two are intertwined in a textual arabesque of paradise lost and found again. Transgression is not entirely absent from this paradise; the narrator's resolution to reject society and devote himself to his work of art will necessarily include "un certain sentiment d'idolatrie [a certain sentiment of idolatry]" (III, 988) directed at the young girls Gilberte is instructed to invite with him. Art is the site of a paschal leap outside time and into the domain of an "allitération perpétuelle [perpetual alliteration]," and yet art cannot afford to exclude the libidinal elements of mystery and the incarnation of beauty. The vision of seduction moves from the medieval painter to the modern one: "comme Elstir aimait à voir incarnée . . . la beauté vénitienne [as Elstir liked to see Venetian beauty incarnated]" (III, 988). Both medieval and modern, in the beginning and ever after, mystery is the theological navel of the "recherche." Despite certain declarations belonging to its fictions, *A la recherche du temps perdu* is the proper name for the impossibility of completely separating love from theology, or, in Proustian terms, desire from art: "antérieur à chacune [each of the girls provoking idolatry] était mon sentiment du mystère où elles baignaient [anterior to each one was my sentiment of the mystery they bathed in]" (III, 988). The inception or origin of Proustian art is articulated in a paradise of paschal and Marian dimensions, figuratively rendered as Combray. At the same time, the religious mystery implicated within artistic representation is not entirely immune from the horrors of idolatry that menace it.

It is therefore impossible to oppose the asceticism of vocation to the world of desire. But if the dimension of idolatry or the menace of unconscious desire cannot be completely eliminated from the revelation of truth anticipated in the acceptance of vocation, then what is the status of the inviolability of that vocation? What is the status of the Proustian conversion as attributed to the narrator of *A la recherche du temps perdu*? Like Augustine, called "the doctor of sin and grace" ("the doctor of confessional narrative and the literature of mystical ecstasy"), Proust makes the exposition and exposure of the infernal regions of desire into a major task taken up in his narrative. Unlike Augustine, however, he finds his turning point toward the dimension of revelation distinguishing the literary accomplishment of the *Recherche* from some previous literary attempts (including *Jean Santeuil* and early short fiction) in the figuration of unholy desire.[19]

Even in the sublime domain of Proust's creation, the narrator is still located within the human realm of misdirection, sin, and desire (exemplified by the ineradicable presence of idolatry), whereas the Augustinian sublime moves beyond the realm of human creation. In the *Confessions*, love and horror are the effect of Augustine's relation to the creator, who vastly transcends both the writing of the *Confessions* and the workings of human love.

Despite some forthright distinctions made by the narrator during his decisive entry into the vocation at the matinée in *Le Temps retrouvé*, it would not be difficult to demonstrate that much of what falls into the domain of Proustian conversion includes love as the inevitable object of vocation. This is true for Swann, the narrator, Saint-Loup, Charlus, and other characters as well. In the Catholic tradition of the literary confession, the trajectory of religious conversion is described as a chronologically ordered itinerary of the soul from sin toward redemption through grace. Confession maintains a double focus, or a dual articulation; Augustine observed that it speaks an avowal of sin and the praise of God.[20]

Regardless of the "factual" autobiographical status of Augustine's confession, the seeds of modern fiction may be located in the incommensurable gap separating these two voices. Augustine writes his avowed "autobiography" of sin and grace by indicating the chronological progression of events in his life leading toward the climax of conversion. After the dénouement, the death of his mother, he enters into a treatise on theological dimensions that may strike the modern reader as inappropriate for an autobiography. A comparison of this structure, centered in a single temporal point of experience, with the framework of the *Recherche* shows that Proust's narrative is definitely modeled on the narrative tradition of conversion. It is also apparent that the Proustian recital of confession implies a conversion with a difference.

Invocare

At the narrator's moment of ecstasy, the instant is found anew in an image of resurrection (III, 872). Privileged instants subtracted from the ruins of time are called symbolic moments of impressions. As signs or "hieroglyphic characters," they are elements of a complex allegorical pattern of resemblances (III, 878). They emerge from the flight of time to become written style in the form of metaphor. As kernels of metaphor that require "déchiffrage [deciphering]" (III, 878), reading, and interpretation within a rhetorical chain, they are both truth and its figuration, "ces vérités écrites à l'aide des figures . . . [qui] composaient un grimoire compliqué et fleuri [these truths written with the help of figures . . . that composed a complicated and florid book of spells]" (III, 879). Their spirals and arabesques are explicitly rendered through aesthetic form and its terms. Like the biblical text in the "Tolle, lege" scene of Augustine's conversion, these instants of "ineffable vision" (III, 875) are singular textual creations; they inscribe the ecstatic vision with a presence that emanates from somewhere else. But these moments function cumulatively rather than punctually in Proust's text, where they form a series starting with the initial "open sesame" of the Petite Madeleine. According to the system established by the text, the vocation would be impossible without it.

Proust's initial opening must be followed by a series of moments of revelation in order to attain a final closure that fictively gathers all the "open sesames" into a definitive conversion. The gesture of closing the circle was essential from the beginning of Proust's conception of *A la recherche du temps perdu*, and it was extended through the "paperoles" (III, 1033) or paper streamers that overflowed the borders of the novel as he had imagined them. The closure of the text consecrates the opening of the vocation to be consummated. But this circle is a fictional one: it is a figure of a circle, since there is no common measure between the authorial scripture as written by Marcel Proust and named "A la recherche du temps perdu," and the inscribed vocation attributed to the narrator. The circle is a fictional image for another reason: the temporal symmetry it adumbrates cannot completely disguise the anachronism of the experience of ecstatic vocation inscribed in Proust's novel.

Proust's edifice of the fictions of temporality depends on a vertiginous twist: time is taken out of the traditional framework of human and divine, lost and found. In Richard Macksey's subtle reading of Proust's Balzacian signposts,[21] this framework of illusions lost in the search for the absolute literally informs the title of the novel. Proust makes use of the rhetorical bravado of this confessional model, but he ultimately refuses it: from the chronologically ec-static "open sesame" of the Magdalene (Madeleine), waiting for the Word to emerge from the grave, the series of deferrals that constitute Proust's writing of the conversion experience seem to point the reader toward an asymmetrical *passage* through hell. In Proustian allegory, this passage makes the narrator a witness of evil and death: hell is the abyss of desire that condemns its subjects to the losses inseparable from human time. Time's shape seems to indicate the impossibility of paradise (III, 870). The moments of ecstasy are punctual indications of an anticipated vocation that does not leave the wasteland of idolatry until the final weave of the loom. Only at the end of the novel can vocation takes its literal stand in an invocation—the effect of the fictional conversion, the crystallization of the book, and the invisible dimension of time (III, 1043–45).

What Walter Benjamin calls Proust's "clasped (or connected) time" ("die verschränkte Zeit")[22] can be seen as essential to the arabesque or figuration of *invisibilia*: the formulation of conversion as style, poetic language, and fiction. The verb *verschränken* is used to describe the crossing or clasping of one's own arms, the teeth of a saw, the steps of a deer. Benjamin appears to invent "verschränkte Zeit" in order to describe Proust's time: "Die Ewigkeit, in welch Proust aspekte eröffnet, ist die verschränkte, nicht die grenzenlose Zeit [The eternity within which Proust opens windows is clasped time, not limitless time]."[23] Benjamin's formulation of eternity seems rather enigmatic: how is it possible to distinguish "eternity" from "time" (as Ramon Fernandez does), and maintain that eternity is not infinite? As if to compound his paradoxical formulation, Benjamin immediately shifts from time to space with the "raumverschränkten Gestalt," the form that clasps the interiority of memory to the exteriority of aging.

The site of this clasped form is not named. It is not the author, but rather the created object, the countless pages of his fiction. One might call it the interior world of the narrator, but only on the condition that the narrator be considered the telescopic heart of the Proustian world, the arena of its day and night. Benjamin's terms seem to exclude the narrator: in the theater of Proustian representation, lived life appears through the hieroglyphics and significations of the dreamworld, far from the fantasmatic projections of psychology. There is only the spun web of the text, and the interlace of aging and memory: "Das Widerspiel von Altern und Errinern verfolgen heisst in das Herz der Proustschen Welt, ins Universum der Verschränkung dringen [To follow the counterpoint of aging and memory in the heart of the Proustian world means to penetrate into the universe of clasping]."[24]

This is the world of resemblance (*Ähnlichkeit*), ruled by *correspondances*. Under the sign of Proustian rapture, Benjamin moves from the similarities that rule the dream world to Baudelairean allegory. "Korrespondenzen," the network of displaced mystical significations, plummet the subject into a universe of hieroglyphics. Benjamin posits "Verschränkung" as the appearance of correspondence in the image of lived life ("in unserem gelebten Leben").[25]

In "Zum Bilde Prousts," "Verschränkung" occurs in several formulations. Benjamin conceptualizes Proustian eternity as the clasping of time; within the context of spatial forms of "Verschränkung," temporality becomes operative. The bearer of lived life or the subject of autobiography is evoked as a point of intersection, the spatial clasping of interiority and exteriority. In spatial terms, the reassuring image of lived life (the autobiographical persona) is reduced to a point, the nearly invisible image of the autobiographical tapestry. On its stage, Proustian temporality is played out in the clasping of memory and aging. The spatial dimension of "Verschränkung" shifts from the autobiographical life to the geography of Proust's remembered world, "wie die Richtung von Guermantes mit der Richtung von Swann für Proust sich verschränkte, da er (im dreizehnten Bande) ein letztes Mal die Gegend von Combray durchstreift und die Verschlingung der Wege entdeckt [As Guermantes' Way clasps/crosses Swann's Way, when (in the thirteenth volume) he evokes the region of Combray for the last time and discovers the interlacing of the Ways]."[26]

In Proust's representation of the writer's vocation, Benjamin singles out a rapture ("Rausch") that characterizes Proustian eternity: "diese Ewigkeit . . . ist rauschhaft [This eternity . . . is rapturous]."[27] The experience of rapture appears to be the mystical, temporal counterpart of the geographical "Verschränkung." At the same time, rapture is the effect of "Verschränkung," "Wo das Gewesene im taufrischen 'Nu' sich spiegelt [Where the past mirrors itself in the dew-fresh 'now']."[28] The image of the past is mirrored in the instant that produces a "Verjüngung" (rejuvenation), the object of Proustian presentification. The clasping of the world with a single human life gives rise to the invisible "now" and its geographical image: "Im Nu springt die Landschaft um wie ein Kind [In the Nu, the landscape springs around like a child]."[29] Benjamin's concept of "Verschränkung" gives an account of the specifically Proustian image of correspondence: the interlace of invisibilia and the emergence of rapturous eternity within the framework of a lived life. The image of the writer's vocation steps out of the flow of time and the flight of images into the light. Clasped and rendered eternal, images of rapture enter Benjamin's text from the concept of vocation that operates in and through *A la recherche du temps perdu*. According to the terms of the novel, Proust's formulation represents rapture as style.

Avec des lignes

Proust illustrates the inscription of rapture through style in the characterization of Bergotte, the writer of fiction admired by the narrator. Like Dante's Vergil, Bergotte disappears before the narrator takes up his own vocation. His paternal role anchors him in the narrator's past, where he glows like the Golden Angel, a harbinger of the ecstatic present tense of vocation. His death is marked by a moment of rapture that is a condensed figure of the turn toward writing. The narrator counterpoints this figure during the matinée, when he alludes to the instants of "an ineffable vision" in terms of a fall or loss of consciousness (III, 875). Bergotte's vision of Vermeer's "View of Delft" is a knot of fiction and autobiography, sifted through the paternity of literary apprenticeship and the *correspondance* of creation. The painting links Bergotte to Swann's role in the narrator's apprenticeship of love and art; at the same time, it recalls the author's formative relationship to Ruskin. Proust considered the "View of Delft" to be the most beautiful painting in the world: "Depuis que j'ai vu au musée de La Haye une *Vue de Delft*, j'ai su que j'avais vu le plus beau tableau du monde."[30] Bergotte's moment of rapture focuses on the style of a single panel of yellow wall framed by spires and chimneys, midway between sky and sea: "'C'est ainsi que j'aurais dû écrire, disait-il. Mes derniers livres sont trop secs, il aurait fallu passer plusieurs couches de couleur, rendre ma phrase en elle-même précieuse, comme ce petit pan de mur jaune' ['This is the way I should have written, he said. My last books are too dry, I should have painted [passer] several layers of color, rendered my sentence precious in itself, like this little panel of yellow wall']" (III, 187).

Bergotte's rapture of style is reminiscent of the effusion of the spire at Saint-Hilaire that voices the passionate sensibility of the narrator's grandmother: "C'était lui qui parlait pour elle [It spoke in her place]." He quotes her remark that if the spire could play the piano, "il ne jouerait pas *sec* [it would not play in a *dry manner*]" (I, 64). This "open sesame" of vocation uncovers the arabesque of *correspondance* linking art, fiction, and love. It is prefigured as light shining in darkness in the paragraphs that present the narrator's vision of the Petite Madeleine. The Proustian wafer bears the proper name of a sinner whose love for the Word led her to a vision withheld from the less effusive apostles: "C'est ainsi que, pendant longtemps, quand, réveillé la nuit, je me ressouvenais de Combray, je n'en revis jamais que cette sorte de pan lumineux, découpé au milieu d'indistinctes ténèbres [And that was how, for a long time, when, awakened at night, I would remember Combray, I never saw anything more of it than a kind of luminous panel, cut out in the midst of indistinct shadows]" (I, 44). The narrator's ecstasy of the Madeleine marks a passage through the illuminated little panel of yellow wall into the fictional revelation of *invisibilia*.

Benjamin's concept of "Verschränkung" unveils Proust's deferral of vocation as evidence of the asymmetry of time. Clasped or crossed, layer to layer, time's weave is interrupted by the knot of an impossible entity—the singular repetition, or a repetition with a difference. Metaphor, too, is a repetition with a difference: "le miracle d'une analogie [the miracle of an analogy]" (III, 871). It allows for an escape from time into the asymmetry of time. The paradoxical figure of metaphor maps out the inviolable singularity of the two entities it brings together for an a-temporal flash of jouissance: "jouir de l'essence des choses, c'est-à-dire en dehors du temps [to enjoy the essence of things, that is to say, outside time]" (III, 871). Proust's strategy of deferral is evident in the telescopic view of the construction of the *Recherche* and in the microscopic display of style. Uniting these two levels of vision is the fictional blank space of *not* writing: the anticipated text requires an effect of belatedness to be written. The effect is an *après-coup*, or the turn of the return. This sign brands the novel with the displacements of mastery, in death, love, and the vicissitudes of creation. Proust shapes language into a *perpetual alliteration*, an ongoing poetic act of fictional crystallization, through a fiction marked by the narrator's desire to return "avec des lignes" (I, 168). This fiction is predicated on the author's invisibility as Marcel Proust. In his image of vocation, the alibi or the lie can only serve to reveal the truth—somewhere else, as the alibi of metaphor reveals the singularity of identity through a fugitive emergence and disappearance.

L'artiste du mal

Through the paradox of symbolic figuration, Proust inscribes this temporal and figural displacement at the heart of fiction. He characterizes the "étrangeté saisissante, la beauté spéciale [striking strangeness, the particular beauty]" of the Giotto allegories (1,82) as the literal effect of a symbol rather than the representation of an idea. Near the end of *A la recherche* this often-repeated opposition occurs in a sentence explicitly opposing representational marking to the letters of figuration that compose the writing of (in)vocation: "Le livre aux caractères figurés, non tracés par nous, est notre seul livre [The book with the figured characters that we have not drawn is our only book]" (111, 879). What is at stake in this poetic interlace of fiction is the object of the invocation—writing itself, the truth of vocation and invocation: "Ces vérités écrites à l'aide des figures [these truths written with the help of figures]" (111, 879). The experience of conversion is inseparable from the act of converting experience, situated beyond the little panel of illuminated wall, into a work of art: "de faire sortir de la pénombre ce que j'avais senti, de le convertir en un équivalent spirituel. Or, ce moyen qui me paraissait le seul, qu'était-ce autre chose que faire une oeuvre d'art? [to bring out of the half-darkness what I had felt, to convert it into a spiritual equivalent. And the means that appeared to me as the only one, was it something other than the creating of a work of art?]" (III, 879). The intensity of enjoyment or jouissance associated with moments of ecstatic experience that punctuate the novel until the matinée gathers them together is posited not only at the initiation moment of the Madeleine but also in the initiation of medieval allegory, Giotto's frescoes of the Virtues and Vices in Santa Maria dell'Arena. The inscription of truth is explicitly related by Proust to "le côté effectif, douloureux, obscur, viscéral, vers cet envers de la mort [the effective, painful, obscure, visceral aspect, to the underside of death]" (I, 82); without this darkness of negativity, the symbolic salvation offered by the moment of "verschränkte Zeit" (appearing in many forms, beginning with the nocturnal kiss) would have no meaning. The elision of alibi, the elsewhere of metaphor, the fiction, and the poetic "blank" implicate the effect of belatedness produced by the writing of transgression in the horror that measures the Proustian dimensions of love.[31]

The "open sesame" of fictionalized transgression leads narrator and reader into two circles of hell from which Proust could not escape: "Je [the narrator]tournais en cercle dans les places noires, d'où je ne pouvais plus sortir [I was going around in a circle in black places that I was no longer able to leave]" (III, 833).

These circles take the form of Jupien's boutique of sadistic homosexuality and "the Jewish question," the identity put to death by French anti-Semitism and dramatized via Swann, Bloch, and the Dreyfus affair. Given the criminal status of homosexuality in the historical context[32] of the Belle Epoque, and the equally tragic dimensions of loss and evil constituting his version of Jewish identity,[33] the only possible escape from the tragic dimensions of Proustian sadomasochism is the scriptural version of Vinteuil's musical paternity. Vinteuil's art was saved by the daughterly evils of homosexuality that put him to death: the narrator's vocation is enigmatically echoed in the uncanny characterization of Bloch and the interlacing of identities that link him to the narrator. An even more important (and much less ambiguous) identification leads the narrator to found his vocation on Swann's failure, finalized in his death and avenged by the narrator's future oeuvre. His work will symbolically honor and resurrect the unmourned Jew, who is silenced, consigned to dust, and otherwise forever lost. Swann's spectacular early social success paled next to his love for Odette; this unhappy love signed his fate. The unusual eloquence he displays shortly before his death is an effect of the retrospective arrangement that allows him to see his fate unfold. His love for Odette caused him the dark suffering of Charité's ardent heart: the detachment that followed could not alter the effects of what Flaubert called "fatality," but it finally allowed him a view of some kind of "other" meaning. Beyond idolatry now, he explores a new area of interpretation.

It all starts with a small musical sentence: "Longtemps, je me suis couché de bonne heure." The little sentence leads to the *petite phrase* that Swann was incapable of displacing from love to its figuration: "Swann qui s'était trompé en l'assimilant au plaisir de l'amour et n'avait pas su le trouver dans la création artistique [Swann who had made the mistake of assimilating it to the pleasure of love and had not known how to find it in artistic creation]" (III, 877). The experience, the desire, and even the revelation of vocation are explicitly attached to Swann (III, 915). He is the patriarch, worldly but ineluctably and increasingly Judaic, of the narrator's world: he is the Moses who does not reach the promised land of aesthetics.[34]

The other source of the narrator's scriptural and sexual authority is his friend and double, Bloch. Instead of Swann's grace and paternal dignity, he bears the weight of anti-Semitism and Jewish self-hatred. His character seems to suffer from the burden of Jewish filiation: after the narrator's first youthful fascination with him, he is cast in an unflattering and comic light whenever he is compared with the narrator. Bloch figures the blocked, blanked-out opacity of the Jew's name, subject to future displacement.[35] Proust's two hells of tragic identification, homosexuality and Judaism, meet in a searing instant of epiphany when Albertine voices her disgust at the pretty Proustian face[36] of Albert Bloch ("Je reconnais qu'il est assez joli garçon, me dit Albertine, mais ce qu'il me dégoûte! [I admit that he's a good-looking boy, but how disgusting he is!]" [I, 880]) only to denounce the verity of his name: "Quand je lui dis, ce premier jour, qu'il s'appelait Bloch, elle s'écria: 'Je l'aurais parié que c'était un youpin' [When I told her that first day that his name was Bloch, she exclaimed: 'I was sure he was a yid']" (I,

881). The knot of naming and transgression doubly inscribes the Christian name (the "petit nom" central to the conquests of Charlus, the explicit bearer of homosexuality in *A la recherche*) of Proust's chauffeur/lover, Agostinelli, in this flash of anti-Semitic horror. It is obvious that Proust's many references to his lover in the fictional portrait of "Albertine" are highly symbolic, but they are often interpreted as straightforward autobiography. Although these stigmata or autobiographical instants repeat an authentic, biographically guaranteed heartache, their integration in the novel makes it imperative to read them as figurative symbols within the fiction. The tacit countersignature of Proustian jouissance at this meeting of love and horror can be found in the name of the narrator himself. Or rather, it may be found in the gesture of naming him, since Proust does not actually do so: the opaque name of Bloch is mysteriously counter-balanced by the blank space of the name the narrator never receives. His baptism is negative: he bears a name, but it is never given to him. It is Albertine, the name of fictionalized sexual transgression confronting the undissolvable and undesired Jew Proust saw in the mirror, who "would have named" the narrator Marcel. In the subjunctive realm of the imagination, the narrator receives the *author*'s "petit nom": "Elle retrouvait la parole, elle disait: 'Mon' ou 'Mon chéri,' suivis l'un ou l'autre de mon nom de baptême, ce qui, en donnant au narrateur le même prénom qu'à l'auteur de ce livre, eût fait: 'Mon Marcel,' 'Mon chéri Marcel' [She found the use of speech again, she said: 'My' or 'My dear,' either one followed by my Christian name, which would have come out to 'My Marcel,' 'My dear Marcel' if the narrator had the same name as the author of this book]" (III, 75). This hypothetical act of naming returns only once in *A la recherche*. Albertine writes it: "'Mon chéri et cher Marcel. . . . Quel Marcel! Quel Marcel! Toute à vous, ton Albertine' ['My dear and dearest Marcel. . . . That Marcel! That Marcel! All yours, your Albertine']" (III, 157). The two names are briefly intertwined in a love letter before they disappear forever: Albertine will soon follow her fugitive act of naming into the total night of death, and the narrator will continue to be nameless.

8

La Charité de Giotto

Même si on savait que notre page sera brûlée aussitôt écrite, on l'écrirait dans la même extase.

[Even if we knew that the page would be burned as soon as it had been written, we would write it in the same ecstasy.] *(CSB 653)*

The writer's translation of autobiographical stigmata into the negative baptism or consecrated blank space of the narrator's name parallels the medieval rendering of the kitchenmaid as a doubly allegorical figure. As "une personne morale, une institution permanente à qui des attributions invariables assuraient une sorte de continuité et identité, à travers la succession des formes passagères en lesquelles elle s'incarnait, car nous n'eûmes jamais la même deux ans de suite [a legal entity, a permanent institution whose invariable assignments insured a sort of continuity and identity, through the succession of passing forms in which she was incarnated, for we never had the same one two years in a row]" (I, 80), she is allegorically typecast in the image of the kitchenmaid ("fille de cuisine"). According to Swann's reading of what the narrator calls "le symbole ajouté qu'elle portait devant son ventre," "la mystérieuse corbeille [the additional symbol that she was carrying in front of her belly, the mysterious basket]" (I, 81; I, 80), she is also an image or incarnation of Giotto's personification of "Caritas," "la puissante ménagère [qui] incarne cette vertu [the powerful housekeeper [who] incarnates this virtue]" (I, 81). The pact of this double allegory is sealed by an additional allegorical dimension, common to both the kitchenmaid and Giotto's "housekeeper"; in both cases, the symbol is repre-

Giotto, *Le Virtu*.
Padua, Cappella degli Scrovegni all'Arena.
Permission: Art Resource, New York.

sented as being so *real* ("comme si réel" [I, 81]) that no traces of awareness of symbolic resonances can be found in the individual woman's facial expression. The guarantee of allegory, like that of the stigmata, takes the form of a "sign" in the flesh, not in thought.

Although Proust emphasizes the fundamental allegorical dimension of his novel as an architectural construction—a church in four dimensions, the site of "perpetual adoration"—he is much less explicit about his use of this symbolic architecture as a frame for a modern version of Giotto's painted allegories. In 1913 the original publication of *Swann* included the announcement that *Le Temps retrouvé* would appear in 1914 and include "The 'Vices and the Virtues' of Padua and Combray." A study of the genesis of *Le Temps retrouvé* reveals the abrupt disappearance of this title.[1] The rough draft of the text attached to this title has only been identified as fragments contained in Cahier 50: the narrator meets the quasi-mythical and comically reduced figure of his desire, the maid of the baronne Putbus, in front of the Arena. She is compared to Giotto's Charity and allusions are made to Combray and Swann's reproductions.[2]

Proust's text locates the relation between the allegorical title and *la Charité de Giotto* in the Virgin's chapel at the Arena Church in Padua. Its interior is covered with Giotto's frescoes, including the series of the Vices and Virtues. In the later version of the text, Proust annuls the meeting with the baronne's chambermaid, leaving intact her mythical/comical status as absent love-object, perhaps in order not to distract from the privileged focus and vehicle of love: *la Charité de Giotto*.

But why should the disappearance of the Vices and Virtues from *Le Temps retrouvé* announced in 1913 be of any particular importance, given Proust's minimal references to Giotto? There are dozens of pages in the *Recherche* concerning cathedrals; their annotations, combined with Proust's letters, translations, and essays, point to the importance of Emile Mâle and especially of John Ruskin.[3] The former was a respected source, the latter was more of a long-distance mentor and aesthetic father figure. Proust's interest in Giotto himself is in part mediated by his reading of Ruskin's "divine oeuvre."[4] In the passage of the novel that revolves around *la Charité* and Giotto, the reader's attention is soon shifted to questions of reading.

L'ardeur de son amour

Proust's introduction to his translation of Ruskin's *Sesame and Lilies*, entitled "Journées de lecture," contains a proto-text of *Combray* and especially of the passage following *la Charité de Giotto*. He seems to construct a dialectical relationship between visibilia and invisibilia—between the realm of pictorial/sculptural representation, the artistic objects discussed in Ruskin's works, and the reading of the young narrator in "Journées de lecture" and *A la recherche*. At the root of this relationship is the portrayal of the Bible in the visible forms of the cathedral.[5] But he uses the two terms of this relationship—the biblical text and its "translation" into medieval allegory—to mask the unspoken third term, between the art discussed by Ruskin and the discovery of the vocation of reading by the young narrator: the initiation into reading and writing of Marcel Proust. Like the Kabbalists' reading of the Bible as black fire on white fire, the writing from the hand of God, this turn toward vocation takes up the invisibilia of the text in the ineffable "invisible vocation" (II, 397) that transcends the master's protective authority over the apprentice. Even as early as "Journées de lecture," it is clear that the theory of reading is a Proustian one, and that the initiation it evokes is inseparable from a certain opposition to the master art historian. The unspoken third term is accompanied by a silent farewell to Ruskin,[6] not as a theoretician/writer/lover of Beauty, but as the adored father of Proustian aesthetics.

The temptation of idolatry is the name Proust gives to his break with Ruskin. It might also be described as the veil concealing what he often calls "réalité": "La réalité que l'artiste doit enregistrer est à la fois matérielle et intellectuelle. La matière est réelle parce qu'elle est une expression de l'esprit

[The reality that the artist must record is at the same time material and intellectual. Matter is real because it is an expression of the spirit]" (CSB, 111). In one of his few allusions to Giotto outside Ruskinian contexts, Proust compares Flaubert's "originalité grammaticale [grammatical originality]," his "révolution de vision, de représentation du monde qui découle —ou est exprimée—par sa syntaxe [revolution in the vision, the representation of the world, that flows from—or is expressed by—his syntax]" to Giotto's revolution in color (CSB 299). Ten years later, in "A Propos du 'style' de Flaubert," Proust eliminates the parallel with Giotto in his description of Flaubert, "un homme qui . . . a renouvelé . . . notre vision des choses . . . [a man who . . . renewed . . . our vision of things . . .]" (CSB 586). The unspoken third term is doubled by a singular silence concerning Giotto. In the manuscript of the *Recherche*, he crosses out yet another evocation of Giotto's colors in the comparison of *la Charité* with the kitchenmaid.[7]

Giotto seems to be emblematic of a new vision in and through art, comparable to Proust's leap outside the domain of reading and translation of others into the fiction of the reading and translation of the self. The text of *Jean Santeuil* indicates a failed attempt to form this new vision, while *A la recherche* marks its success. Between the two? An unspoken revelation. Proust's talkative dissemination of the voices of Mâle and especially Ruskin, his constant quotation of their interpretation of Giotto, is the silence of Penelope; he weaves and unweaves Ruskin's description of Giotto's frescoes into his own reading. While he endlessly discusses dogmatic frames, cathedral constructions, and so on, his silence on the subject of Giotto speaks volumes.

Through the failure of his earlier attempts, Proust formulates the writing of "reality." He learns to convert the invisible weavings of the self into the figuration of reality—the figuratively *real*, according to his usage of the term—the infinitely symbolic structure of allegory. It is only in this sense that the narrator's quest for vocation may be read as a figural rendering of the "recherche" attributed to Marcel Proust himself. "La place de la Madeleine" is the fictional altar of transubstantiation, where the forgotten is converted into memory. In the second phase of Proustian conversion, the allegory of art is constructed around it.

Proust highlights "La pauvre charité de Giotto, comme l'appelait Swann [Poor Giotto's Charity, as Swann called her]" as the predominant virtue, "la Vertu de Padoue" (I, 121). The narrator refers to the kitchenmaid by the allegorical name that integrates "le symbole giottesque de cette vertu [Giotto's symbol of this virtue]," Giotto's Paduan allegory, in *A la recherche*. Introduced as one of the "passing forms" of the kitchenmaids, Giotto's Charity is distinguished by her "état de grossesse déjà assez avancé quand nous arrivâmes à Pâques [condition of rather advanced pregnancy when we arrived at Easter]" (I, 80). The first term of Proust's version of Giotto is the clothing that covers the "mystérieuse corbeille," the "forme magnifique [mysterious basket, magnificent form]": "Ceux-ci rappelaient les houppelandes qui revêtent certaines des figures symboliques de Giotto dont M. Swann m'avait donné des photographies [These [smocks] recalled the ample cloaks worn by some of Giotto's symbolic figures in photographs that M. Swann had given to me]" (I, 80). It was in this sentence that Proust had evoked Giotto's colors, and then erased them. The narrator describes the resemblance between the maid and the "vierges . . . matrones plutôt, dans lesquelles les vertus sont personnifiées à l'Arena [virgins . . . matrons rather, in whom the virtues are personifiéd at the Arena]" (I, 81). Within this frame of the double allegory mentioned earlier, he evokes "le symbole" that is "représenté comme si réel," Giotto's symbol painted to look so real.

The artist represents this reality in the allegorical image rather than in thought:

> Par une belle invention du peintre elle foule aux pieds les trésors de la terre, mais absolument comme si elle piétinait des raisins pour en extraire le jus ou plutôt comme elle aurait monté sur des sacs pour se hausser; et elle tend à Dieu son coeur enflammé, disons mieux, elle

le lui 'passe,' comme une cuisinière passe un tire-bouchon par le soupirail de son sous-sol à quelqu'un qui le lui demande à la fenêtre du rez-de-chaussée. [Through the painter's beautiful invention she tramples on the treasures of the earth but absolutely as if she were pressing grapes underfoot to extract the juice or rather as she would have climbed on sacks to raise herself up; and she holds out to God her heart in flames, or rather, let us say that she 'passes' it to him the way a cook passes a corkscrew through the cellar opening to someone at the ground floor window who asks her for it.] (I, 81)

Despite the prosaic evocation of the corkscrew and the cook, it is clear that Giotto's Charity in Combray as in Padua is the symbol or allegorical emblem of the essence of Proustian activity. Bearing human suffering, "tous les malheurs de la terre [all the misfortunes of the earth]" (I, 121), she incarnates love as the ultimate gift by literally offering her ardent heart to God.

Proust quotes the source of this passage, Ruskin's *Stones of Venice*, in the notes to *En mémoire des églises assassinées* (CSB 97):

A la chapelle de l'Arena elle se distingue de toutes les autres vertus à la gloire circulaire qui environne sa tête et à sa croix de feu. Elle est couronnée de fleurs, tend dans sa main droite un vase de blé et de fleurs, et dans la gauche reçoit un trésor du Christ qui apparaît au-dessus d'elle pour lui donner le moyen de remplir son incessant office de bienfaisance, tandis qu'elle foule aux pieds les trésors de la terre (CSB 744). [In the Arena Chapel she is distinguished from all the other virtues by having a circular glory round her head, and a cross of fire; she is crowned with flowers, presents with her right hand a vase of corn and fruit, and with her left receives treasure from Christ, who appears above her, to provide her with the means of continual offices of beneficence, while she tramples underfoot the treasures of the earth.] (X: 397)

Proust also quotes a passage that he and his editors attribute to *The Eagle's Nest*, another work by Ruskin: "à Padoue la Charité de Giotto tend dans sa main son cœur à Dieu, foule aux pieds des sacs d'or, les trésors de la terre, et donne seulement du blé et des fleurs (CSB 745) [in Padua the Charity of Giotto gives her heart to God, while she tramples upon bags of gold, the treasures of the earth, and gives only corn and flowers]" (XXVII: 130; X: 397). Proust's translations of Ruskin's representation of Giotto's Charity include yet another version quoted at the end of a non-fictional text, without a reference other than quotation marks. It is the most "Proustian" of the three passages, i.e. it most closely approximates Proust's formulation in *Combray*: "cette figure de la Charité que Giotto a peinte à Padoue . . . et dont Ruskin a souvent parlé dans ses livres, 'foulant aux pieds des sacs d'or, tous les trésors de la terre, donnant seulement du blé et des fleurs, et tendant à Dieu, dans ses maux, son coeur enflammée' [the figure of Charity that Giotto painted in Padua . . . and that Ruskin often mentioned in his books, 'while she tramples upon bags of gold, all the treasures of the earth, and gives only corn and flowers; and from the depth of her sufferings, she gives to God her heart in flames']." The allegorical rendering of *La Charité de Giotto* emphasizes a certain form of *passion*. Ruskin's different readings of Giotto's Charity reveal the mystical confluence of giving and receiving; this ambivalence is justified by iconographic tradition and by the attitude of Giotto's Charity herself. But there can be no doubt about what Ruskin calls "l'ardeur de son amour [the glowing of her love]" (CSB 744), and Proust's translations of Ruskin echo the same words, quoted from another author: "M. Mâle a dit admirablement: '*La Charité* qui tend à Dieu son coeur enflammé . . .' [M. Mâle has said it admirably: 'Charity who offers to God her heart in flames . . .']" (CSB 745).

Among the elements borrowed from Ruskin's description of *La Charité* the crucial one is most evident in the third version quoted above. As the *chute de phrase*, it stands out from the rest of the sentence: "son coeur enflammé [her heart in flames]." The "enflamed" (impassioned) heart of Charity is offered to God. Given Ruskin's importance for Proust, as well as the key role played in Ruskin's aesthetic by *La Charité de Giotto*, Proust's use of this source is hardly surprising. A closer reading of the sentence, however, reveals subtle but important differences between Proust's translation and the description he incorporates in the *Recherche* through the fictional voice of the narrator.

In the most "Proustian" of Ruskin's descriptions of Charity, three verbs in the form of present participles structure the sentence: "foulant," "donnant," "tendant." Proust's sentence (on I, 81, quoted above) reproduces them in the present indicative, with minor changes: "foulant" becomes "foule," "tendant" becomes "tend." The latter, however, becomes the second in a series of three verbs, and instead of "donne," Proust writes "passe." He brings this verb into relief by using it twice, once with the feigned artificiality of superfluous quotation marks that underscore the metaphorical quality of the image, and a second time in the literal, material meaning of "give." He expands the sentence with another tripartite structure, the three similes. Given Proust's predilection for a somewhat pedantic tone in certain descriptive passages of the novel (an unconscious echo of the master, perhaps?), it would be difficult to defend the hypothesis that the hyperbole and the conversational tone or prolixity of this sentence form a deliberate imitation of Ruskin's style. I would suggest, however, that this sentence offers an example of *serious* parody or imitation of Ruskin (in contrast to the comic version, exemplified by Proust's pastiche entitled "La Bénédiction du sanglier. Etude des Fresques de Giotto représentant l'Affaire Lemoine à l'usage des jeunes étudiantes du Corpus Christi qui se soucient encore d'*elle, par John Ruskin* [The Benediction of the Wild Pig. Study of Giotto's Frescoes Representing the Lemoine Affair for the Use of the Young Students of Corpus Christi who are Concerned with *it, by John Ruskin*]").

The master of metaphor builds this strategic sentence with the repetition of "comme." In "A Propos du 'style' de Flaubert," Proust writes: "je crois que la métaphore seule peut donner une sorte d'éternité au style [I believe that metaphor alone can give a kind of eternity to style]" (CSB 586). Where then lies the *Proustian* eloquence of the sentence in question? Ironically, it would seem that the Ruskinian prolixity displayed in the similes and parallel verbs acts as a disguise for the truly Ruskinian core of the sentence, its jewel of metaphor: "et elle tend à Dieu son coeur enflammé [and she gives to God her heart in flames]." For "donnant" read "passe": the gift is a passage. At the core of the mystical offering of "Caritas" is the core of Proust's sentence: the heart. Proust evokes and translates Ruskin's image of it in a text entitled "Pèlerinages ruskiniens en France [Ruskinian Pilgrimages in France]," published in *Le Figaro* on February 13, 1900 (and signed "Marcel Proust"):

> Tel qu'il fut, chrétien, moraliste, économiste, esthéticien; renonçant à sa fortune, donnant la beauté au monde, mais soucieux aussi d'y diminuer l'injustice et donnant son coeur à Dieu, il fait penser à cette figure de la Charité que Giotto a peinte à Padoue et dont Ruskin a souvent parlé dans ses livres, 'foulant aux pieds des sacs d'or, tous les trésors de la terre, donnant seulement du blé et des fleurs, et tendant à Dieu, dans ses maux, son coeur enflammé.' [As he was, Christian, moralist, economist, aesthetician; renouncing his fortune, giving beauty to the world, but concerned as well about diminishing injustice in it and giving his heart to God, he evokes the figure of Charity that Giotto painted in Padua, and about which Ruskin spoke often in his books, 'while she tramples upon bags of gold, all the treasures of the earth, and gives only corn and flowers; and from the depth of her suffering, she gives to God her heart in flames.'] (CSB 443–44)

This obituary marks the site of an aesthetic and scriptural transmission camouflaged and preserved as an act of "passage" in *A la recherche*.

Proust's ambivalent adoration and condemnation of Ruskin are reflected in the allegorical figures of Charity and Idolatry. In this eloquent obituary, however, the author's identity and judgment are veiled in silence. He may be found receiving the Ruskinian transmission somewhere between "giving beauty to the world" and "giving his heart to God," in the anticipated role of the artist. The heart of Ruskin/Charity concludes the obituary that began with a comparison of Ruskin's soul—and particularly its immateriality, contrasted with the body laid to rest at Coniston—to the focus of Romantic necrology, the heart of the poet. Proust writes:

> je propose à ses amis de France de célébrer autrement le 'culte de ce héros,' je veux dire en esprit et en vérité, par des pèlerinages aux lieux qui gardent son âme (tel ce tombeau d'Italie qui s'intitule le tombeau de Shelley et qui du poète, dont le reste du corps fut consumé par la flamme, ne contient que le coeur) et qui lui confièrent la leur, pour qu'en la faisant passer dans ses livres, il la rendît immortelle. [I propose to his friends in France that they celebrate otherwise the 'cult of this hero,' I mean in spirit and in truth, with pilgrimages to the places that possess his soul (like the grave in Italy that bears the name of Shelley and that contains of the poet, consumed in the rest of his body by flames, only the heart) and that entrusted their soul to him, in order that by filtering it [la faisant passer] into his books, he render it immortal.] (CSB 441)

The centerpiece of Proust's intertextual tribute to Ruskin (the description of *La Charité de Giotto* in the *Recherche*) is the heart of Proust's revelation of allegory: "et elle tend à Dieu son coeur enflammé [and she passes to God her heart in flames]." Through the image of the poet's heart and its passage through flame, Proust prefigures the connection between Giotto's Charity and Ruskin that ends the obituary. The hero's soul and its truth meshes with the poet's heart in a striking comparison that concludes with a passage of the soul/heart duality into the writing of books. The exchange between place and spectator, the offering of souls, concludes with immortality: if Proust's remarks are read retrospectively, in light of the *Recherche* and in particular its remarks about Charity, the heart of the poet, and immortality, then perhaps it is the suffering heart, caught up in material reality and desire—the "saisissant" and the "frappant" of the "effectivement subi [effectively suffered]" (I, 82)—that passes through form to give its power to allegory. The passage in question recalls Flaubert's "adieu to the personal": the heart is dissolved in the eternity of ink.

Allegory is inseparable from the revelation of the weaving and unweaving of time, its invisible substance theorized by Proust and Benjamin. Its effects are marked with the stamp of *Nachträglichkeit*, belatedness:

> Mais plus tard j'ai compris que l'étrangeté saisissante, la beauté spéciale de ces fresques tenait à la grande place que le symbole y occupait, et que le fait qu'il fût représenté, non comme un symbole puisque la pensée symbolisée n'était pas exprimée, mais comme réel, comme effectivement subi ou matériellement manié, donnait à la signification de l'oeuvre quelque chose de plus littéral et de plus précis, à son enseignement quelque chose de plus concret et de plus frappant. [But later I understood that the startling strangeness, the particular beauty of these frescoes depended on the large space that the symbol occupied in them, and that the fact that it was represented, not as a symbol since the symbolized thought was not expressed, but as real, as effectively suffered or materially handled, gave to the meaning of the work something more literal and more precise, to its teaching something more concrete and striking.] (I, 82)

Proust establishes his singular version of allegory through the fictional role of Giotto's Charity, a figurative portrait that illustrates the artistic weight of the symbol and its representation of the real. Proust's explanation points to the convergence of allegory and metaphor, image and language, in "quelque chose de plus littéral [something more literal]." The style and vision of the *Recherche* can be seen as the effect of this gap between thought (or the idea) and the letter.

In this framework, Proust's three interjections, the similes qualifying *La Charité de Giotto*, may be read in terms of their allegorical resonances. The extraction of juice from earthly grapes, the act of raising the self toward God, the "passing" of the corkscrew—these images, in the context of Giotto's fresco, are figures of the sacrament founded in the Passion. Christ's love, the offering of flesh and blood, gives rise to transubstantiation, the central term in Proust's aesthetic. Although it is unspoken here, transubstantiation is the miracle of style exemplified by Vermeer's *View of Delft*, and the little panel of yellow wall that performs an uncanny "open sesame" for Bergotte. The symbol and the real add up to something literal—poetic truth, unhindered by the mysteries and veils of idolatry.[8] Ruskin's transmission has been enacted. Transubstantiation may now occur: "Il fallait bien que ces Vertus et ces Vices de Padoue eussent en eux bien de la réalité puisqu'ils m'apparaissaient comme aussi vivants que la servante enceinte, et qu'elle-même ne me semblait pas beaucoup moins allégorique [These Virtues and Vices of Padua must have contained within themselves quite a lot of reality since to me they appeared to be as lifelike as the pregnant maid, and she herself did not seem much less allegorical]" (I, 82). Proust's version of *La Charité de Giotto* may be considered as a portrait of the artist who creates the incarnation of allegory.

Art marks the mystical passage of the enflamed heart, the Passover leap of the angel, the pillar of light. This privileged moment enters the creation of Combray from the liturgy of Easter. Proust underscores the mystical character of Charity when he quotes Mâle: "'*La Charité* qui tend à Dieu son coeur enflammé est du pays de St François d'Assise' [The Charity who holds out to God her heart in flames is from the region of St Francis of Assisi]" (CSB 745). The aesthetic consequences of mystical love are confirmed in a quotation from *The Stones of Venice*: "'La beauté propre à la plupart des conceptions italiennes de la Charité est qu'elles subordonnent la bienfaisance à l'ardeur de son amour, toujours figuré par des flammes'" (CSB 744) ['The peculiar beauty of most of the Italian conceptions of Charity is in the subjection of mere munificence to the glowing of her love, always represented by flames'\]" (X: 397). The complex layering of fiction and aesthetics revolves around the living allegory of Charity. Her portrait introduces the representation of symbolicity and the rhetoric of allegory into the construction of Proust's cathedral, where the dimensions of the letter take the irreducible aesthetic form of a medieval fresco. At the same time, this artistic vision is rooted in a moral and ethical constellation intimately linked with the cathedral structure of *A la recherche*. Proust "translates" Giotto's revelation through color of the visible into a revelation of the invisible—reading, imagination, subjectivity, time—through the letter.

Chosen from among the Vices and Virtues of Padua, Charity is the vehicle not only for the allegory of reading, but for the symbolic proportions of the Proustian enterprise as well. In the context of the turn or conversion that founds the artist's vocation, Proust's insistent repetition of the term of "incarnation" is doubled or tripled in the unfolded layers of reading that illustrate the operative effects of allegory. A kitchenmaid takes on the form of Giotto's matron, and then the incarnation of Giotto's Charity: she becomes this double incarnation because of a third form, (pro-)creation. The narrator enters the world of reading, thereby taking up forms that deliciously blur and suspend his own so-called identity. This is the first step toward his incarnation of reading: the book to be written out of his own life, the creation infinitely transmitted or offered to other readers.

Even when she finally gives birth, *La Charité de Giotto*, now called by her allegorical name, is still associated with her basket, filled with the asparagus described through the exquisite details and colors of the flowers "dans la corbeille de la Vertu de Padoue [in the basket of the Virtue of Padua]" (I, 121). Her affect is still "douloureux, comme si elle ressentait tous les malheurs de la terre [sorrowful, as if she felt all the misfortunes of the earth]" (I, 121); among the stars and azure crowns of the asparagus, she seems to evoke the angels painted in the Scenes at Padua. They too are "douloureux," mourning the death of Christ with a show of emotion that instantly displaces the hieratic poses and the Byzantine formalism of the painter's contemporaries. Giotto offers a possible model for Proust's own rendering of subjectivity, displaced from the codes of the nineteenth century, inaugurating literary modernity. With Dante and the Proust of *la Charité*, Giotto renders medieval vision through the intensely personalized identity of the modern subject. *La Charité de Giotto* suffers, "très malade de son accouchement récent [very ill from her recent childbirth]"; she stays in bed ("ne pouvait se lever" [I, 121]); her ever-present basket of asparagus provokes asthma attacks (I, 124). . . .

Les vices et les vertus

Unlike Swann, Françoise, Mme Sazerat, and so on, "la Charité de Giotto" is not a character; she is pure allegory. Her place in the text is predicated on her "condition of pregnancy." Like her suffering, her sorrowful air, and her eventual disappearance due to violent attacks of asthma, her pregnancy resonates on the level of what is called "autobiography," or what I would prefer to call indirect autobiography, the fictional portrait of the artist. The narrator's vision of creation becomes *material* or *real* through the pregnancy of "la Charité," the allegory of spiritual fecundity and "accouchement." In this particular instance, Proust's vision of the real prefigures Lacan's "Réel." By definition, the "Real" eludes the psychic agencies and conceptualizations of the Imaginary and the Symbolic. Like Proust's investigation of reality and its sexual ground, Lacan's elaboration of the Real is often related to the subject of maternity.[9]

In an empty interior space, a non-conceptual "trou" or hole, the narrator places the object of future exaltation; the mystical moments of vision give rise to a future *Magnificat*, an offering to God of a fiery heart. The single real pleasure of the narrator's life, these visionary moments are contrasted with the futility and "sterility" that previously haunted him: "cette contemplation, quoique d'éternité, était fugitive. Et pourtant je sentais que le plaisir qu'elle m'avait, à de rares intervalles, donné dans ma vie, était le seul qui fût fécond et véritable [this contemplation, although of eternity, was fleeting. And yet I had the feeling that the pleasure it had given to me at rare intervals in my life was the only one that was fruitful and true]" (III, 875). Later, he remarks: "On peut presque dire que les oeuvres, comme dans les puits artésiens, montent d'autant plus haut que la souffrance a plus profondément creusé le coeur [One can almost state that oeuvres, as in artesian wells, rise higher the more deeply suffering has hollowed out the heart]" (III, 908) As creation, Charity's childbirth opens the universe of reading for the narrator. The narrator's understanding and appreciation of Giotto's allegory occur belatedly (*nachträglich*), and the transition from the universe of reading to the interior creation of the book is also belated. The offering of beauty and the heart is delayed until the narrator's vision will have taken its belated effect: "La valeur objective des arts est peu de chose en cela; ce qu'il s'agit de faire sortir, d'amener à la lumière, ce sont nos sentiments, nos passions, c'est-à-dire les passions, les sentiments de tous [The objective value of the arts is modest in that respect; the things that must be brought out, held up to the light, are our sentiments, our passions, in other words, the passions, sentiments, of everyone]" (III, 907). This comment about the narrator's preference for the company of Albertine rather than Elstir recalls Swann's preference for Odette rather than his aesthetic "object," the painting of Giotto, Botticelli, Vermeer.

    The gift of the heart and the heart's gift of beauty in aesthetic form repeatedly link Proust's figure of Charity to the figure of the Virgin. Climbing on "sacks" in order to raise herself up, Proust's *Charité de Giotto* rises through the earthly treasures of the flesh to a symbolic domain that is paradoxically linked for all time to a passage through jouissance and death . . . an incarnation. The immeasurable distance between the voice of God and the unspeakable fall into the materiality and corruption of flesh maps out the territory of the impossible—the point of incarnation and its counter-signature, resurrection. Mary's *Magnificat* answers the Annunciation (Luke 1:35): *Exaltabo*, she begins, My soul doth magnify the Lord. A pure fire of love and her paradoxical flesh without sin raise her like Charity to the heights of divine poetic voice and ear—another name for what is generally called mystical love. In this context, it might appear that critics who repeat the narrator's statements about Swann's idolatry are playing into the hands of Proust's fiction, while Swann "himself," a vehicle of allegory who bears allegorical reproductions, stands for a Proustian inseparability of love and creation. In this sense, the representations of the narrator and Swann can only be separated on certain fictional levels and in terms of the messianic structure of the *Recherche*.

According to the terms of this structure, then, Swann's fatal mistakes form the theater for the narrator's apprenticeship. He founders in aesthetic idolatry and displaces his focus on aesthetic creation to an investment in love. Doubly negated, Swann's vision of art figures a kind of photographic negative of the double gift of creation according to *La Charité de Giotto*, who offers beauty to the world and her heart to God. Swann abandons all hopes of Ruskinian gifts of beauty when he falls in love with Odette, and offers his heart to a paragon of feminine corruption and evil. Does she represent the keeper of the treasures of the earth? the monster symbolizing Idolatry at Amiens?[10] The ungodliness of both Odette and Albertine is such that true words cross their lips only by mistake, either when they lose track of their own intricate lies or when innate vulgarity gives them away. Odette turns Swann's potential for creation into a double negation: not only does she become a substitute for his Ruskinian vocation, she destroys all memory of him after his death. When she consigns Swann to silence and erases his name, her behavior recalls the sadism of Françoise who effects the literal disappearance[11] of *la Charité de Giotto* by torturing the kitchenmaid until she gives notice.

But Swann's gift of allegorical reproductions is ultimately a gift of allegorical reproduction itself. Charity is doubled by the Virgin, the gift of the enflamed heart is doubled by the powers of allegorical writing in the book the narrator will write to save Swann from oblivion, and the words of the *Magnificat*:

Swann possédait une merveilleuse écharpe orientale, bleue et rose, qu'il avait achetée parce que c'était exactement celle de la Vierge du *Magnificat*. Mais Mme Swann ne voulait pas la porter. Une fois seulement elle laissa son mari lui commander une toilette toute criblée de pâquerettes, de bleuets, de myosotis et de campanules d'après la Primavera du *Printemps*. Parfois, le soir, quand elle était fatiguée, il me faisait remarquer tout bas comme elle donnait, sans s'en rendre compte, à ses mains pensives le mouvement délié, un peu tourmenté de la Vierge qui trempe sa plume dans l'encrier que lui tend l'ange, avant d'écrire sur le livre saint où est déjà tracé le mot "Magnificat." [Swann possessed a marvelous Oriental scarf, blue and pink, that he had bought because it was exactly the one worn by the Virgin in the *Magnificat*. But Mme Swann did not want to wear it. Only once she allowed her husband to order a dress covered with daisies, cornflowers, forget-me-nots, and bellflowers like the one worn by la Primavera in *Spring*. At night sometimes, when she was tired, he remarked to me in a very low voice that without her knowledge, her pensive hands took on the loosened and slightly tormented movement of the Virgin who dips her quill in the inkwell held out to her by the angel before writing in the holy book where the word "Magnificat" already has been traced.] (I, 617)

Odette refuses Swann's vision of art, and his displaced vocation leads him to renounce the heights. He would be forever silenced, fallen "very low," were it not for the comments he makes in a hushed voice to the narrator. Proust's allegory indicates that only the narrator can take up the Virgin's pen and redeem the fallen Swann.

Given the proliferation of allegory in the *Recherche*, how can the disappearance of "The 'Vices and the Virtues' of Padua and Combray" from *Le Temps retrouvé* be explained? In other words, what is the status of Proustian allegory, simultaneously offered and retracted, disseminated and yet erased? The split between vice and virtue, Padua and Combray, already informs the evocation of *La Charité de Giotto*. In the completed typed draft and published version of *Combray*, an additional split enters the picture. Invisible rather than pictorial, it elaborates the temporal rhetoric of allegory. Proust writes: "Mais plus tard j'ai compris . . . [But later I understood . . .]" (I, 82). Understanding occurs as a belated effect of the narrator's apprenticeship to Swann: he bears the mystery and resonant code of allegory, and he offers it as a gift of hieroglyphics. Like Flaubert's modern allegories of antiquity, the code of *La Charité de Giotto* is suspended in the framework of modern fiction.

The infinitely meaningful dimensions of allegory are the belated effect of its status as an emblem, a display of hidden meaning. Its splendor is never completely revealed, and as an aesthetic object it can never be fully mastered by the "limits" that define its significance. Out of mystery, then, comes belated understanding. The abyss of time takes shape in the foreplay of pleasure, a symbolic jouissance caused by the narrator's eventual "understanding" of the Giotto fresco. In the context of knowledge and enjoyment, the manuscripts show that Charity originally hung in the narrator's bedroom before he displaced the scene of apprenticeship to the "salle d'études [study]."[12] Later the narrator moves out of the bedroom where his love for Albertine held them both hostage. As he attained allegorical understanding by moving beyond the death that devours Swann, he passes beyond Albertine's death to take a trip with Maman.

Here the reader discovers a doubling of the *Nachträglichkeit* that characterized the narrator's appreciation of Giotto's Charity: the excursion to Padua was once supposed to take place during the narrator's childhood. In addition, Proust gives a particularly virtuoso performance of belatedness when he proposes the trip to Padua as an occasion "pour revoir ces 'Vices' et ces 'Vertus' dont M. Swann m'avait donné des reproductions, probablement accrochées encore dans la salle d'études de la maison de Combray [in order to see again those 'Vices' and 'Virtues' of which M. Swann had given me reproductions, probably still hanging in the study of the house at

Combray]" (III, 648). Because of these temporal layers, the explanation of the disappearance of "Les 'Vices et les Vertus' de Padoue et de Combray" from *Le Temps retrouvé* must be delayed until after a brief summary of the textual history reconstructed by genetic studies.[13]

The question of the Vices and Virtues is present in various stages of *Combray* and *Le Temps retrouvé*, including the early manuscripts of *Contre Sainte-Beuve*. The first evocation of these allegories in the novel occurs in the narrator's description of *La Charité de Giotto* in *Combray*: "Et je me rends compte maintenant que ces Vertus et ces Vices de Padoue lui ressemblaient d'une autre manière [And I realize now that these Virtues and Vices of Padua resembled her in another way]" (I, 81).

The narrator's appreciation of the reproductions of the Vices and Virtues, a gift from Swann, is delayed until an unspecified "later," but his understanding seems to have already occurred when the allegories are explicitly evoked in the account of a trip to Padua (*La Fugitive*, III, 648). According to Bernard Brun's genetic reconstruction of *A la recherche*, *La Prisonnière* and *La Fugitive* are rooted in the project of *Le Temps retrouvé*. The discussion of Giotto comes to light as a reflection of the "original" Giotto motif: Padua inversely mirrors Combray, i.e. it repeats the image of Combray, but time has turned it inside out and revealed its structural role as a point of origin. The reproduction is the source of *La Charité de Giotto*. When the narrator enters the chapel of Santa Maria dell'Arena, Proust returns to the reproduction and builds the chapel as a repetition of that small image of Charity, an allegory of an allegory of an allegory. I will return to this spiraling image and its role in the interpretation of Proust's allegorical landscape following the genetic commentary on the evolution of the Giotto motif.

Proust makes extensive use of materials from the *Sainte-Beuve* project, notably the "matinées," the sounds and odors of the street, and the article published in *Le Figaro* (III, 9, 16, 567).[14] Proust seems to displace material from the matinée with Maman to a later time in the novel. Despite the labyrinthine silences that characterize Proustian "chronology," the temporal layering in this instance is not simply double (lost and found), since the insertion of this material prior to the matinée of the Princesse de Guermantes creates a third temporal focus.[15] The third layer, however, is located in the mysterious silence of the Proustian tapestry or in an unlocalized temporal cloud. In contrast to this silence of writing, fiction loudly proclaims the two terms of Venice and Combray, Saint-Marc and Saint Hilaire. The narrator comments: "J'y goûtai des impressions analogues à celles que j'avais ressenties si souvent à Combray, mais transposées sur un mode différent et plus riche [There I enjoyed impressions analogous to those that I had felt so often in Combray, but transposed into a different and richer mode]" (III, 623). There are other doubles: Madame Sazerat reappears, and the narrator takes the trip to Italy that he nearly took as a child (III, 630, 623 ff.).

The object of scholarly genetic studies seems to take a Romantic form through an organic model of textuality. In Proust's case, the fiction of a quasi-organic internal spiral of art and life strangely parallels the genetic model. The effect of genetic studies resonates on the symbolic level of Proust's doubles: the genetic term of "bipartition" indicates a form of sexual reproduction by meiosis that is an effect of Swann's reproductions of the Vices and Virtues, including *la Charité de Giotto*. Allegory gives rise to more allegory—not by chance is the model for Proustian reproduction a sexual one. Lost and found: the repetition of life is inseparable from death. Contrary to common opinion, the doubled or messianic structure is a response to that knowledge rather than a repression of it.

The function of reproduction in Proust's fiction may be the cause of the particular bipartition (division) affecting the Vices and Virtues. The result of cutting and pasting is a doubling of Proust's allegorical dimensions à la Giotto that occurs late in the chronology of Proust's composition, on a typed manuscript. The kitchenmaid, Swann's gift, and the trip to Padua originally composed an undivided ensemble[16] until Proust crossed out the trip to Padua and wrote "cut here." Although *La Prisonnière* and *La Fugitive* were not conceived before World

War I, when he had this version typed, he had already imagined another trip to Venice and Padua. According to a recent study,[17] he planned to insert this second trip prior to the text of *Le Temps retrouvé*.

The earliest evocations of the voyage to Italy and the allegorical art the narrator admires there are presented in a Proustian form of allegory as emblematic spirals of meaning, symbolic doubles or layers, and fragments independent of the fictional plot. The Venetian motif is founded in Cahier 3 (1908), among the Cahiers Sainte-Beuve, and Cahier 5 includes a visit to Santa Maria dell'Arena. A narrative link does not occur until Cahier 8, when the episodes of Françoise and the grande-tante, Eulalie's visits, and so on, appear in coherent narrative form. This text[18] is now considered to be the first rough draft of *Combray*.

The current and definitive form of the episode appears in Cahier 10. The two pages concerning the trip to Padua have been cut out. (In the typed version, the passage is simply crossed out.) The description of the frescoes and their symbolism is missing from Cahier 10, however, and has been located in an autograph classified as the "Proust 21."[19] As if in tacit accord with the symbolic stratification typical of allegory, the manuscript layers multiply. Proust inserts another copy in the form of a note that contains this description of the frescoes, and then he adds an additional copy of the trip to Padua. He annuls the crossing-out made previously and joins this passage to the rest of the typed version according to Cahier 10. In 1911 he crosses the trip out of the typed version of *Combray*, and in 1916 he cuts it out in order to include it in the composition of *La Fugitive*.

Bernard Brun concludes that the voyage to Padua is first linked to the reproductions at the time when Proust introduced a "message" into the work; the breaking of this link was a second step, a rupture and a displacement, related to the creation of *Le Temps retrouvé*. He describes the introduction of the message and its later reappearance as revelation in terms of an "initiatory progression" and a "final message."[20] The reader is struck by a resemblance between the vocabularies of the genetic study and Proust's fiction; the division of Giotto's Padua emblematizes the doubling of the Vices and Virtues, the allegory that enters the ground of writing. Once again, however, the doubles are threatened by a third element that cannot be easily assimilated into the structure of "bipartition." The origin of the narrator's vision of Giotto, and within the fictional realm of the *Recherche*, the origin of the Giotto paintings themselves, is the site of a displaced or perverted origin that is doubly allegorical: the narrator's Charity is not the original fresco in Padua, but rather its reproduction. The silence of the realization ("later I understood [Mais plus tard j'ai compris]") is related to the perversity of a mediation that falsifies guaranteed origins. One could name this essential phenomenon of belatedness the Swann effect.

A la fin d'un roman.

The question of why Proust erased "The 'Vices and the Virtues' of Padua and Combray" from *Le Temps retrouvé* still remains unanswered. In the light of this disappearance, is it possible to claim that Proust's enterprise is steeped in allegory? If the reader concedes that Proust's work is inseparable from allegorical representation, then what is the status or interpretive weight of that blank space preceded by a crossing-out? To answer these questions, it will be necessary to read the doubling of the text, the subterranean continuation of *la Charité de Giotto*. Marked by "bipartition"—a rupture, a repetition, an after-effect—this paradoxical continuation may be a form of forgetting as well, the "oubli" essential to Proust's invention of "involuntary memory."

He marks the tempo of the two pages introducing the trip to Venice (III, 623–24) with the repetition of "as in Combray." The narrator describes his impressions of the beauty of Venice: "j'y goûtai des impressions analogues à celles que j'avais si souvent ressenties autrefois à Combray, mais, transposées . . . [There I enjoyed impressions analogous to those that I had felt so often in Combray, but transposed . . .]." Saint-Hilaire is compared to Saint-Marc, daily life in Venice is no less real than daily life in Combray: "comme à Combray le dimanche matin. . . . comme à Combray les bonnes gens de la rue de l'Oiseau . . . [as in Combray on Sunday mornings. . . . as in Combray the good people of the rue de l'Oiseau . . .]," and so on. Proust's Padua takes the form of a self-contained extension of Venice (although in terms of allegory in the *Recherche*, Venice might have grown out of Padua). On the fictional level, he locates the narrative episode of the Venice trip under the sign of the opposition between Combray and Padua/Venice. Since the ecstasy of involuntary memory opens and closes the *Recherche* with the revelation of two places—Combray at the beginning, during the matinée with Maman, and Venice at the end, during the "matinée held by the princesse de Guermantes"—this opposition is particularly important for the fictional experience of conversion. The question remains, however, whether this opposition concerns the allegory of the Vices and Virtues.

Within the Venetian episode, the continuation of *la Charité de Giotto* takes the form of a visit to Giotto's chapel in the "real" Santa Maria dell'Arena. The central panel in a miniature triptych (III, 648), this visit is preceded by an evocation of art and the narrator's "travail" à la Swann (III, 645–47)—à la Ruskin: "un travail que je faisais sur Ruskin [some work I was doing on Ruskin]" (III, 645). It is followed by an evocation of life in the world (the farewell to Padua, letters announcing the two marriages, a dialogue concerning these marriages [III, 655–59]). Like the *Recherche* itself, the trip to Venice is under the sign of the pulsation of desire, its rhythm of alternation. Irreducible to a mimetic mechanism, this phenomenon is inscribed earlier in the *Recherche* as "the intermittences of the heart." Love is inextricably linked to death: consecrated by absence and made permanent, it vanishes beneath the cloud of lost time and identity, leaving its only traces in the symbolic death that paradoxically marks its disappearance. The narrator's trajectory of love takes him through the loss of his grandmother and the presence of Albertine to Venice. This city is the site of a complex layering or palimpsest of absences; indeed, it is Albertine's absence, if not her death, that makes it possible for the narrator (held captive by his "prisoner") to travel to Venice at all. The palimpsest of feminine deaths includes an element of temporal depth: Albertine's ascendance coincided with the effacement of the mother and the disappearance of the grandmother, whereas the trip to Venice is placed under the sign of the presence of the mother and the definitive disappearance of Albertine. This return to the original love of the narrator (his tête-à-tête with Maman) is marked by the turn or return of the narrator's vocation.

As Swann's love for Odette consigned his own symbolic disappearance, the narrator's love for Albertine confirmed his inability to engage in a search for his own vocation. Maman occupies the opposite pole in this structure, since she will create the conditions necessary for the revelation of "involuntary memory." Under her watchful eye, the narrator marks the birth or return of his vocation in the Baptistery of Saint-Marc.

The sacrament of baptism is central to the narrative of the life of Christ and his prophetic vocation. In the early Christian church, the ceremony of baptism occurred at the climax of the conversion experience, during the vigil of Holy Saturday. Its Judaic antecedents, or rather the Christian borrowings from Judaism, include both the ceremony of naming and a Passover tradition of re-enacting the paschal night of sacrifice, Exodus and the pillar of fire. Venice/Padua joins Balbec (the pillar of fire at Rivebelle) and Combray ("Holy Week") as a privileged site of Proustian memory and vocation, subtly harmonized through the liturgical motif of Easter/Passover. In order to take notes for his work on Ruskin, the narrator explains, "Nous entrions, ma mère et moi, dans le baptistère . . . [We would enter, my mother and I, the baptistery . . .]" (III, 646). The excursion to Saint-Marc opens the first panel, focusing on art, of the miniature triptych representing Giotto's Padua at its heart. Following his insistence on the parallel between Venice and Combray, Proust emphasizes the symbolic importance of the Baptistery. It resonates through the named architectural symbolism, the scenes of Christ's baptism, and the mosaic art that figures the narrator's conversion in an unarticulated *tolle, lege*. He takes up the book in "la précieuse reliure, en quelque cuir de Cordoue, du colossal

Evangile de Venise [the precious binding made of some Cordoba leather of the colossal Gospel of Venice]" (III, 646). Engaged in reading it, he lingers: "Voyant que j'avais à rester longtemps devant les mosaïques qui représentent le baptême du Christ, ma mère, sentant la fraîcheur glacée qui tombait dans le baptistère, me jetait un châle sur les épaules [Seeing that I would have to linger for a long while before the mosaics that represent Christ's baptism, my mother, feeling the chilled freshness that was falling in the baptistery, would throw a shawl over my shoulders]" (III, 646).

The passionate and virginal maternal figure ("la ferveur . . . de la femme âgée qu'on voit dans la *Sainte Ursule* de Carpaccio [the fervor . . . of the elderly woman who is seen in Carpaccio's *Saint Ursula*]") brings the narrator out of his narrative context and into the future of a present tense: "Une heure est venue pour moi où, quand je me rappelle le baptistère, devant les flots du Jourdain où saint Jean immerge le Christ . . . il ne m'est pas indifférent que . . . à côté de moi, il y eût une femme drapée dans son deuil avec la ferveur . . . [An hour has come for me when, remembering the baptistery, in front of the Jordan waters where Saint John immerses Christ . . . it is not a matter of indifference . . . that next to me, there was a woman draped in mourning with the fervor . . .]" (III, 646). He contrasts his pleasure of mourning, increased by the previous visit to Saint-Marc with his mother, to that same pleasure mentioned by Albertine at Balbec and dismissed as a pure illusion on her part. The microscopic opposition between Albertine and Maman is rooted in the Venetian art of Carpaccio. But the extension of this artistic comparison clearly opposes the mother's abnegation to Albertine's worldly desires for luxury that had caused the narrator's financial ruin. Maman is identified with the mosaics of Saint-Marc, but Albertine is recalled wearing the Fortuny overcoat that disappears with her after a visit to a monument of worldly pleasures, Versailles ("elle avait jeté sur ses épaules un manteau de Fortuny qu'elle avait emporté le lendemain et que je n'avais jamais revu depuis dans mes souvenirs [she had thrown over her shoulders a Fortuny coat that she had taken the next day and that I had never seen since then in my memories]" [III, 647]).[21] Rendered permanent in Saint-Marc, Maman's virtue is contrasted with the vice of Albertine, twice fugitive. Her flight ended in her death and in another "fuite," the disappearance of the narrator's love for her, his "retour vers l'indifférence [return toward indifference]" (III, 643).

Hovering between the fin de siècle terms of art and life, the quasi-nameless narrator lingers in the Baptistery. His namelessness, described earlier as negative baptism, guarantees Proust's own vocation even as it walks the borderline between fiction and an unverifiable moment of "autobiography." Negative baptism suspends the narrator's identity between creator and creation. It marks this fictional identity (as fiction and in fiction) with the stigmata of indirect autobiography, and takes on the decisive proportions of the writer's vocation in Saint-Marc.

> Une heure est venue pour moi où, quand je me rappelle le baptistère devant les flots du Jourdain où saint Jean immerge le Christ . . . il ne m'est pas indifférent que dans cette fraîche pénombre, à côté de moi, il y eût une femme . . . et que cette femme . . . que rien ne pourra plus jamais faire sortir pour moi de ce sanctuaire doucement éclairé de Saint-Marc où je suis sur de la retrouver parce qu'elle y a sa place réservée et immuable comme une mosaïque, ce soit ma mère. [An hour has come for me when, remembering the baptistery in front of the Jordan waters where Saint John immerses Christ, . . . it is not a matter of indifference that in the fresh half light, next to me, there was a woman . . . and that this woman . . . whom nothing will ever be able to take out of the softly lit sanctuary of Saint Mark where I am sure to find her because her place there is reserved and as immutable as a mosaic, is my mother.] (III, 646)

The messianic hour indicates a definitive separation from the narrator's mother. Sidetracked once during childhood at Combray, this separation or loss haunts an entire (fictive) life lived under the sign of the goodnight kiss. Feminine losses multiply. In Venice, the mother mourns the loss of the narrator's grandmother, whose appearance and character she takes on in a gradual transformation. The narrator has lost Albertine, and he anticipates the loss of his mother For an uncanny instant, Albertine is returned to him (when he receives a telegram he thinks she has sent [III, 641]) and then lost again, in the doubled twilight of nightfall: "'deux fois crépusculaire, puisque la nuit tombait et que nous allions nous quitter' ['like a double twilight, since night was falling and we were going to leave each other']" (III, 647).

At this particular moment in Proust's fiction, the density and multiplication of feminine losses are presented as a web of countless repetitions. Proust gives the reader already afflicted with vertigo a final dizzying spin when he echoes the doubled twilight of Albertine's last letter (III, 468) with the doubling of her letter in Italy (III, 647). The narrator's last nightfall with her was a kind of double negative, according to her written account of it. In the wake of Albertine's death, clearly underscored in the Italian *ricorso*, this double negative is unveiled in the infinite dimensions of negativity. Proust's metaphoric constellation of nightfalls and separations, Egyptian dark nights and moments of loss and forgetting, seems to be inseparable from the negativity that gives them their power and form (and forever dismisses the reading of Proust as a precious fin de siècle gentleman writer). Indeed, one of his dizzying virtuosities appears in the form of a simultaneous evocation of aesthetic pleasure and the disappearance of its beholder into the abyss. Albertine's correspondence and its double negative echo the double negative of Swann's creation —the gift of beauty and the gift of the heart—in the form of Odette as Botticelli's *Primavera*. An idolatrous substitute for vocation, Swann's art of love consigns him to the abyss. Botticellian beauty and all, Odette bears a certain resemblance to the Grim Reaper, and Albertine's double negatives are no less threatening.

In the Venetian baptistery, the narrator's mother (unlike Albertine) takes her place and finds form among the allegories of the Gospel. Accessory to the narrator, self-effacing and almost hidden, Maman becomes part of Saint-Marc: "her place there is reserved and as immutable as a mosaic." Out of the vertiginous impossibility of the real, out of reality as flesh and absence, creation and death, Maman steps into art: compared to a mosaic in Saint-Marc, she becomes a permanence that maintains the negativity of mourning and death without erasure. This paradoxical structure is repeated on the temporal level. Within the time sequence of the visit to Saint-Marc (in the imperfect tense), the narrator inserts a deictic present tense ("Today") with a messianic hour: "An hour has come for me" (III, 646). In allegory, a future past moves into the permanent presence of resurrection.

In the opposition of Albertine to Maman that unfolds in the baptistery, the narrator inverts the allegorical process that renders his mother's virtue in the marble and glass of mosaic, the beauty of allegory. The common ground of Carpaccio shows the division between Maman as Saint Ursula and the body of Albertine, evoked (along with the narrator's love for her) in "*Le Patriarche di Grado exorcisant un possédé* [*The Patriarchs of Grado Performing an Exorcism*]" (III, 646). Maman as the patron saint of the 11,000 virgins is opposed to—Albertine the possessed? her son the possessed? the devil himself, exorcised during the Catholic ceremony of baptism? All three, perhaps, since the infinite dimensions of negativity do not lend themselves to easy demarcations or simple oppositions.

Under the narrator's "cover," the illusory parallelism of the two women, loved and lost through death, Proust inverts the process of allegory that moves Maman from the realm of the real into the realm of art. The narrator admires the paintings that will lure him into seeing the images of his desire:

> Tout à coup je sentis au coeur comme une légère morsure. Sur le dos d'un des *Compagnons de la Calza*, reconnaissable aux broderies d'or et de perles qui inscrivent sur leur manche ou leur collet l'emblème de la joyeuse confrérie . . . je venais de reconnaître le manteau qu'Albertine avait pris pour venir avec moi en voiture découverte à Versailles, le soir où j'étais loin de me douter qu'une

quinzaine d'heures me séparaient à peine du moment où elle partirait de chez moi. [Suddenly I felt something bite lightly at my heart. On the back of one of the *Calza Brothers*, recognizable in the gold and pearl embroideries that inscribe their sleeve or collar with the emblem of the carefree brotherhood.... I had just recognized the coat that Albertine had taken to come with me in an open carriage to Versailles, that evening when I was far from the knowledge that scarcely fifteen hours separated me from the moment when she would leave my house.] (III, 647)

This is not a coincidence, but rather an extension of allegory, since the Venetian designer of Albertine's coat detached it from Carpaccio's painting: "Or c'était dans ce tableau de Carpaccio que le fils génial de Venise [Fortuny] l'avait pris . . . pour le jeter sur celles de tant de Parisiennes [Now it was from this painting by Carpaccio that the brilliant son of Venice [Fortuny] had taken it . . . to throw it over the shoulders of so many Parisian women]" (III, 647). Fortuny's design moves out of the emblematic spiral of aesthetic permanence in Carpaccio's painting to Albertine's shoulders, on the night of her first (and ultimately definitive) disappearance. The motif of art steps into the real; a forgotten past is resurrected, but only for an instant. Albertine's coat goes with her, and both evaporate from the narrator's memory. In Venice his love is nearly resurrected, but not quite; desire and melancholy are "bientôt dissipé" after only a few moments. Proust's allegorical inversion here marks the resurrection as momentary. The "forms" of Albertine move from art to the real, and then they vanish forever. Within the domain of allegory, virtue remains triumphant and vice is condemned to its own silence.

The visit to Padua is the center of the triptych created or re-created by Proust: "pour revoir ces 'Vices' et ces 'Vertus' dont M. Swann m'avait donné des reproductions [In order to see again those 'Vices' and 'Virtues' of which M. Swann had given me reproductions]" (III, 648), the narrator (accompanied by his mother) enters the Arena chapel. The center of Proust's miniature triptych unfolding the Vices and Virtues maps out the explicit return to the Giotto allegories of Combray. Within this rendering of repetition and its actualization—its "réalisation" as a literal entry into the realm of allegory, "'les Vices et les Vertus' de Padoue et de Combray" —Proust introduces two new elements. One of them echoes the identifications made in the baptistery, through the images narrating the life of Christ and the Virgin. The narrator/son and his mother move through narrative from the baptistery, the place of naming and the site of conversion, to the Marian chapel of allegory. The new element within this return to the source of Combray and Swann's reproductions is narrative itself, the vocation as fiction—fictitious and true, through fiction and its writing.

The other new element literally heralds and introduces the first ("des fresques qui retracent l'histoire de la Vierge et du Christ [frescoes that retrace the story of the Virgin and Christ]"): "Dans ce ciel transporté sur la pierre volaient des anges que je voyais pour la première fois, car M. Swann ne m'avait donné de reproductions que des Vertus et des Vices [In this sky transported onto stone flew angels that I was seeing for the first time, for M. Swann had given me reproductions only of the Virtues and the Vices]" (III, 648). Within this declared domain of allegory, placed under the sign of the Virgin, Proust inscribes Giotto's angels and relates them to the literal reality of Giotto's Charity. Their flight impresses the narrator: "Hé bien, dans le vol des anges, je retrouvais la même impression d'action effective, littéralement réelle, que m'avaient donnée les gestes de la Charité ou de l'Envie [And so in the angels' flight I was finding the same impression of action taking effect, literally real, that the gestures of Charity or Envy had given to me]" (III, 648). The Proustian highlights of virtue and vice, *la Charité et l'Envie*, locate the angels as pure allegory, and therefore as what Proust calls "literally real": they create a reality effect in Giotto's painted sky, and they enter reality through the radiant instant of the letter. This effect could be described as the agency of the letter,[22] in order to emphasize its insistence, its ineluctable alterity, and the tendency of allegory to create figures or images.

Proust's aesthetic chapel displays the angels that the narrator sees for the first time when he enters the territory of his vocation as the promised land denied to Swann. Swann gave him the Virtues and Vices, but the realm of negative baptism and the flight of allegory were destined to be confronted by the narrator alone. Like Dante's Vergil, the narrator's initiator may not enter paradise, figuratively rendered in the painted sky of the chapel and the new flight of angels.

Veils of Fiction

Swann's flight, his effect of "reality," and the effect of the real on him (including the retrospective arrangement of consciousness that lends him a prophetic voice shortly before his death) were consummated as disappearance long before the narrator encountered these "volatiles [winged creatures]," Giotto's angels. Although Swann did not introduce the narrator to the painted "créatures réelles et effectivement volantes [real and effectively flying creatures]," the Proustian "reality" of Giotto's angels is precisely that allegorical representation of death and the soul's departure from the earthly realm of so-called reality, through flight: "on les voit s'élevant, décrivant des courbes, mettant la plus grande aisance à exécuter des 'loopings,' fondant vers le sol la tête en bas . . . et ils font beaucoup plutôt penser à une variété disparue d'oiseaux ou à de jeunes élèves de Garros s'exerçant au vol plané [one sees them rising up, drawing curves, displaying the greatest ease in their performance of 'loopings,' heading toward earth in a nose dive . . . and they bring much more to mind some type of bird that has disappeared than young students of Garros practicing their flying]" (III, 648). The reality that strikes the narrator subtly echoes his vision of the airplane seen with Albertine at Balbec and reinscribes her death within its Italian context (the telegram, Carpaccio, Fortuny, and so on). But the uncanny aeronautics of Giotto's angels seem to be designed primarily to mark this passage as an instant of fictional autobiography. The angel who disappears in a series of "loopings" practiced "vol plané" under the name of "Marcel Swann" and flew to his death ("heading toward earth in a nosedive"); Proust evokes the flight of "Marcel Swann" in a note to *En Mémoire des églises assassinées* (CSB 66). The instant of autobiography signs the allegory of the real with the unavowed name of Alfred Agostinelli.

What constitutes the "real" in this passage? This question receives a double answer: flight and death. Throughout *A la recherche*, Proustian angels are privileged in their exclusively allegorical status. They anchor reality in the letter and in invisibilia, since their capacity as messengers does not classify them within the enforced representability of creatures of flesh and blood. Angels bear the allegorical message of allegory; they represent something like allegory squared. In this sense, they guarantee the rhetorical flight of Proust's allegory from its inception in Swann's *la Charité de Giotto*.

They thus guarantee the portrayal of the Virtues and Vices, continued in the final panel of the miniature triptych. When the narrator suddenly stages a repetition of the fugitive's flight, his mother is condemned to repeat the role of Albertine, although in a virtuous mode. At the moment of her departure a porter brings three letters (III, 652), left unread until after the narrator's reunion with her in the train. Until that moment, however, the narrator's desire to remain in Venice suddenly returns him to the sufferings of separation and a repetition of loss: "je n'étais plus qu'un coeur qui battait [I was nothing more than a beating heart]" (III, 653).

The suffering heart repeatedly replaces the narrator under the sign of *la Charité de Giotto* and her love. Every allegorist knows, however, that allegory is not a unilateral conception and that the subject of jouissance has at least two answers to every question. Proust's representation of the adieu to Padua can only be rendered as a permanent setting for the allegory essential to his *Recherche*. It may be for this reason that the final panel of the Padua triptych includes a repetition of the characteristically Proustian drama of the suffering heart, victim of separation. In this context, however, the identification with Charity cannot protect the suffering heart from negativity. Proust's portrait of the narrator pins him through the heart and displays him between the two wings of flight; the fugitive of Virtue (Maman), both first and last, and the intermediary fugitive of Vice (Albertine), whose first flight became her last, in death.

Proust's inscription of the abyss of negativity tacitly returns to the moment of infinite solitude created by the death of his beloved fugitive. The messianic hour of allegorical resurrection perceived in Saint-Marc is linked with the zero hour of total loss. The terms describing the mother's departure cast it in a permanent form: "Ma solitude irrévocable était si prochaine qu'elle me semblait déjà commencée et totale [My irrevocable solitude was so near that it seemed to have begun already, and to be total]" (III, 652). The anticipated death of the narrator's mother sets the scene for the farewell to Padua and the reading of letters in the train.

Once he catches up with Virtue, the narrator discovers that the telegrammatic resurrection of Albertine was an interpretive error; the enigmatic message had been sent by Gilberte. Wedding bells are still in the air but not for the narrator, despite the apparent ambiguity of the telegram. Maman is alive for the moment, and Albertine has returned to her abyss; the opposition of Virtue and Vice is reaffirmed. This stability is confirmed by the letter to the narrator from Gilberte, announcing her marriage to Robert de Saint-Loup (III, 656). The two sides of Méséglise (chez Swann) and Guermantes come together in the cathedral arch of Proust's oeuvre. This marriage is a kind of retrospective time capsule for the *Recherche* as a cathedral of allegory leading from Combray and Swann through the final matinée, while the trajectory of the narrator's anticipated oeuvre brings together Swann's death and the creation of the final matinée, death and resurrection, in the form of Mlle de Saint-Loup. Gilberte's wedding announcement is also a letter from Proust to the reader, announcing the structure and span of his novel.

The other letter received by the narrator's mother locates Proust's oeuvre at the crossroads of plot, character, temporality, and vocation—the elements of allegory that turn the theme of vice and virtue into a representation of the Vices and the

Virtues. Another marriage has been arranged to stage the oppositions built into the cathedral frame; like Gilberte's marriage to Saint-Loup, it brings together the two "côtés," the lower classes and the Guermantes aristocracy. The young Cambremer will marry Jupien's niece, adopted by Charlus and given the title of Mlle D'Oloron.

The conversation between the narrator and Maman aligns the two marriages according to the arches of Proust's beautiful fiction, the cathedral of *A la recherche*. Time has undermined the stability of the narrator's childhood categories and twisted their oppositions and correspondences into a spiral of allegory. One opposition leads to another: "la grande aristocratie" and "les petits bourgeois," the king and the shepherd-girl —Cambremer and Jupien's niece, Swann and the courtesan Odette, Saint-Loup and the daughter of the socially diminished Swann, and so on. The narrator's mother verbally confronts the fictions of Combray, i.e., the stability of social classes, and casually anticipates the "real" revelation of truth in the mixed blood of "le sang de la mère Moser qui disait: 'Ponchour Mezieurs' et le sang du duc de Guise! [the blood of old lady Moser who used to say 'Ponchour Mezieurs' (Bonjour Messieurs) and the blood of the Duke of Guise!]" (III, 659) Always too high or too low (III, 659), the narrator and his mother are caught at the crossroads of social terms, while the *real* convergence of the allegorical archways occurs at the unmistakable point of allegorical truth—the existence of Mlle de Saint-Loup, who enters the narrator's territory of time and desire during the matinée.

The allegory of the Proustian cathedral brings the two ways together in an unpredictable series of encounters. In the representation of the marriage of two minor characters, Cambremer and Mlle d'Oloron, the Virtues and the Vices come face to face. This marriage is typical of those that take place in the *Recherche*. Love is inseparable from the jealousy suffered by a heterosexual partner and caused by the irreducible alterity founding the desire of the (homosexual) beloved. Through the combination of love and suffering, the perfectly Proustian heart of Mlle d'Oloron identifies her with the narrator and

Giotto's Charity. The two sides are juxtaposed in a moment of allegorical marriage that includes the marriage of allegory, Virtue and Vice: "'C'est la récompense de la vertu. C'est un mariage à la fin d'un roman de Mme Sand,' dit ma mère. 'C'est le prix du vice, c'est un mariage à la fin d'un roman de Balzac,' pensai-je ['It is the reward of virtue. It's a marriage at the end of a novel by Mme Sand,' said my mother. 'It is the cost of vice, it's a marriage at the end of a novel by Balzac,' I thought]" (III, 658).

Proust presents the two worlds together in this brief exchange that recapitulates the major symbolic layers of the *Recherche*. Sustained by the author of *François le Champi* and the innocent Maman, the lost paradise of Combray is inscribed under the sign of Virtue. Through the narrator's illicit knowledge and sexual apprenticeship, however, paradise has been lost. The hellfire of *Sodome et Gomorrhe* focuses on the (homo)sexual blackness of desire that displaces the Proustian site from Combray to Paris and Balbec, and shifts the domain of love from Maman and the worshiped Gilberte to Albertine and the Balzacian world of Charlus. Fiction moves from factitious innocence and the namelessness of origins (François le Champi) to *Illusions perdues*. At the same time, Proust remains faithful to the sign of Giotto's Charity hovering over the world: if the unforeseeable Mlle de Saint-Loup is the product of one allegorical marriage, the premature death of Mlle d'Oloron is the result of the other (III, 671). Consumed by a suffering heart, Mlle Douleur is a martyr to vice. Like the kitchenmaid at Combray, she is silenced and will vanish soon after the wedding.

The allegorist must capture passing forms within the permanence of representation. Distracted from art and lured into the evanescent apparitions of desire, Swann succumbs to idolatry. His renunciation of the allegorist's detachment led him away from his Ruskinian artwork, while the narrator has gone full circle (or rather, beyond the circle) to discover his vocation, projected as a conversion to writing that will lift him beyond good and evil. The allegorist stands apart from representation, in the vision opened up by the "adieu au personnel" and the sublime passage of the suffering heart. By entwining the narrator's altered relation to allegory with Swann's downfall, Proust uncovers the perils of silence underlying the scriptural vocation.

The Padua triptych implicates Swann in the double inscription of allegory: as the initiator of *la Charité de Giotto*, he is the counterpart of its belated effect on the narrator. Anchored in the rhetoric of writing and allegory, Swann thus appears as the mediator for the narrator's vocation. At the same time, the doubling of the Giotto allegory explains the mysterious disappearance of the allegorical title from *Le Temps retrouvé*. Proust's doubled reference to Giotto's allegory in Padua seems to be the correlative of its erasure from the title in *Le Temps retrouvé*: allegory leaves the domain of explicit titles and enters Proustian invisibilia.

In the beginning, Proust wrote of Combray's *Charité de Giotto* and the visit to Padua/Venice in *La Fugitive (Le Temps retrouvé)* at the same time. The reference to Padua originally occurred in the context of the narrator's childhood visit to Padua. Proust later deleted this trip, and in its place he fashioned Swann into the provider of images of the Vices and Virtues. As a result of Proust's deletion and alteration, what was once united is divided in both form and temporality as "Combray" and "Padua." The cut that splits Proust's Giotto into two parts swallows the allegorical title once destined for *Le Temps retrouvé*. In light of Proust's doubling of Combray/Padua, the original title ("Les 'Vices et les Vertus' de Padoue et de Combray") could no longer be applied to a single chapter (*Le Temps retrouvé*); the allegorical trajectory of the entire novel represents the "Vices and Virtues." The text itself is the allegory.

Proust may have decided to erase that title (along with his early project of a tryst with the chambermaid of the Baronne Putbus, and so on) because it seemed to be too obviously allegorical, or transparently didactic. His entry into the secret turns of the labyrinth separates allegory into Combray and Padua. This division extends the paired structure of the allegorical image beyond its apparent symmetry to introduce in allegorical terms the narrator's singular discovery—the invisibility of time. The return of time within a cyclic configuration is a return with a difference; "le temps *re-trouvé*" shows the fundamental asymmetry of Proustian repetition. The cyclic configuration is a thin veil of fiction, hovering over the invisibility of temporal passage.

Comme Madeleine

Proustian time cannot be reduced to a binary simplicity of lost and found; its asymmetry is related to the revelation of invisibilia, the object of the conversion to writing. This revelation delineates the site of the speaking subject as the marks on the doors of the Hebrews inscribed their monogram as subjects of the Lord and his Passover. If an "object" is the "thing" that answers desire, a goal, or the incarnation of the other, then revelation in the Proustian sense is an "object" inseparable from its "subject": translation, transfiguration, *correspondance*, container/contained, and "forme et fond" all indicate the connection, inscribed in the vocabulary of Flaubert and Baudelaire. The Hebrews' passage out of Egypt and its mode of polytheistic proliferation is adumbrated in the narrator's conversion to writing: "une joie pareille à une certitude, et suffisante, sans autres preuves, à me rendre la mort indifférente [a joy that was like a certainty, and that sufficed, with no other evidence, to render death indifferent]" (III, 867). Beyond the symmetry of life and death, subject and object are connected when the conversion to writing takes the possibilities instilled by the speaking voice of the subject to their logical Judeo-Christian conclusions, away from nature. It will give the narrator an unnatural asymmetrical insight into the domain of invisibilia—the heart and soul of immortality, resurrection, and writing.

This vision is anticipated in a moment of textual layering that illustrates the step taken by the narrator outside the clear-cut symmetries of life and death, good and evil, truth and falsehood. The allegorist of the Vices and Virtues, Proust displays the narrator under the sign of Giotto's Charity, surrounded by the angelic bearers of invisibilia and the letter.

But they remind the reader of Old Testament angels who bring with them the double edge of jouissance offered under the law. When Robert de Saint-Loup introduces the narrator to his beloved mistress, the narrator's realization that she is none other than "Rachel quand du Seigneur [Rachel-when-from-the-Lord]" is quite literally overseen by an allegorical messenger, the angel of allegory itself, translated from the biblical site of Sodom: "un mystérieux voyageur, arrêté pour un jour dans la cité maudite, un ange resplendissant se tenait debout [a mysterious voyager, stopped for a day in the cursed city, a shining angel was standing]" (II, 161). Like the "deux anges aux portes de Sodome [two angels at the gates of Sodom]" (II, 631), the angel who becomes visible in the form of a flowering pear tree unmasks the truth in an instant of vision.

The narrator stresses the instantaneity of recognition: "je reconnus à l'instant 'Rachel quand du Seigneur'" (II, 158). Presented earlier in the *Recherche* as "la juive [the Jewish one]" in a bordello, Rachel is derisively nicknamed by the narrator. "Rachel quand du Seigneur" recalls Halévy's *La Juive* and the well-known aria sung to her by Eleazar, the Jewish figure of fatherhood; the madam presents Rachel as an object of supreme sexual delight, while the narrator's nickname opposes her to *la Juive* as vice to virtue. The two arches of Proust's cathedral of allegory come together in a vision of the two versions of Rachel. Vice silently confronts virtue, the narrator's view encounters the fiction created by Robert, and the truth of love—Giotto's Charity, or Halévy's Charity-like figure of Rachel—meets its opposite in Robert's Rachel, a living assortment of vices. On an allegorical level, Rachel recapitulates and anticipates an end point or conclusion ("un aboutissement," according to Proust's text) of two infinities, Virtue and Vice. At the peak of mystery, their mystical meeting is another version of the Proustian cathedral, the line-by-line inscription on thin paper of the meeting of the ways, Swann and Guermantes:

> L'immobilité de ce mince visage, comme celle d'une feuille de papier soumise aux colossales pressions de deux

atmosphères, me semblait équilibrée par deux infinis qui venaient aboutir à elle sans se rencontrer, car elle les séparait. . . . Robert et moi, nous ne la voyions pas du même côté du mystère. [The immobility of this thin face, like that of a piece of paper, caught between the colossal pressures of two atmospheres, seemed to me balanced between two infinities that found their end-point in her without meeting each other, for she separated them. . . . Robert and I, we did not see her from the same side of the mystery.] (II, 160)

The truth of love and beauty takes on the Proustian form of *la Charité de Giotto*, but the suffering that inhabits her allegorical forms appears to open the door to "*l'artiste du mal* [the artist of evil]." Rachel is a minor artist of this kind: her nickname combines the purity of the virginal *Juive* with the corruption of the whore ironically named "Rachel quand du Seigneur" by the narrator. The consequences of Saint-Loup's illusions about Rachel's virtue play out the mortal truth of the narrator's witty nickname for her. The allegorist portrays the intertwining or correspondence of virtue and vice as the quintessential mystery of *Rachel quand du Seigneur*. Its fatal message is the law of desire that subjects even the virtuous to sexuality and death, and that makes all subjects into walk-on characters or "figurants" for what Proust originally called *le bal des têtes* ("la matinée given by la princesse de Guermantes"). Even in innocence, the Proustian angel has its eyes wide open.

The passing form of the flowering pear tree appears to the narrator. As a metaphor or a term of beauty, the pear tree disappears within the invisibilia of its splendor—the angel. The beautiful image ("the splendor of poetry") marks the site where the elements of allegory resonate in unnatural fragments broken by the vision of beauty, the apocalyptic messenger of mystery and divine judgment. At the end of *A la recherche*, Proust writes: "L'art est le vrai Jugement dernier [Art is the true Last Judgment]" (III, 880). The innocence of this angel and the promise of joy offered by "l'Ange d'or du campanile de Saint-Marc [the Golden Angel of the campanile of Saint Mark]" (III, 623) are linked obliquely to Proust's version of the Fall. He turns the angels of Genesis into innocent voyeurs, witnesses of *le bal des têtes* [*the unmasked ball*]," and purveyors of judgment, much like the narrator himself.

The pear tree returns in full beauty, illuminating the darkness of a double-edged mystery: allegory is both fiction and jouissance. "Rachel quand du Seigneur" is the Jew as a feminine incarnation of the narrator's image of Vice, allegorized in his ironic application of Halévy's image of Virtue. Robert's quasi-virginal goddess is the narrator's undesired whore, according to the immeasurable terms of an architectural mystery: the paper-thin separation of the two "sides," Swann's Méséglise and Guermantes, wandering Jews and French aristocrats, Judaic femininity and its presumably innate scandal of sexuality in contrast to the authority of Catholicism.

Rachel in the eye of the angel obliquely leads back to the beginning, when Proust creates a centripetal allegory and the narrator's sources for the conversion of writing. The vision of the narrator leads him to extend the metaphor of the angel in terms that hold memories of Combray, the long afternoons of reading, the "perpetual alliteration" on the banks of the Vivonne and the promise he made to return "with lines": "les grandes créatures blanches merveilleusement penchées au-dessus de l'ombre propice à la sieste, à la pêche, à la lecture, n'était-ce pas plutôt des anges? [*the great white creatures marvelously leaning above the shadow favorable to siestas, fishing, reading, were they not angels?*]" (II, 160). Back to the beginning, not yet *retrouvé*, not yet *re*-found: back to reading. In the beginning was allegory, and Swann was its dark night, the ground of its shining stars. He catalyzes the translation into emblems and biblical models of desire: Abraham and Isaac (the father and the narrator); Zephora, the wife of Moses (Odette in the photograph kept by Swann); *la Charité de Giotto* (offered and named by Swann through the reproduction and the kitchenmaid), remembered in *his* name at Padua. As a figure of scriptural paternity, Swann is overdetermined—the Judaic father of desire is also Gilberte's Jewish father. The narrator's black vision of the catastrophe of desire, the judgment of Rachel guaranteed by the shining beauty of the angelic "pear tree in flower," recalls the pre-Fall vision of Gilberte and the flowering hawthornes in "the month of Mary."

The central moment of Proustian time is Easter: "ne m'étais-je pas trompé comme Madeleine quand, dans un autre jardin, un jour dont l'anniversaire allait bientôt venir, elle vit une forme humaine et 'crut que c'était le jardinier'? [had I not been mistaken like Mary Magdalene when, in another garden, on a day whose anniversary was coming soon, she saw a human form and 'believed that it was the gardener'?]" (II, 160) In this instant of transformation at some point after the beginning (Combray) and before the return or "retrouvailles" of time, the unfolding of the paschal allusion to Christ's body, no longer flesh but not yet resurrected in glory, focuses the question of form and scriptural identity. The return of time is promised by the angelic pear trees, "Gardiens du souvenir de l'âge d'or [guardians of the memory of the golden age]" (II, 160). Much later the golden angel of Venice (III, 623) will appear as a guardian like the pear tree angels, "garants de la promesse que la réalité n'est pas ce qu'on croit, que la splendeur de la poésie, que l'éclat merveilleux de l'innocence peuvent y resplendir [guarantors of the promise that reality is not what we think it is, that the splendor of poetry, the marvelous luster of innocence can shine in it]" (III, 160). After the angelic guarantee of invisibility and the cluster of revelations of "reality," the heraldic signs of Proust's angels will point toward the possibilities of reappropriating the lost paradise, and the narrator will be led to "ces vérités écrites à l'aide des figures [these truths written with the help of figures]" (III, 879). The revelations of privileged moments counter the loss of time, but it can only be *re*-trouvé *through* figuration, or the arabesque of writing.

The dimensions of the loss of time unravel the symmetry of "lost" and "found." The return of what was once possessed and lost does not reinstate the object of that loss. For example, the narrator at the final matinée does not re-become the child he was at Combray; the retrieval is a symbolic one. The deferral of return is related to a transference to writing:

something has been transported, displaced, or linked through correspondence. In Proustian terms, one might say that analogy is the closest one can ever get to singularity. In the dimensions of poetic language, the image—analogy or metaphor—is always located in an "elsewhere," it is always somewhere else, an alibi of invisibilia. Through the act of transference inherent in Proust's writing (III, 890), the image articulates the mysterious language of "perpetual alliteration" that turns an interior tablet covered with figures ("un grimoire compliqué et fleuri") into more figures: "these truths written with the help of figures." Proust the invisible takes on the miracles of transubstantiation. He filters and crystallizes, converting the invisible into the visible "saturation" of desire and form. Through the "re-" with a difference, the repetition of deferred and waylaid reading (III, 879), loss is repeatedly displaced and subsumed in the interpretive act, and "reading" becomes "creation." The losses of time, flesh, love, and life itself—the "accidents" of corporeality—are mysteriously interpreted, converted, and made into a work of art (III, 879) that emerges from the interiority or the invisibility of "an ineffable vision" (III, 875). This vision is mystical and therefore requires a revelation (III, 878). Like Proust's angels, the mystery or the mysterious vision does not deny reality; it is in fact the ultimate form of reality, acted out in the domain of "truths."

At the end of the novel Proust finally defines reality in the terms that turn him, through fiction, toward the *Recherche*; "in the direction of" (or "à la recherche") is inscribed in the turn of a repetition with a difference. The terms of reality and repetition describe or create writing, in the mouth of the narrator. For him and his creator, reality is as literary and mystical as the doctrine of *correspondance*. Proust explains it in a sentence filled with Baudelairean resonance: "Une heure n'est pas qu'une heure, c'est un vase rempli de parfums, de sons, de projets et de climats. Ce que nous appelons la réalité est un certain rapport entre ces sensations et ces souvenirs [An hour is not only an hour, it is a vase filled with perfumes, sounds, plans, and climates. We give the name of reality to a certain relation between these sensations and memories]" (III, 889).

Reality is a singular relationship between the subject and the time-ravaged realm of the flesh (encoded as the unmasked ball, and later as the "matinée chez la princesse"), translated and resurrected as "beautiful style" (III, 889). Moving from the accidental relation to something described as a "common essence," the writer operates a mysterious and indescribable leap from translation to creation. In order to resurrect objects or moments in the beauty and permanence of language, the writer must find ("retrouver") the correspondence that links them. Their poetic liaison, *correspondance*, takes precedence over the objects or moments themselves.

What is specifically Proustian about this formulation of *correspondance* is that beautiful style is both the vision of reality and its resurrection, both the terms of absolute evanescence ("two sensations") and their resurrection "à jamais," for all time, in the permanent glory of "essence commune." The vision of the world beyond, the "là-bas" of visionary experience, includes a return through fleeting sensation to the memories it evokes from the past, buried under clouds of forgetfulness. Reality, "un certain rapport entre ces sensations et ces souvenirs [a certain relation between these sensations and memories]," is the "rapport unique que l'écrivain doit retrouver pour en enchaîner à jamais dans sa phrase les deux termes différents [unique relation that the writer must find to forever connect in his sentence the two different terms]" (III, 889).

The paradox of Proustian correspondence is that the "common essence" described by the narrator, the permanence of "beautiful style," is the result of the encounter or "rapport" between two contingent sensations, two instants of fleeting feeling. This permanence is evanescence squared, or what Proust calls metaphor. The artist "dégagera leur essence commune en les réunissant l'un et l'autre pour les soustraire aux contingences du temps, dans une métaphore [will bring out their common essence by uniting the one and the other in order to subtract them from the contingencies of time, in a metaphor]" (III, 889). Here and beyond, sensation and memory: these binary oppositions open out toward metaphor, the third term of the Proustian trinity. The writer translates through substance. Transubstantiation makes reading into a creation and takes the instant of experience and the turn or return to memory out of the retrospective glance and the ravages of time. Through the ongoing figuration of metaphor, the visionary power of style (III, 895), it enters the fullness of time: "Je crois que la métaphore seule peut donner une sorte d'éternité au style [I believe that metaphor alone can give a kind of eternity to style]" (CSB, 586).

Autobiographies of Style

Le son de la trompette est si délicieux,
Dans ces soirs solennels de célestes vendanges,
Qu'il s'infiltre comme une extase dans tous ceux
        Dont elle chante les louanges.

The trumpet sound tastes of such delight
In sky-risen wine harvests' awed evenings
That like an ecstasy it infiltrates
        All those whose praise it sings.

(Oeuvres complètes, vol. 1, p. 172;
my translation)

9

La Vocation Artistique

Ne pas oublier qu'il est un motif qui revient dans ma vie, plus important que celui de l'amour d'Albertine, et peut-être assimilable au chant du coq du Quatuor de Vinteuil, finissant par l'éternel matin, c'est le motif de la ressouvenance, matière de la vocation artistique. . . . Tasse de thé, arbres en promenade, clochers, etc.

[Not to forget that there is a motif that returns in my life, more important than the motif of the love of Albertine, and perhaps assimilable to the cockcrow of Vinteuil's Quartet, ending with eternal morning, it is the motif of remembering, the material of the artistic vocation. . . . Cup of tea, trees on an outing, bell towers, etc.][1]

Motive and leitmotif

Within life, a motif returns repeatedly: memory, the material of vocation. As a "motif," it is the artfulness that goes beyond the borders of "life": as a life-rooted "matière," it escapes the realm of representation, "art." Vocation is spelled out in an alphabet of individual objects that bear an ecstasy, ravishment, or felicity. Integrated in the architecture of Proust's novel, they are held together from within like the individual lozenges of a rose window.[2] The fictional projection of memory into time and space figured through metaphor turns "ressouvenance" into the material of artistic vocation. At its source, Flaubert's art of temporality turned "ressouvenance [remembering]" into the motif of "the story of an entire life"; Emma, Salammbô, Schahabarim, and Julien emblematize an "adieu to the personal" that brings "life" face to face with the "abyss" through the excess of Art. Flaubert's fiction focuses on a representation of the trajectory from sentiment to the sea of ink. This passage of the heart slips into the background of Proust's remark in the *Cahiers* quoted above as the essential element in a constellation of style. The "remembered" and the "eternal" enter the fabric of Proust's novel from an image of modernity created by Flaubert and Baudelaire. Discussed in "Passing Forms," the role of the "eternal" in Proust's aesthetic construction of *A la recherche du temps perdu* is substantiated by its importance in his criticism, particularly in "A Propos du 'style' de Flaubert."[3] This essay develops the view of style that appeared in the polemic against Sainte-Beuve in Proust's early essay on Baudelaire and later reappeared in the novel. Proust inscribes it in the layers of fiction that implicate the life stories of the painter, the art critic, and the composer, and the resonances of artistry—writing, painting, and music—within the narrator's experience. The association of the "eternal" with Vinteuil and the resurrection of the artist through art is central to the aesthetics of *A la recherche du temps perdu*, as well as to its structure of vocation—linking art and love, the narrator and Swann, the mysterious and allegorical promise associated with the narrator's discovery of Vinteuil's Septuor and the "little phrase" that anchored Swann's love for Odette and his own "motif of remembering" in the music later cherished by the narrator. This link to Swann is related through Albertine and Mlle Vinteuil to another chain of transgression, memory, and pleasure.

The remark quoted from Proust's Cahiers does not take up the question of the enunciation. On this level, Proust's account of his style remains far more enigmatic than either Flaubert's statements about style or Proust's interpretation of Flaubert. While Proust elucidates the elements of Flaubert's rigorous syntax (as Flaubert often did in detailed letters to friends), his Modernist strategy of clasping life and art together in the terms of vocation gives rise to an aesthetic (including a vocabulary of style) that seems to exclude an explanation of how he reformulated Flaubertian elements of style in the construction of his own language. In the novel and elsewhere, Proust makes many declarations about "structure" on the scale of "architecture" or the "oeuvre d'art," but he says comparatively little about the minimal unit of construction. It is characteristic of Modernism that the identity of this unit cannot be taken for granted: Flaubert and Baudelaire both make this clear in conceptions of poetic prose that provide a new framework for genre and rhetoric.[4] Flaubert's unit of construction was the Sentence, while there were several significant units for Baudelaire: the verse, the image, the sentence, and the poem. Since Proust posits his role as a descendant of the poet as well the novelist, the shifts or fluctuations of Baudelaire's strategic use of individual units of construction may have induced Proust to maintain an air of mystery around the question of style. At the center of Proust's aesthetic, the sublime and the infinite resonate in Augustine's terms of theological mystery. Its miraculous apparitions, sublime delights, and mystical resurrections guarantee the "avenir poétique [poetic future]" leading to the eternity of beautiful representation. Since Proust's aesthetic emerges in *A la recherche* within the terms of fictional style, beautiful representation is at stake in the novel on its own ground, beyond the purely theoretical concerns of the critical writings.

If the reader of *A la recherche*, its antecedents, and Proust's criticism were to single out an explicit unit of construction that operates on the level of the enunciation (rather than on the scale of architectural "structure") he would have to name metaphor as the essential element of Proustian rhetoric, the touchstone of vocation. It marks the convergence of time and memory, art and love, the poetic image and what it translates from a fiery heart into writing: "le seul livre vrai, un grand écrivain n'a pas . . . à l'inventer . . . mais à le traduire [the only true book, a great writer does not . . . have to invent it, . . . but to translate it]" (III, 890). This translation of interiority and "remembering" also implies another form of translation; Proust reinvents the style of both Baudelaire and Flaubert through the ideal and form of "éternité du style" (CSB 586). This stylistic eternity could be imagined as Proust's focus on the Baudelairean image: "Une heure . . . c'est un vase rempli de parfums, de sons, de projets et de climats [An hour . . . is a vase filled with perfumes, sounds, projects, and climates]" (III, 889). Proust combines this form of *correspondance* with Flaubert's palette of time, the painted image of vision and temporality: "le style pour l'écrivain, aussi bien que la couleur pour le peintre, est une question . . . de vision [style for the writer, as much as color for the painter, is a question . . . of vision]" (III, 895); "cette matinée . . . marquerait . . . dans celle-ci [mon oeuvre] la forme . . . du Temps [this matinée . . . would mark . . . in it [my work] the form . . . of Time]" (III, 1045). The two come together in Proust's decisive dénouement and its projected *après-coup*, the belated effect of the "coup de théâtre" or dramatic turn of events; outside the self and time, the narrator's ecstatic experience and his projection or construction of a style that captures sensations interiorized by memory within representation coincide at the matinée.

In this context, the eloquence of Flaubert's "blank" turns syntax into the composition of a "Symphony in White Major." Its poetic forms are guaranteed by the aesthetics of poetic prose. An equation for Proust's style might sound like this: Baudelairean correspondence plus Flaubert's painting of temporality equals the miracle of analogy, transubstantiation, or Bergotte's meditation on style elicited by the little panel of yellow wall, the most sublime example of "le vernis des maîtres." Weighted on a celestial scale, the writer gives life, on one side, for the work of art—Baudelaire's "sky-risen wine harvests"—on the other.

As "memory" and "sensation" (III, 889), Proust's statements on the unit of construction combine the "motif," representatively framed in the Cahier quotation above, with the "matière de la vocation." Memory and sensual impression, or the motif and the material that composes it, add up to the figure of metaphor. Proust's image invokes the term of allegory discussed earlier: writing as painting verbally renders "ressouvenance" through the convergence of sensations like shades of color. The "imparfait éternel" of Proust's Flaubert and the *correspondance* of Baudelaire are forms of the transromantic allegory that unites "souvenir" and "sensation." In this sense, although Benjamin's essay does not link it to Baudelaire, his interpretation of Proust's style as "Verschränkung" (clasping) would mark Proust's writing as a contemporary extension of the modern allegory that clasps together the form and content of the nineteenth century in Baudelaire.

Proust's aesthetics turn time into "le Temps," the essential form of allegory. This Proustian elixir of invisibilia is decanted (or precipitated: brought into appearance) through the clasping or convergence of time, in the fruitful encounter between the past and the present. Concentrated into an essence and transparent, saturated and crystallized, the explicit figure that appears in Proust's fictional sentences (shaped as self-reflection) and his aesthetics (voiced in the novel and reflecting an imaginary text outside it) is the enigmatic term of "perpetual alliteration." Invoked in the episode of the "Vivonne carafes," it is the figure for Proust's figural unit: metaphor.

The Vivonne episode[5] appears in the final section of Combray, during an excursion "along the Guermantes Way." It will lead to the discussion about the duchess and the dreams of writing pursued in an account of the spires of Martinville; it follows the incident at Montjouvain and its drama of scandal and desire. Within the Vivonne episode, the crucial paragraph containing "perpetual alliteration" is framed by two representations of repetition. They appear to comment on the textual effect of alliteration, the figure of repetition of sounds in lines of poetry that "combines analogy and contiguity," according to Genette's formulation. Proust's text reserves a few surprises for partisans of contiguity: the paragraph following "allitération" describes the misfortune of metonymy that afflicts an isolated water lily, "eternally" crossing and recrossing the river (I, 168–69). This tortuous repetition is associated with neurotics, tante Léonie, and the "malheureux [unfortunates]" Dante sees in hell. The paragraph that precedes "allitération," however, presents the repetition of a simple innocent happiness in the numerous "boutons d'or" ["gold buds," i.e., buttercups] near the river (I, 167–68). Unlike the freshness of the Vivonne water, their golden surface does not drift toward the pleasures of the palate; it formulates an early lesson in names and other forms of "useless beauty" that anticipate an aesthetic based on metaphor. The passage concludes with a Flaubertian echo; the flowers maintain "un poétique éclat d'Orient [a poetic brightness of the Orient]" that lingers through the visual emphasis of the next sentence:

> Je m'amusais à regarder les carafes que les gamins mettaient dans la Vivonne pour prendre les petits poissons, et qui, remplies par la rivière où elles sont à leur tour encloses, à la fois "contenant" aux flancs transparents comme une eau durcie et "contenu" plongé dans un plus grand contenant de cristal liquide et courant, évoquaient l'image de la fraîcheur d'une façon plus délicieuse et plus irritante qu'elles ne l'eussent fait sur une table servie, en ne la montrant qu'en fuite dans cette allitération perpétuelle entre l'eau sans consistance où les mains ne pouvaient la capter et le verre sans fluidité où le palais ne pourrait en jouir. [I was entertained by looking at carafes that children would put into the Vivonne to catch little fish, and that, filled with the river where they in turn are enclosed, at the same time a "container" with transparent sides like hardened water and a "contained" plunged into a larger container of liquid and running crystal, evoked the image of freshness in a more delicious and irritating manner than they would have done on a dinner table, by showing only its flight in this perpetual alliteration between the water without consistency in which hands could not capture it and the glass without fluidity in which the palate could not enjoy it.] (I, 168)

The poetic brightness associated with the Orient of style will emerge to challenge Genette's observation that the contiguity of liaison is the most important figural element in this passage.

Proust's elaborate container/contained relation uses the baroque artifice of reciprocal metaphor[6] to emphasize the metonymic tangle of water, glass, and the movement of the current: "hardened water" and "liquid and running crystal."

This complex "image of freshness" is suddenly "in flight," however, and the two reciprocal metaphors are now disentangled from the course of metonymy to form a new constellation. It preserves the reciprocal metaphors, but in the form of two negations that stand in a kind of chiasmatic relation to each other: "water without consistency" and "glass without fluidity." Unable to stop the "flight"—incapable of grasping or enjoying ("capter," "jouir") freshness, the carafes point to "perpetual alliteration." The ambiguous flight into (or between) water and glass that Proust is describing as poetic repetition brusquely stops metonymic movement with its complex cluster (or "supersaturation") of metaphors: they constitute its textual act of poetic repetition. Movement shifts to a symmetrical mirroring extended from the reciprocal metaphors to the sound shape of "alliteration perpétuelle": all/elle, té/ét, and ra/er form an aural mirroring reinforced by the graphic repetitions of p and t, and particularly of the vowels and liquid consonants that transform water and metonymy into the figured "other" of the letter of style: eternal and continuous, alliteration anticipates the "perpetual adoration" that Proust conceived as the crowning glory of metaphorical style, revealed at the end of the novel.

The "poetic Orient dazzle" that introduces the visual dimension into this paragraph also bears a principle of inedible beauty. If the current of metonymy leads to carnal satisfaction,[7] then the many notations of denied satisfaction in the "perpetual alliteration" sentence imply either that metaphor is more sublime than the stringing along of metonymy or that the jouissance in question is "other" than carnal. This double view is taken up in another strange discrepancy between what Proust's sentence offers and what it delivers: the poetic gaze is suddenly sidetracked by the question of the pleasure of catching fish: "Je me promettais de venir là plus tard avec des lignes; j'obtenais qu'on tirât un peu de pain . . . j'en jetais dans la Vivonne des boulettes qui semblaient suffire pour y provoquer un phénomène de sursaturation, car l'eau se solidifiait aussitôt autour d'elles en grappes ovoïdes de têtards inanités qu'elle tenait . . . en dissolution, invisibles, tout près d'être en voie de cristallisation [I promised myself to come back there later with lines; I got permission to have a little bread taken out

... I threw into the Vivonne little pellets of it that seemed sufficient to set off a phenomenon of supersaturation, for the water immediately solidified around them in ovoid clusters of famished tadpoles that it held in dissolution, invisible, close to being on the way to crystallization]" (I, 168). A sequence of first person imperfect verbs shifts from the poetic gaze ("je m'amusais à regarder les carafes") to a promise of lines ("je me promettais . . ."), and then to an active strategy of fishing ("j'obtenais . . . j'en jetais"). Like Rosanette at Fontainebleau in *L'Education sentimentale,* the narrator looks at the acting out of desire that crystallizes the invisible into "supersaturation": "Pendant un quart d'heure, elle jeta des morceaux de pain dans l'eau pour voir des poissons bondir [During a quarter of an hour, she threw pieces of bread into the water to see the fish leap]" (ES 322–23).

The major difference between the two accounts of the saturation of desire is that Proust emphasizes the clustering process of condensation and the visible representation of the invisible tadpoles. Proust's account extends this representation to the invisible vocation, associated with "Le Temps" and the discovery of metaphoric style at the end of the novel.

This moment in the water of life at Combray emblematizes the fictional curve of vocation in the sequence leading from the childhood view of Combray, the promise of the poetic lines to come later, and then the vision of what was previously invisible that occurs when the ecstatic moments are clasped together at the matinée. The promise bears a metaphorical relation to the "invisible vocation" and the Proustian "transubstantiation" it requires: the narrator adds bread to the water of life, and the transfiguration of the invisible occurs. The accomplishment of metaphor strangely reflects the deferral of satisfaction described in the account of perpetual alliteration: the narrator offers the "provisions" of the "snack" and cancels out the double negation linked to the hand and the palate. Suddenly, he receives consistent water and fluid glass: suddenly, he gets a taste of "alliteration perpétuelle."

Like the apostrophized woman in Baudelaire's "A Une Passante," the letter falls into the abyss of the past; its evanescence is paradoxically preserved through the emergence of another letter in its place. The difference between the liquid letter of speech and the writing of a metaphor, however, is the difference between the "Passante" seen by the narrator of Baudelaire's poem and the fulfilled promise of Proust's narrator who will return to alliteration "with lines": he will write the "work of art," the result of his invisible vocation.[8] Baudelaire's "Jamais!" follows the paradoxical contours of allegory by building a monument to the woman's evanescence, and rendering it permanent in a kind of "toujours." This "never ever" is at the heart of allegory: its rhetorical model (and miniature version) is metaphor. The word becomes a passing form: replaced by the signifier that emerges in its place, the first signifier falls away.[9] Perpetuated, preserved, integrated as fiction in *A la recherche*, it is the source of its allegory.

Proust discusses elements of the metonymic process (syntax and the unit of the sentence) in the criticism of Flaubert and Baudelaire, whereas in his remarks about his own writing (and the anticipated oeuvre of the narrator), metonymy is consistently overruled by metaphor. Perhaps he emphasizes his personal use of metaphor because he has used it to guarantee the aesthetic originality of the novel. When the narrator discovers its function in memory, the figure of metaphor slips from form into content on the level of narrative "récit" as well as "écriture." As the foundation of poetic style and the kernel of allegory, the figure of metaphor is turned into fiction. *Le Temps retrouvé* shows this to be literally true, when the narrator's ecstatic vision takes the form of a three- or four-way convergence of previous moments of rapture; in this sense, the narrator's vocation consists of the correspondences of metaphor.

As a fiction that purports to tell all about art and life. the narrator's complex weave of metaphor is a veil worn by Proust himself: the sublime veil in the Flaubertian manner of Tanit ("the nocturnal muse" [III, 914]) and the veil of the undecidable and undecipherable, autobiographical fiction of the "not always me." The landmark status of the oeuvre that became *A la recherche du temps perdu* does *not* reside in its presentation of an author's aesthetic through autobiography and its identification of writer and text, as is often supposed; Proust's image of modernity captures the undecidable and mysterious connection between a masked authorial identification and the aesthetic that emerges from the author's work. Obliquely presented through fiction as a discovery of style, his aesthetic is portrayed in the perpetual difference of the letter of metaphor, slyly or at times tragically marking the complicity of the abyss of lost time and the eternity of resurrection through two different sensations polarized as a "content" rising into "form." Although Flaubert conceives of the relation of "forme" to "fond" without the emphasis on metaphor that Proust will develop, the clasping of "sensation" and "memory" is essential to Flaubert's allegory and its version of poetic continuity or perpetual difference. As I have shown, Flaubert's mature fiction disguises or veils this aesthetic; the author allows it to hover between the lines. Proust, however, uses the medium of fiction to codify the aesthetic that will shape the oeuvre of the narrator: fiction is covered with a veil of aesthetics, and what wavers between the lines is something like the limits of fiction, the subtle disguise of a "not always me" that threatens to evanesce in the representation of a desire to attain the permanence of art.

Sensory impressions occur in the double flight of time and words: time makes them disappear instantly, and words fail to produce a verbal equivalent for them or a name to invoke their presence. Proust articulates Flaubert's many "disappearances" and "silences" in his own terms: at one point in the novel, an impression is described as "vanished" and "imperceptible" (I, 209). Impressions are interiorized in Flaubert's vocabulary as "stupor" or "melancholy"; their Proustian counterparts lose their sharpness through a process of forgetting. They can only re-emerge fortuitously, as involuntary memories that distance the original impression from consciousness and its sentiments; they are therefore depersonalized, and ready to reflect on representation. "The work of style" (Flaubert's expression) gives rise to an aesthetic of correspondences that must be understood in the terms of allegory

—the encounter between material form and the meaning visited upon it, or the encounter between the unquiet heart occupied with the reality of death and the emblem it carries without knowing it.

When Proust discusses the structure of his novel in "A Propos du 'style' de Flaubert," the parallel he draws between Flaubert's use of syntax and his own use of memory allows him to elide an explicit attribution of "Proustian" remembering to Flaubert. The path that leads Flaubert through stupor to the image of memory marks a "resurrection of the Past" and enters the Sentence; it sets the pattern for Proust's impression, which succumbs to forgetting before the resurrection of remembering turns it into the beautiful "image." The difference between the two seems to lead back to the famous symptom of Flaubert's black illness: his images threatened to submerge him in an interior overflow, and tightly controlled syntax was his only possibility for eluding them in the "other" images of Style. Proust's asthma appears to be a perfect counter-symptom; perhaps the extended arabesques of his sentences were the only antidote for shortness of breath.

This oblique structure of "remembering" and "sensation" is brought into relief by the larger sense of Proust's allegory; the relation of form to content interlaces the artist's "oeuvre" (the allegorical work) with the oblique, invisible revelation of its allegory of conversion. When the enigmatic operations of the artist are successful, the two are mysteriously and impassibly woven together into a beautiful veil of art. An allusion to it can be seen in the mystical exchange of art and life that doubly transforms the kitchenmaid, allegorically identified as "La Charité de Giotto"; life seems to thrust its inappropriate forms upon art, while art inexplicably enters life, making it "not less allegorical."

Proust's Cahier entry bares the fictional construct of "my life" as an entity of style joining the two extremes of the "motif." According to the *Petit Robert*, this term used by Proust to qualify the origin of remembering is the cause, pretext, or "mobile" of the text; "motif" derives from the Latin form of "mobile," defined as that which puts something into motion. As a "motif," however, Proust's "remembering" also includes the sublime final destination of that origin. One modern meaning of "motif" is "leitmotiv," defined as a musical phrase that goes beyond music and enters the dramatic realm of significance. Proust combines this Wagnerian reworking of "motiv" with several of its earlier resonances, including the visual sense of design in painting (the drawing, surface, and image that occupy space) and the aural sense of musical design (the "phrase," "harmony," and "arabesque" that occupy time). The fictional leitmotiv announces the "beyond" of the text as the absolute Other of language, the permanence of "the eternal." This final destination is already present in Flaubert's aesthetic as the "resurrection of the Past" of the travel journals; taken up in Proust's fiction as the resurrection of the artist, it is signaled by the Golden Angel of Venice.

Between the beginning of "motif" and its end, other meanings anchor it in the domain of the symbolic image: sketch, drawing, figure, and musical phrase. All of these figures cluster together as metaphor in Proust's weave of allegory. In his novel, the beginning and the end of "motif" ultimately converge: the beginning is something like an ecstatic revelation of the retrieval of time, while the end recalls the episode of the Petite Madeleine and thus embraces the beginning. Proustian time telescopes the two temporalities as the narrator makes use of Flaubert's continuous imperfect tense to recall Combray and "cette sonnette qui tintait encore en moi [this doorbell that was still ringing inside me]," "la petite sonnette qui annonçait qu'enfin M. Swann était parti et que Maman allait monter [the little doorbell announcing that at last M. Swann had gone and that Maman was going to come up]" (III, 1046). The term of "motif" indicates the span of the Proustian enterprise: in the beginning, the Latin "mobile" locates God as the mover of men and the force that puts the allegorical pleasures of the text into motion: "You stir a man to delight in praising you because you made us oriented toward you."[10] In the most modern development of "motif," Proust saw Wagner's invention of the "leitmotiv" as an influence on Baudelaire's epithet of the delicious trumpet sound in "L'Imprévu" (CSB 623). Proust points out that the "mystical meaning" and the "strange happiness of the chosen" of Baudelaire's poem were inspired by "a memory of the passionate admirer of Wagner" (CSB 623). His casual remark about the writer's "useful reveries" inspired by other arts gives a clue to the relation between the emphasis on the musical phrase in *A la recherche* (accompanied by many references to Wagner), the synaesthetic image anchored in Baudelaire, and the particular invention of mystical moments of Souvenir. The Cahier passage quoted in the epigraph gives the formula for this relationship: "cup of tea, trees on an outing, steeples, etc." It is developed outside literary criticism, in the novel: "quelque chose comme un mystique chant de coq, un appel, ineffable mais suraigu, de l'éternel matin . . . On aurait dit que, réincarné, l'auteur [Vinteuil] vivait à jamais dans sa musique [something like a mystical cockcrow, a call, ineffable but high-pitched, of the eternal morning. . . . One could have said that, reincarnated, the author lived forever in his music]" (III, 250, 253).

Ces phrases mystérieuses

In the chapters devoted to Flaubert, I indicated how the images of allegory as well as the uncontrollable, disquieting bouquets or constellations of images associated with hallucinatory moments of "the black illness" are transformed into art. Endless but untainted by the floods of hallucination, the Sentence is Flaubert's aesthetic object. At the same time, however, the image as the cause and effect linking impression and memory in Flaubert's allegory is central to his aesthetic. The status of the image is artistic as well as psychoanalytic; like the "frémissement" described by both Baudelaire and Flaubert, the vibrating nerve is also the violin string of the allegorist.[11]

What is the status of the image and the Sentence in Flaubert's Modernist aesthetic? Hints of synaesthesia infuse some of Flaubert's beautiful sentences with the allegorical capacity of the image itself as the source of fluidity, beauty, and the sentiments that solicit writing. Flaubert gives a trans-romantic account of this rather Romantic version of the image in

L'Education sentimentale, where Frédéric's vocation blends art and love together. In spite of Frédéric's profile as a typical Romantic, Flaubert's vision shines through his comments on the character's interest in music and especially painting: "la surface des choses l'appréhendait, et il voulait peindre [the surface of things would seize him, and he wanted to paint]" (ES 15). He hesitates between writing and painting until he decides that painting will allow him to approach Madame Arnoux. Although this irony has not escaped Flaubert's contemporary readers, it seems to have overshadowed the oblique self-representation that Flaubert inscribes in his allegory of conversion. He presents Frédéric's interest in writing in a framework similar to his own youthful attempts, before his particular vision of the allegorical image—the apprehension of the surface of things—led him to transform the Romanticism of his youth into the new style encoded as "peindre [painting]" and the other key terms of his aesthetic.

The fluid and synaesthetic qualities of the image take the stage once more when the account of Frédéric's first soirée in the presence of Madame Arnoux integrates a subtle portrayal of Flaubert's lyricism within the ironic twists of the text. Like Proust's narrator, Frédéric is affected by the impressions that are in the realm of Baudelairean correspondence, somewhere beyond the meaning of words. At the lyrical peak of the evening, the singing of his beloved affects him through specific images of sound, voice, and liquid melody ("la mélodie revenait amoureusement, avec une oscillation large et paresseuse [the melody came back amorously, with a wide and lazy oscillation]") rather than through meaning: "Frédéric ne comprenait rien aux paroles italiennes [Frédéric did not understand any of the Italian lyrics]" (49). The images of melody and water continue, interiorized at the moment of his "vocation": "Son coeur débordait . . . il sentait monter du fond de lui-même . . . un afflux de tendresse qui l'énervait, comme le mouvement des ondes sous ses yeux [His heart was overflowing . . . he felt rising from deep within himself . . . a rush of tenderness that enervated him, like the movement of waves before his eyes]" (49–50). These images arising in

Frédéric's lyrical solitude lead the narrative into a visionary domain, "où il vous semble qu'on est transporté dans un monde supérieur [where it seems that you are transported to a superior world]" (50). From "the surface of things" to the apprehension of an interior wave of rising emotion, this moment of Frédéric's vocation allegorizes the turn from the visible to the visionary world of invisibilia, where images are melted into the object of vocation, the Modernist "object" rigorously created by Flaubert: the Sentence.

In Proust's aesthetic, image and sentence appear to have a more ambiguous status: emphasis is placed on the image as metaphor, while at the same time, the author's highest praise is reserved for the controlled effects of Flaubert's syntax. The liquid, musical, and melodic qualities of the image permeate the sentence that emerges from Vinteuil's music: "la petite phrase" is accompanied by "ces phrases mystérieuses qui hantent certains quatuors [the mysterious phrases that haunt certain quartets]" (III, 381). The difficulty of mapping out the relationship between Proust's image and sentence is indirectly confirmed by literary criticism. Although they run along parallel tracks, two extensive studies based on broad concepts of style[12] arrive at opposite conclusions: Ullmann's *The Image in the Modern French Novel* privileges the image, and Spitzer's "Le Style de Marcel Proust" emphasizes the sentence. The latter work focuses on Proust's sentence without placing the image in its context, and the converse is true of Ullmann's study.

Spitzer's brilliant monograph on Proust's novel describes its object through what might be seen as the quintessential trait of Modernism, "the strangeness of style."[13] An examination of *A la recherche* leads him to highlight the following: "great periodic sentences" (398), "the art of the sustained periodic sentence" with a "meandering outline" (399), and "polyphonic periodic sentences" including an "interior expansion" (404). Extended, sustained, meandering, or layered with interiorized voices, characterized by both spatial and temporal complexity, the motif of the sentence is Spitzer's focus. Ullmann, on the other hand, evokes the strangely artificial or unnatural images of art (172–74) and synaesthesia.[14] He emphasizes the following: the dominant role of the image for Proust (238); the "development of an image" (226); the sequences and recurrences of images (228–29); the layering of "concurrent images" (227); and the interior expansion of the image (226), studied earlier by Ramon Fernandez.[15]

Proust's rendering of "beautiful style" (III, 889) refrains from an opposition between image and sentence. Unlike Flaubert, he does not use the sentence to exert aesthetic control over the fluid, the synaesthetic, or the melodic. On the contrary, the motif implicates a musical phrase within the vocation for writing and the ideal of style; in the "incitements" of allegory, the liquidity of language becomes the site for the sublime height of style, announced as eternity, or "the eternal morning." The "perpetual alliteration" of the Vivonne carafes episode demonstrates the relation between metaphor, motif, and the invisible liquid element necessary to bring about "the eternal morning"; another account of this relation occurs in a central passage on style at the end of the novel.[16] The studies by Spitzer and Ullmann present a remarkable parallelism, despite their divergent approaches to the Flaubertian "excess" of Proust's style. Neither discusses the status of the nonprivileged element of Proust's style, because neither interpretation can give an account of what it has excluded from its conceptual framework. Spitzer's central focus on the sentence and Ullmann's study of the image offer concurring evidence of Proust's stylistic effects, but neither takes up the question of what is at stake in the new version of Modernism.

Only the aesthetic of allegory can "explain" or interpret the traits of Proust's style without concentrating exclusively on either the sentence or the image. In *A la recherche*, the image explodes the confines of the sentence: it overflows from within the borders of conventional sentence structure. Adopted by Fernandez, Spitzer's term of "interior expansion" gives an account of its interiority. This "débordement" (Flaubert's word for Frédéric's lyrical state) indicates that Proust's image controls syntax by shaping it from the inside, according to an ideal based on the relation between "sensation" and "memory." This is Proust's version of allegory as the sublime. For Flaubert, however, the relation between image and sentence appears to be inverted, since syntax "controls" the images. The complex relationship between the "school of style" in the "gueuloir" and the image that fascinates and threatens its viewer turns the sentence into the central entity of Flaubert's sublime.

As a narrative account including the allegory of conversion, the ravishing overflow or the ideal of style is borrowed from *L'Education sentimentale* (49–50). Proust takes it up in the resonances of a rush of tenderness that oscillates like the waves Frédéric contemplates. At the beginning of the *Recherche*, this moment of inner overflow makes an appearance as a ravishing, ecstatic effect of memory in the first version of the Petite Madeleine: "je sens tressaillir en moi quelque chose qu'on aurait désancré, à une grande profondeur . . . cela monte lentement [I feel leaping inside me something that could have weighed anchor, at a great depth . . . it rises slowly]" (I, 46). This image recalls the rising lyrical intensity of the ravishing "rush" staged by Flaubert in Frédéric's double vocation of art and love. The possibility of resurrecting this intensity floats throughout the later sections of *L'Education sentimentale*. At the same time, Frédéric's lyricism is an anticipation of a lasting encounter between Art and Reality—the sublime jouissance inherent in the vocation of Romantic love, according to the terms developed in the novel. When this vocation has not been fulfilled later in the text, lyrical intensity is directed toward a Flaubertian "resurrection of the Past."[17]

In a sense, Proust literalizes this crucial point of Flaubert's allegory by locating resurrection in the complex folds of forgetting and remembering. Through memory and style as the art of temporality, Proust invests the theological sense of resurrection with an aesthetic meaning: "Et peut-être la résurrection de l'âme après la mort est-elle concevable comme un phénomène de mémoire [And perhaps the resurrection of the soul after death can be conceived as a phenomenon of memory]" (II, 88). This enigmatic resurrection of the soul rather than the body is confirmed within the novel by the account of Bergotte's death and outside it by the obituary for Ruskin.[18] The "soul" returns in the offering of an ardent and unquiet heart that bears the writing of allegory—the book that preserves the revelation of the invisible within its clasped correspondences. The isolated instants described by the narrator in terms of "enjoying the essence of things" and "the miracle of an analogy" are "these resurrections of the past" (III, 871–72). The reciprocal metaphors of the Vivonne episode are figures that allude to the "Verschränkung" of correspondences, rendered visible in the narrator's discovery of style late in the novel when ecstasy spells out the promise of metaphoric lines to come.

The analogy between resurrection and memory is confirmed and explained by the eternity of the work of art. Its truth and aesthetic essence, the form and content of style, focus on the resurrection of memory and the past. A theological figure marks the death of Bergotte: "On l'enterra, mais toute la nuit funèbre . . . ses livres . . . veillaient comme des anges aux ailes éployées et semblaient . . . le symbole de sa résurrection [He was buried, but during the entire funeral night . . . his books . . . kept watch like angels with spread wings and appeared as . . . the symbol of his resurrection]" (III, 188). Here too, metaphor subtly enacts a "miracle of analogy" that dissolves and refines Proust's theological vocabulary in his aesthetics.

The nth and final version of the Petite Madeleine is placed near the end of the novel as a belated ecstasy, an *après-coup*: the narrator looks back at the different pasts that progressively covered up the first layer of past time, childhood at Combray, while they were gradually obscured by new present tenses. He also looks back to the unlocalizable Past of the Madeleine experience itself. This belatedness occurs after all the moments of ecstasy are gathered in a bouquet at the final matinée. Through the "dramatic turn of events" (III, 920) that stages time's corrosive power to ruin memory by destroying the palimpsests that rendered it possible, Proust demonstrates that moments of ecstasy may not be assimilated to a positivist rebirth or resurgence. Under the sign of Madeleine, they are a kind of "renaissance" that emerges out of the negativity that threatens it. "Lost time" is not the subject of simple repetition; it is the mystery of loss and death that can only be sought as loss. The work of art alone can retrieve it in the belated form of symbolic creation. Proust's commentary on this mystery and the sublime spirituality of symbolic creation emphasizes a revelation of invisibilia: "cette matinée . . . marquerait . . . dans celle-ci [mon oeuvre] la forme que j'avais pressentie autrefois dans l'église de Combray, et qui nous reste habituellement invisible, celle du Temps [this matinée . . . would mark . . . in it [my oeuvre] the form that I had sensed long ago in the church of Combray, and that habitually remains invisible, that of Time]" (III, 1044–45).

Un style qui serait beau

Where can the subject of invisibilia be located? At the eloquent ineffable "blank," the space on the page where time led the narrator to the pillar of fire of the Hebrews? Saint-Loup saved him from the dusty laments of the Jew mourning on a roll of exile's carpets, and cleared a path for light: can the subject of invisibilia be found in the margin of beauty, at Rivebelle? Or is it inscribed on the "grimoire" (I, 47–48) that translates Proust's roses, hawthornes, and geraniums into the flowery arabesques of a tablet covered with signs, the aesthetic translation of sensual impressions onto paper?

The ecstatic revelation of a passionate excess that overflows edges and borderlines is figured by the miraculous opening of Japanese paper pebbles into aquatic flowers; it operates "like love" in the episode of the Petite Madeleine. The subject of invisibilia moves along a path that separates this revelation from the belatedness of forgetting and silence in the text that follows it. The invisible presence of "Marcel Proust" is guaranteed in the terms of the invisibility of Time, the counterpart of the mysterious feminine Unknown who offers her precious essence to the narrator from the lines of Vinteuil's Septuor. Proust's evocation of the height of beautiful style as the artful expansion of time through a blank space—the visual revelation of the invisible and the silent fourth dimension that became the object and subject of the dramatic turn at the final matinée in *Le Temps retrouvé*—may be a secret allusion to Flaubert, who wrote: "Ce que l'on sent le mieux reste flottant sur le blanc du papier [The things that one feels the most remain floating over the blank page]."[19] In "A Propos du 'style' de Flaubert," the inscription of invisibilia through style takes place through the artfully arranged "blank" of syntax. Rendered eternal, it might be called white metaphor.

Proust's impersonal subject of invisibility is the supposed "autobiographer" covered by a veil of fiction: his vocation will arise as a revelation and translation of invisibilia. Taken from Flaubert's blueprint, the Proustian project is another "book about nothing": instead of making the writer into a "character" or an omniscient representative of the writer's psychology, style turns him into the veiled and masked purveyor of allegory. This allegorist represents the aquarium of memory and forgetting, alliteration and inscriptions that promise to return "with lines" in the crystallized saturations of "l'oeuvre d'art." Since Flaubert's aspirations brought beauty into focus for him as a book "in which the subject would be practically invisible,"[20] the subject inherited from him is twofold—allegory and the artist, or the rhetorical subject and the speaking subject.

Flaubert's new subject of invisibilia is intimately related to a hybrid genre of writing that became a central innovation of modern style. Through a subversion of the literary tradition that included the Romanticism of the 1830's,[21] this invention gave an account of the altered dimensions of writing and founded the domain of "questions of writing." With the development of Modernism into the twentieth century, however, the upstart genre whose origins are attributed to Aloysius Bertrand and Maurice de Guérin has spread far beyond any generic limits. In one sense this is not surprising, because its subversive quality was linked to its essential freedom from the boundaries of genre, described by Baudelaire as "dangereuse comme toute liberté absolue [dangerous like all absolute freedom]."[22] In a work written after *Les Fleurs du mal*, he raised it to the highest literary status.²³ Despite its recognized greatness, however, the singularity of this work and its baroque combinations of opposites appeared problematic to several generations of critics. Even the author could not imagine the solution he soon would discover: in the *Notes Nouvelles sur Edgar Poe* (1857), Baudelaire maintained the difficulty of crossing from truth to beauty and clasping them together. Several years later, a newly invented abyss of "form and content" allowed him to arrive at a solution of enduring modernity in *Le Spleen de Paris*.

This abyss of style discovered in Modernism is Flaubert's central predicament: the infinite difficulty of clasping beauty to truth. In fact, it is another version of the invisible subject, another angle on the central problem of "form and content." It is hardly a coincidence that Flaubert anticipated Baudelaire's invention. His aesthetic formulation of this new "solution," demonstrated in his oeuvre, can be found in some private correspondence to Colet. In 1853, ten years before Baudelaire's dedication of *Le Spleen de Paris* to Houssaye, Flaubert writes:

> J'en conçois pourtant un, moi, un style: un style qui serait beau . . . qui serait rythmé comme le vers, précis comme le langage des sciences, et avec des ondulations, des ronflements de violoncelle, des aigrettes de feu, un style qui vous entrerait dans l'idée comme un coup de stylet; et où votre pensée enfin voguerait sur des surfaces lisses, comme lorsqu'on file dans un canot avec bon vent arrière. La prose est née d'hier, voilà ce qu'il faut se dire. [But I can conceive of one, a style: a style that would be beautiful . . . that would be rhythmic like verse, precise like the language of the sciences, and with the undulations, the throbbing of a cello, with crests of fire, a style that would intrude in your idea like the thrust of a stiletto; and in it your thought would sail along on smooth surfaces, the way one glides in a canoe with a fair wind. You must tell yourself that Prose was born yesterday.]²⁴

Interlaced with Flaubert's emphasis on the ideal of style is an explicit aspiration toward a lyrical writing outside the formal range of poetry.

The rhythmic flow of beautiful prose emerges at the heart of what Flaubert would call modernity. As he progresses in the writing of *Madame Bovary*, he confirms his remark on the new sublime style in another account of the aesthetics at the root of the first great Modernist novel: "Vouloir donner à la prose le rythme du vers (en la laissant prose et très prose) et écrire la vie ordinaire comme on écrit l'histoire ou l'épopée (sans dénaturer le sujet) [Wanting to give to prose the rhythm of verse (while leaving prose alone, and very prosaic) and to write ordinary life the way one writes history or epic (without misrepresenting the subject)]."[25] The concept of a poetic prose is firmly anchored in the exigencies of the "book about nothing," the beautiful story about a life of banality and "false poetry," inherited from a tepid and stereotyped Romanticism. Flaubert's description of poetic prose takes lyricism out of the domain of sentimentality: his contempt for what Emma represents pales when compared to some of his letters about Musset and Lamartine. Lyricism plunges into the infinite, dangerous, vertiginous realm of allegory that submits it to an open-ended and personal series of restrictions, paradoxically culminating in impersonality: rhythmic, precise, oscillating, with deep musical resonance and flashing images of fire. Form enters content with the violence of a knife; like Baudelaire's writing, Flaubert's poetic prose assembles a whirl of synaesthetic images.

In the preface to *Le Spleen de Paris*, Baudelaire contrasts his new work with the picturesque writing of Aloysius Bertrand, and he locates the center of prose poetry in the Modernist sublime. Baudelaire's account of style is remarkably similar to Flaubert's description:

> Quel est celui de nous qui n'a pas . . . rêvé le miracle d'une prose poétique, musicale sans rythme et sans rime, assez souple et assez heurtée pour s'adapter aux mouvements lyriques de l'âme, aux ondulations de la rêverie, aux

soubresauts de la conscience? [Who among us has not
. . . dreamed the miracle of a poetic prose, musical without rhythm and without rhyme, supple enough and abrupt enough to adapt to the lyrical movements of the heart, the undulations of revery, the jolts of conscience?][26]

Like Flaubert writing *Madame Bovary*, Baudelaire places his project in the frame of "la vie moderne, ou plutôt d'*une* vie moderne [modern life, or rather *one* modern life]" and criticizes the traditional "subject" of the novel; he provocatively dismisses it as "le fil interminable d'une intrigue superflue [the interminable thread of a superfluous plot]."[27] The crossings of modern life are as decisive for *Le Spleen de Paris* as they were for *Les Fleurs du mal*: they run parallel to the allegorical painting of Rouen in *Madame Bovary* that sets the stage for the recreation of Carthage, Paris, and so on, in later writings. Baudelaire writes: "C'est surtout de la fréquentation des villes énormes, c'est du croisement de leurs innombrables rapports que nait cet idéal obsédant [It is above all from frequenting enormous cities, from the crossing of their innumerable relations that this obsessive ideal is born]."[28] This remark could serve as an epigraph for Benjamin's writings on the nineteenth century: allegory arises at the crossroads of history, sociology, economics, urban architecture, and politics. Their paths and arcades map what he calls capitalism, transformed into the allegorical forms of Baudelaire's art. On another level, Baudelaire's comment locates modernity in the crossings of writing that link the image, correspondence, synaesthesia, and signification with the allegorical effects of the city. Modern subjectivity provides the interior passageway or subterranean *correspondance* where the cityscape of allegory takes shape in a poetic voice. The crossing of "relations" in the modern city gives rise to the effects of the necropolis-carnival represented in Baudelaire's "Le Cygne." Monuments and disguises go underground: they live on in the sanctum of memory. The viewer's impressions of the city enter memory: evanescence is made permanent in the effects of style.

The correspondence or clasping of "rapports" in impressions of the city, in the temporality of the remembered and the evanescent, and in the writing of life stories ("*one* modern life")—the elements that combine to form the Modernist aesthetic represented in "poetic prose"—emerge independently in the work of Flaubert and Baudelaire. Proust's aesthetic shapes these elements into a third form. He hints at his version of poetic prose in the narrator's description of the style that he will seek for his written "work of art" (III, 870). Like Flaubert and Baudelaire, he emphasizes its "great difficulties," its complexity, its capacity for rendering contrasts, its miraculous qualities ("le miracle d'une analogie" [III, 871]):

> Car j'en devrais exécuter les parties successives dans une matière qui serait bien différente de celle qui conviendrait aux souvenirs de matins au bord de la mer ou d'après-midi à Venise, si je voulais peindre ces soirs de Rivebelle où, dans la salle à manger ouverte sur le jardin, la chaleur commençait à se décomposer, à retomber, à déposer, où une dernière lueur éclairait encore les roses sur les murs du restaurant tandis que les dernières aquarelles du jour étaient encore visibles au ciel,—dans une matière distincte, nouvelle, d'une transparence, d'une sonorité spéciales, compacte, fraîchissante, et rose. [For I would have to execute the successive parts in a material that would be quite different from the one that would be appropriate for memories of seaside mornings or Venetian afternoons, if I wanted to paint those evenings at Rivebelle where, in the dining room opening onto the garden, the heat was beginning to decompose, fall away, settle, where a last gleam still lit the roses on the restaurant walls while the last watercolors of daylight were still visible in the sky—in a distinct new material of a particular transparence and resonance, compact, refreshing, and pink.] (III, 871)

This key sentence may be the most important remark about writing in the entire novel; I will return shortly to the emblems it displays as a constellation of style. The materiality of art described in Proust's sentence will become the narrator's "obsessive ideal" in the Modernist clasping of "the question of writing" or the difficulty of style. From the chance impressions of lived life that filter through memory into description, the invention of style is formulated as a "new substance." Distant and yet inseparable from art, life offers the material of its execution. This ideal problematizes the artist's desire to create by turning it into an aesthetic event on the threshold between passage and permanence, the double vision of allegory. Proust's mysterious Sentence takes the billowing and unfolded form of a line by Baudelaire; it is painted with the images of a Flaubertian pane of colored glass, echoed in the narrator's description of the bookcases at Balbec (I, 805). Consecrated to form, the necessity of style ("les anneaux nécessaires d'un beau style" [III, 889]) marks a detachment from sentiment characteristic of modern allegory. It opens the door to Baudelairean cruelty, Flaubert's "anatomy of style," the "thrust of the stiletto," and Proust's "Novel of the unconscious."[29]

The violence associated with this necessity—the cruel blow inflicted by the sufferer, the scalpel wielded by the patient, and the stiletto used by the murderer—receives a different emblem in Proust's aesthetic, but the ravages of the unconscious are not less deadly than the verbal and artificial means invoked by Baudelaire and Flaubert. Proust's use of metaphor includes its complicity with the brutal and depersonalizing force of forgetting; indeed, the ecstatic benefits of metaphor (its reappearances that "correspond" with each other and with earlier disappearances) are inseparable from the power of negativity, the abyss that swallows time. It may be for this reason that metonymy cannot attain the status of metaphor in Proust's aesthetic and style. An illustration of the negative power associated with metaphor can be seen in the "faire catleya" passage. Swann's timid caresses began with an "arrangement of the catleyas" worn by Odette; its metonymic extension to "'faire l'amour'" was encoded as "'faire catleya.'" But the metonymic origins were soon forgotten: "quand l'arrangement . . . des catleyas fut depuis longtemps tombé en désuétude, la métaphore 'faire catleya,' . . . survécut dans leur langage, où elle le commémorait, à cet usage oublié [when the catleya arrangement had long fallen into disuse, the metaphor of 'make catleya' survived in their language, commemorating it with the forgotten usage]" (I, 234). Forgetting destroys metonymic connections and leads to a structure based on metaphor.[30]

In the Modernist frame of "prose poétique," it becomes possible to approach sentences criticized according to the "too much of a muchness" criterion[31]—too much imagery, too precious, too recondite, and too artsy. Encoded as "unnaturalness" or "artificiality," the allegorical elements that elicit Hindus's uneasiness are widely condemned in Romantic and post-Romantic criticism, precisely because they exclude an effortless continuity between materiality and language, or life and art. The "matière nouvelle" of allegory reflects retrospectively on another mysterious sentence, located close to the beginning of the work. In a context framed by love and writing, the narrator remembers the church of Combray:

> Le soleil . . . donnait une carnation de géranium aux tapis rouges et sur lesquels s'avançaient en souriant Madame de Guermantes, et ajoutait à leur lainage un velouté rose, un épiderme de lumière, cette sorte de tendresse, de sérieuse douceur dans la pompe et dans la joie qui caractérisent certaines pages de *Lohengrin*, certaines peintures de Carpaccio, et qui font comprendre que Baudelaire ait pu appliquer au son de la trompette l'épithète de délicieux. [The sun . . . gave a geranium fleshtone to the red carpets on which the smiling Madame de Guermantes advanced, and added to their nap a velvety pink, a skin of light, the kind of tenderness and serious sweetness in majesty and joy that characterize certain pages of *Lohengrin*, certain paintings of Carpaccio, and that indicate how Baudelaire was able to apply to the sound of a trumpet the epithet of delicious.] (I, 178)

The reference to Baudelaire's image takes up the stanza from "L'Imprévu," quoted earlier.[32] In his writings on Baudelaire,[33] Proust discusses style as a ground for strange encounters that are captured by an imagery filled with resonances of delight and cruelty, beauty and heartlessness. The sentence about the church of Combray is framed by Proust's criticism of Baudelaire; the poet's use of synaesthesia masks the cruelty that Proust's commentary tied to the eternal beauty of his style, inseparable from the impersonality and impassibility of allegory. In *A la recherche*, the counterpart of this cruelty slowly unfolds the horrors of desire and love (except for maternal love); Virtue suffers at the hands of Vice, but the boundaries become blurred when the sufferer's strategy leads him or her into vice in order to curtail pain (e.g., Swann or the narrator), and when the torturer, the figural representation of Vice, attempts to renounce pleasure (e.g., Albertine, Mlle Vinteuil).

Proust's reference to other forms of style also reflects Baudelaire's Modernism. An evocation of music and art leads back to the poet's attentive admiration for Wagner's opera (CSB 623). The elements in this sentence form layers of influences and correspondences, focused on the writing of "certain pages" —leitmotiv, painting, opera, and Renaissance allegory. The synaesthesia of the poet's *correspondance* is re-created through images of aesthetic materiality.[34] The context literally illuminates art, flooding it with light; its beauty and deliciousness are the effect of the narrator's passion for Madame de Guermantes. The majesty of the sentence and the red glow of sublime flesh[35] ("carnation de géranium") shift to the images that unfold from the narrator's dreams of "a poetic future" (I, 178) prefigured by "a velvety pink": the Baudelairean color of beauty is the color of a mysterious miraculous "new substance" found in the poetics of prose and the conclusive account of style. Proust's "carnation" of light, color, texture, and image will render eternal the prose style of the "poetic future"; it will translate the book into the "melting" beauty of form discovered on the other side of the little panel of yellow wall.

Félicité, ravissement, beauté

> Elle appartenait à un ordre de créatures surnaturelles et que nous n'avons jamais vues, mais que malgré cela nous reconnaissons avec ravissement quand quelque explora-

teur de l'invisible arrive . . . à l'amener, briller quelques instants. . . . C'est ce que Vinteuil avait fait pour la petite phrase. . . . Elle avait disparu. [She belonged to an order of supernatural creatures that we have never seen, but that nevertheless we recognize with ravishment when some explorer of the invisible succeeds . . . in bringing it to shine for a few instants. . . . That was what Vinteuil had done for the little phrase. . . . She had disappeared] (I, 351).

In Proust's "Novel of the unconscious," invisibilia and invisible vocation take the stage and become visible when Time lost re-emerges in a "found"—a recognized return that shines for a few instants and disappears. Evanescent, passing, and violently torn from its origin, the object altered by Time is given back on the terms of that alteration and loss. Unforeseen, sudden, and gratuitous, the fragile essence of the impossible "object" appears in a flashing instant. A figure for the loss of time, it becomes the subject of spiritual happiness: "spiritual joys" (in Bergotte's words), "felicity" (the narrator), "ecstasy" (Proust). Through a form of grace, resurrection will offer a symbolic compensation for loss and death in allegory à la Flaubert. The artist's "object" makes form and content inseparable through time, memory, and vision: the "jamais" of death, evanescence, and modernity is tied to the "toujours" of writing. The interiority of remembered subjectivity leads to the lines of "eternity" or permanence. The allegory of conversion represents this link between "form and content" in fiction, as ecstasy and style.

The correspondence between ecstasy and style unfolds in the aesthetic of fiction on three levels: the ideal of the sublime, represented through narration or attributed to fictional characters; allegory as the combination of memory and images, the "poetic prose" of the writer's style; and, finally, the act of turning the ideal and the style of allegory into an ongoing stylistic creation. Interiorized, the sublime ideal of style moves through style—through the text—in an act of "perpetual alliteration."

Although the term is Proust's invention, its meaning in his novel derives from Flaubert's writing; "perpetual alliteration" marks the anticipation of the correspondence between ecstasy and style in *Combray*, where the Petite Madeleine has already set up the opening of memory and vocation that will be confirmed at the closing point of *Le Temps retrouvé*. Toward the end of *L'Education sentimentale*, the melancholic fruit of Frédéric's "education" gives an account of the clasping of ecstasy and style. Beyond the limits of Romanticism and the irony often interpreted as Flaubert's unambiguous distance from it, this clasping inscribes Flaubert in the text of transromanticism. The double vocation of art and love promised in the early scene on the Pont-Neuf (49–50) has not been fulfilled: neither poet or painter, Frédéric had lost all hope of possessing Madame Arnoux. Because of her, he renounced the loves of sensual pleasure (Rosanette) and ambition (Mme Dambreuse), but not before he tarnished his ideals in the realities of these other involvements.

Following his act of double renunciation, Frédéric suddenly sounds like the bitter-lyric, mournful Flaubert of the correspondence: "Il voyagea. Il connut la mélancolie des paquebots . . . Il revint . . . il eut d'autres amours encore. Mais le souvenir continuel du premier les rendait insipides [He voyaged. He came to know the melancholy of ships . . . He returned . . . he had other love affairs. But the continual memory of the first one rendered them dull]."[36] Memory marks the return of the sublime ideal to the apprehended surface of the present, now haunted by "the first"—a paradise never quite possessed, but lost during the process of "education" that maintained it as an impossible ideal. Memory recalls lost intensity and disfigures the present: "et puis la véhémence du désir, la fleur même de la sensation était perdue [and then the vehemence of desire, the flower itself of sensation was lost]" (419). Throughout the text this flower of desire or impression links the ravishment of love with beauty through Madame Arnoux. Beauty is inseparable from style: "tout ce qui était beau . . . l'allure d'une phrase, un contour, l'amenaient à sa pensée d'une façon brusque et insensible [all that was beautiful . . . the bearing of a sentence, a contour, would bring her to mind in an abrupt and imperceptible way]" (69). The two ravishments are clasped together by that other "fleur," Frédéric's sublime love object. She has become the focus for the intensity of sensation even when she sleeps "tranquille comme une fleur endormie [serene as a flower asleep]" (76).

The first (original) intensity arose "like an apparition" (4). Madame Arnoux appears at the beginning of the novel, when she sets Frédéric's "sentimental education" in motion. Like Proust's Petite Madeleine, the flower will reappear after a long journey through time—loss, melancholy, and allegory—to mark the return of lost time in literary language. Ravishment is repeated, accompanied by Flaubert's self-inscription of the delights of writing.

At the other end of the novel, near its close, Madame Arnoux arrives unexpectedly in Frédéric's room. Belated and literally *après-coup*, her presence is highly allegorical. She confesses her temptation of many years ago, and suddenly, the flower of sensation comes alive again for Frédéric in "un saisissement de volupté [an access of sensual delight]" (420). Shocked to see that her hair has turned white, he describes his old image of her, his love-image of "délices," "parfums," "infini," "belle à éblouir," "musique," and "splendeur" (delights, perfumes, infinity, dazzling beauty, music, and splendor), in language that Flaubert has ironized by concentrating and exaggerating it. This lyrical confession conveniently elides all of the disappointments, compromises, and anti-lyrical effects of corruption that composed Frédéric's "education." In spite of Flaubert's ironic distance, however, this poetic prose uses his own words for the images of Art and its sublime ideal.[37] While Madame Arnoux listens in "ravissement pour la femme qu'elle n'était plus [in rapture for the woman that she no longer was]" (422), Frédéric is no longer a passive audience for allegory. He has become the Flaubertian allegorist: "Frédéric, se grisant par ses paroles, arrivait à croire ce qu'il disait [Frédéric, growing intoxicated at his own words, succeeded in believing what he was saying]" (422). Between mourning and melancholy, the ravishment of words erects a false monument to the falseness of lyricism and a true monument to the sublime sentiment that has now been so ironically "educated." Frédéric's faculty of fictive intoxication is borrowed from Flaubert's depersonalized emotion of writing, his personal ravishments of allegory: "Seulement quand je lui écrivais, avec la faculté que j'ai de m'émouvoir par la plume, je prenais mon sujet au sérieux mais seulement pendant que j'écrivais [Only when I was writing to her, with my faculty for excitement induced by the pen, was I taking my subject seriously but only while I was writing]."[38]

At the pole opposite "autobiography," writing provides the script for life by turning back to life and representing it in fiction. The intoxication of words effects a return of lost time. Allegory, beauty, and Romantic dazzling ravish Frédéric in his own voice. The flower of sensation countersigns the literary act of "Frédéric, growing intoxicated at his own words": "il était repris par une convoitise plus forte que jamais, furieuse, enragée [He was repossessed by a lust that was stronger than ever, furious, raging]" (423). Like Baudelaire's "passante," Madame Arnoux disappears as suddenly as she had arrived: "Elle monta dedans. La voiture disparut. Et ce fut tout [She climbed in. The carriage disappeared. And that was all]" (423). Out of invisibilia comes the shining object of ravishment; like the mysterious unknown, "the little phrase by Vinteuil," it soon disappears.

When the impersonal ideal of style has been scaffolded and structured in the literary text and its created world, the double inscription of the artist and his fiction in a poetic future neither risks nor compromises the fictional enterprise. When Proust on his deathbed rewrote the episode of Bergotte's death that leads through the panel of wall Proust had loved and admired above all other paintings, the fictional quality of the character Bergotte was guaranteed by narrative omniscience. The mastery of the narrator who knows mediates between author and writer-character or veils the author with a camouflage disguise linked to the "not always me." The narrator seems to know what he knows only because of the invisibility of time and the miraculous effects of memory slipped into style. His invisible appearance and the magical powers of opening the doors of the forgotten and reading the hieroglyphs of lost time allow for "figuration" and "translation"; Proust's self-inscription of ravishment through style is filtered through an aura of mystery. While Flaubert was writing *Madame Bovary*, his ambitious attempt was threatened by an overdose of lyricism and an infiltration of personal sentiment: the boundaries between life and fiction were blurred to the point where he was taken over the edge of delicious jouissance and into the other, vertiginous domain of the image associated with "the black illness." While writing the love scene between Emma and Rodolphe, Flaubert wrote to Colet: "au moment où j'écrivais le mot *attaque de nerfs*, j'étais si emporté, je gueulais si fort, et sentais si profondément ce que ma petite femme éprouvait, que j'ai eu peur moi-même d'en avoir une [at the moment of writing *nervous attack*, I was so carried away, I was yelling so loudly, and feeling so deeply what my little woman was suffering, that I was frightened of having one myself]."[39]

In this context, it is possible to understand why Flaubert extended his passion for style to Emma in the early version of the novel and took it out of the final version. Like Flaubert and Colet during this period, Emma and Rodolphe exchanged frequent love letters. She suddenly begins to sound like her creator, rewriting prose in view of an ideal of style that cuts away excess: "Emma s'allongeait donc le sentiment, en le passant ainsi au laminoir du style [Emma drew out her sentiment in putting it through the mill of style]."[40] In the first *Education sentimentale*, Flaubert's identification with Jules portrays the hero's preoccupation with the "école du style" as the counterpart of a new (and rather artificial) mastery of passion culminating in the departure for Flaubert's beloved Orient.[41] With *Madame Bovary*, however, the author's identification with his heroine includes the threat of falling into sentimental intoxication of love and lyrical aspiration that will end in death, the final form of "the black illness."

Although brief, Emma's foray into writing anticipates the fictional interiorization of the rapture of style in *Salammbô*, *L'Education sentimentale*, and its culmination in *La Légende*.

Infinite, uncontrollable, whirling and hallucinatory images are mysteriously transformed into the equally infinite but far more pleasurable "objets d'art," invented by Flaubert as both Object and Art. The adventure-Sentences of fictional creation turn the black image of estrangement and its deathly fireworks, described in the letter to Taine of November 1866, into the mastery of style. Beautiful representation of evanescence and the haunting return of the image is the essence of allegory. Through sensation, memory, and horror, Flaubert's necropolis of imagery is converted into the other images of allegory that evolve and explode on paper as what Proust will call "perpetual alliteration."

In view of the convergence of ecstasy and style in Flaubert's fictional allegory, Proust's commentary on Flaubert and Baudelaire confirms the narrator's vision of style in *Le Temps retrouvé*. The "not always me" of the novel and its truth entails a fictional portrait of the narrator engaged in an intimately Proustian process of elaborating a theory of style through an ecstatic experience. Through Flaubert, Proust's enigmatic portrait of the narrator inscribes the combination of "sensation" and "memory" of involuntary memory within the ideal of style. When rapture enters theory, theory anticipates a poetic future: the poetic prose of *A la recherche du temps perdu* effects this transformation.

Several paragraphs of *Le Temps retrouvé* gather the narrator's ecstatic experiences together in a final decisive set of correspondences (III, 867, 868, 872). Venice and Combray are clasped together with Balbec, the narrative go-between for Virtue and Vice. Distanced from the ways of Combray and the labyrinths of the city, it becomes the stage of desire for the "girls in flower," and especially Albertine. Proust transposes Swann's pursuit of aesthetic, amorous, and social pleasures into the narrator's experience at Balbec: the correspondences of sky and sea develop the allegory of desire and love through Elstir's modern painting, the narrator's impressions of light and color, and the potential of the visual image to enter the beautiful writing of allegory.

The allegorical imagination turns the jouissance of something absent into beauty. The "varnish of the masters" theorized by Proust is not an object, a concept, or a content ("le fond"); it is "le fondu," the beautiful convergence of style. It is not a coincidence that the Ruskinian Swann is drawn toward the study of Vermeer (until the all-consuming pursuit of Odette turns his aesthetic ambition into idolatry), or that the dying Bergotte has a final vision of beautiful style at a Vermeer exhibit like the one Proust attended shortly before his death. The narrator describes the style of his anticipated "oeuvre d'art" in terms that extend from Proust's new style while they confirm the lineage of the Vermeer ideal within the fiction of *A la recherche*. The narrator's "jouissance immédiate, chaque fois que le miracle d'une analogie m'avait fait échapper au présent [immediate enjoyment, each time the miracle of an analogy had allowed me to escape the present]" (III, 871) takes Vermeer into the domain of beautiful writing associated with Flaubert's luminous ravishment and painted images. The colored surface of allegory recalls the panes of colored glass that compose the stained glass of style.

What is this new style? Its fictional representation unfolds in a series of correspondences that link it to rapture. Like the initial Petite Madeleine ecstasy that spreads to contain the threefold parallels of the baptistery (evoked by the cobblestone), the three trees outside of Balbec (evoked by the spoon), and the "serviette" of Balbec (evoked by the starched napkin), the metaphorical elements of the narrator's new "material" of style in the sentence on III, 871 explicitly recall Bergotte's vision of the layers of color on Vermeer's "little panel of yellow wall" and its rendering of impressions clasped together in the "passage" of "couleur" like coats of paint. The future oeuvre is composed of a new material distributed in layers of difference: allegory. Although these layers do not derive from the mystical reading of Scriptures, they are as mysterious as Dante's allegory. Vinteuil's "mysterious phrases" and the rediscovered "world of mystery" of literature (III, 883) lead the narrator toward the extra-temporal miracle of style, "felicity" of "diverse blessed impressions" and, ultimately, the resurrection of Bergotte's "joys of spiritual life" (871) in writing.

"Distincte, nouvelle" (III, 871), the new material is the modern absolute of style. It unfolds like a fan to display the clasped elements of "sensation" and "souvenir," the manifold connections between memory and "immediate jouissance," and the correspondence of metaphor. These elements produce a temporal image of morning, afternoon, and evening, that corresponds to Balbec, Venice, and Rivebelle; its triadic structure runs parallel to the ecstatic triad at the matinée (cobblestone, spoon, and starched napkin), linked to Combray and the "first" revelation of a past that tied art and love together forever in the taste of the Petite Madeleine.

This sentence substantiates the glimmerings of an aesthetic throughout the novel and the narrator's final explanations of metaphor, ecstasy, and time. Although its "parties successives" create images of style that anticipate the parts of the work to come, the narrator's style emphasizes the nocturnal angle ("ces soirs de Rivebelle") borrowed from his dark hours of writing, and the passage of heat ("se décomposer . . . à retomber . . . à déposer") into the strange funereal images of "matière" falling into dust. Like Elstir's Whistlerian painting, the last light inverts the artificiality of painted roses with the natural colors of the sky: "encore, les roses sur les murs," "les dernières aquarelles du jour étaient encore visibles" (III, 871). These daylight paintings are watercolors: they recall the Venetian water labyrinth associated with the fugitive and Carpaccio, the sea at Balbec associated with Albertine and Elstir, and the passage through darkness of the weeping Jew. He followed the pillar of fire to the margin of beauty, Rivebelle: its wallpaper roses faded in the night like the magical images of the magic lantern, brightly entering and escaping vision.

Proust's water images and layers of color paint the invisible through the "fondu" of representation ("d'une transparence . . . spéciale" [871]). On an impressionist canvas where colored form evades its contours, the "roses sur les murs" become beautiful layers of color; painted in the nocturnal shadows of passage, death, and invisibilia, they bear the wild roses of Gilberte and the "mois de Marie," the roses of aesthetics. Like the roses displayed in certain church festivals, the "rose" that ends this sentence is the pink tint of the resurrection: the flowering of eternal life emerges from memories, the glassy petrification of the allegorical. Through flowers, poetry, and painting, the color "rose" returns to the delicious pleasures of beauty. The Venetian school of Renaissance painting used pink as a dominating shade in its effervescent palette, described by art historians as lighter and brighter than the colors of other schools. These beautiful pinks persisted through Vivarini, Crivelli, Carpaccio, and into the eighteenth century, with Tiepolo, whose particular pink Proust borrowed for the lining of Albertine's Fortuny dress (III, 394). From the "incarnation" of style beginning with *La Charité de Giotto* to the end and its anticipated resurrection, this marvelous sentence spells out Proust's ultimate synaesthetic ecstatic image of style. It inscribes the writer in the passage through death and the spiritual, joyful resurrection of the flesh presided over by angels who bear the promise of mysterious Sentences. The miracle is resurrection—the permanence of immediate jouissance, enjoyment of the essence of things, in some space beyond evanescence, temporality, and ruin. Style awakes and breathes like Carpaccio's resurrected virgins: new, transparent, musical, compact, refreshing, and pink.

Notes

2 The Image of Modernity

1. Flaubert described himself to Turgenev in these terms. See Victor Brombert, *The Novels of Flaubert* (Princeton: Princeton University Press, 1966), p. 129. All translations are my own unless I have indicated another source.
2. Letter of June 13, 1857, from Flaubert to Baudelaire, *Correspondance de Flaubert*, ed. Jean Bruneau (Paris: Bibl. de la Pléiade, 1980), vol. II, p. 745.
3. Letter dated Oct. 21, 1857, from Flaubert to Baudelaire, in reference to Baudelaire's article on *Madame Bovary* (published in *L'Artiste* of Oct. 18, 1857, and reproduced in *Oeuvres complètes* [Paris: Bibl. de la Pléiade, 1979], vol. 2, pp. 76–86) and in *Correspondance de Flaubert* II, p. 772.
4. *A Future for Astyanax* (New York: Columbia University Press, 1969), p. 66.
5. "Déguisements du moi et art fragmentaire" in *Recherche de Proust* (Paris: Seuil, 1980), p. 17. It is noteworthy that he can do so only by conceding an undeniable unity or parallelism: "Marcel seems to have a Flaubertian preoccupation with correspondences between languages and reality."
6. Ibid., pp. 10–11.
7. Ibid., p. 7.
8. Emile Zola, *Oeuvres complètes*, ed. Henri Mitterand (Paris: Cercle du livre précieux, 1966), vol. 11, pp. 99, 97.
9. Ibid., p. 97.
10. See "Erzählen oder Beschreiben?" This essay was first published in 1936 and later reprinted in *Begriffsbestimmung des Literarischen Realismus*, ed. Richard Brinkmann (Darmstadt: Wissenschaftliche Buchgesellschaft, 1969), pp. 33–85. Part of this article, including the discussion of French literature, is translated as "Narrate or Describe?" in Georg Lukács, *Writer and Critic and Other Essays*, ed Arthur D. Kahn (New York: Universal Library, 1971), pp. 110–48.
11. Ibid., p. 36.

12 Ibid., p. 42.
13 Ibid., p. 39.
14 Ibid., p. 40.
15 Ibid.
16 Ibid., p. 44.
17 Ibid., p. 39.
18 Ibid., p. 60.
19 Letter of Jan. 16, 1852, to Louise Colet, *Correspondance de Flaubert*, ed. Jean Bruneau (Paris: Bibl. de la Pléiade, 1980), vol. II, p. 31. From now on I will refer to this edition as *Corr.* I or *Corr.* II. References to the Conard edition of the correspondence will be followed by Arabic numerals designating volumes, except for the *Suppléments*.
20 Letter dated Feb. 8, 1852, to Colet, ibid., p. 43.
21 Letter dated Feb. 27, 1853, to Colet, ibid., p. 252.
22 Letter dated Jan. 31, 1852, ibid., p. 41.
23 Letter of May 5, 1857, in *Corr.* II, p. 710. Victor Brombert documents Flaubert's defense of Romanticism and discusses the problematic aspect of the label of "realism." He discusses Flaubert's "Romantic heredity" in *The Novels of Flaubert* (Princeton: Princeton University Press, 1966).
24 I will return later to the question of Baudelaire's aesthetics and its relevance for a reading of fiction.
25 "Un des premiers états de *Swann*" (1908–9), reproduced in *Marcel Proust: Textes retrouvés*, eds. Philip Kolb and Larkin B. Price (Urbana: University of Illinois Press, 1968), p. 176.
26 *Contre Sainte-Beuve*, eds. Pierre Clarac and Yves Sandre (Paris: Bibl. de la Pléiade, 1971). Repeated page references to works included in this edition (abbreviated as CSB) will be in parentheses in the text.
27 "A Propos de Baudelaire," CSB 628–29.
28 Lukács, pp. 59–60.
29 This remark is quoted by Sartre and discussed by David Mendelsohn, *Le Verre et les objets de verre dans l'univers imaginaire de Marcel Proust* (Paris: José Corti, 1968), p. 216.
30 In *Mimesis: The Representation of Reality in Western Literature* (trans. W. R. Trask [Princeton: Princeton University Press, 1973], p. 482, Erich Auerbach writes: "In Flaubert realism becomes impartial, impersonal, and objective." Auerbach quotes a passage from *Madame Bovary* and writes: "To be sure, there is nothing of Flaubert's life in these words, but only Emma's: Flaubert does nothing but bestow the power of mature expression upon the material which she affords" (ibid., p. 484). In a later chapter dealing with *A la recherche du temps perdu*, Auerbach describes the Proustian narrator as an autobiographical character whose "interiority" makes him identical with the persona of Proust himself: "There is to be noted in this a fusion of the modern concept of interior time with the neo-Platonic idea that the true prototype of a given subject is to be found in the soul of the artist; in this

case, of an artist who, present in the subject itself, has detached himself from it as an observer and thus comes face to face with his own past" (ibid., p. 542).
31 "Flaubert: Spleen and Ideal" in *Flaubert: A Collection of Critical Essays*, ed. Raymond Giraud (Englewood Cliffs, N.J.: Prentice-Hall, 1964), pp. 73–74.
32 Ibid., p. 73.
33 *Narcisse romancier* (Paris: José Corti, 1972), pp. 16–17. This remark refers to *La Vie de Marianne*, but it is equally valid for Proust's novel.
34 Ibid., p. 17.
35 CSB 586–600. Proust's essay was first published in January 1920 in the *Nouvelle Revue Française* in response to an article by Albert Thibaudet in the November 1919 issue. Thibaudet's article, entitled "Une querelle littéraire sur le style de Flaubert," was followed by another in March 1920, entitled "Lettre à Marcel Proust sur le style de Flaubert." Thibaudet refers often to his controversy with Proust in *Gustave Flaubert* (Paris: Gallimard, 1935).

3 The Allegory of Conversion

1 Saint Augustine, *Sermons pour la Pâque*, ed. Suzanne Poque (Paris: Cerf, 1966), Sermon 59, p. 193.
2 See chapter 4, "Necropolis and Carnival," for an interpretation of this essay and its consequences for an interpretation of both Flaubert and Proust.
3 Letter dated late December 1875 to Sand, *Corr*. 7, p. 280.
4 Freud's emphasis on the theory of the unconscious anchored the psychoanalytic concept of truth in a domain usually so inaccessible to consciousness as to be "impersonal." Through the Freudian relation between the unconscious and the subject's truth, Lacan locates the domain of the ego as "méconnaissance," thereby indicating the dimensions of the abyss separating impersonal "vérité" from personalized consciousness.
5 Benjamin contrasts it to Baudelaire's theory of modern art, which he considers to be Baudelaire's least successful portrayal of modernity: "Keine ihrer ästhetischen Reflexionen hat die Moderne in ihrer Durchdringung mit der Antike dargestellt, wie das in gewissen Stücken der 'Fleurs du mal' geschiet [None of Baudelaire's aesthetic reflections represented modernity in its interpenetration with antiquity the way certain pieces of 'Les Fleurs du mal' do]." *Charles Baudelaire. Ein Lyriker im Zeitalter des Hochkapitalismus* in *Gesammelte Schriften*, I. 2, 1974, p. 585.
6 Ibid., p. 586.
7 A key example of this aesthetic use can be found in "Le Mauvais vitrier" (Baudelaire, pp. 285–87). The narrator exclaims to the glassman: "'Comment? vous n'avez pas de verres de couleur? des verres

roses, rouges, bleus, des vitres magiques, des vitres de paradis? . . . vous n'avez pas même de vitres qui fassent voir la vie en beau!' [What? you have no panes of colored glass? pink, red, and blue glass, magic windowpanes, glass from paradise? . . . you don't even have panes that make life look beautiful!']"

8   *Madame Bovary: nouvelle version précédée de scénarios inédits*, eds. J. Pommier and G. Leleu (Paris: Corti, 1949), p. 216. The quotations in the paragraphs that follow will be taken from pp. 215–17 of this edition.

9   *Corr.* II, p. 89. See Pommier/Leleu, p. xix.

10   Letter of Aug. 23, 1846, to Colet, *Corr.* 1, p. 309.

11   Letter of June 7, 1844, to Louis de Cormenin, *Corr.* 1, p. 208.

12   Genette hypothesizes that this passage (despite Flaubert's avowed satisfaction with it) was cut according to Bouilhet's recommendations; according to Bouilhet, episodes in the novel that did not contribute to its plot were to be eliminated. In the case of this passage, however, Flaubert may have thought it inappropriate for Emma to take his own allegorical distance, within the framework of an episode (the ball at La Vaubyessard) that will later have so many allegorical resonances for her. In "Silences de Flaubert" (*Figures I* [Paris: Seuil, 1966], pp. 223–43), Genette interprets what Sartre has called "le grand regard pétrifiant des choses" through a reading of Flaubert's simultaneous suspension of plot and dialogue. Genette concludes with a diagnosis of Flaubert's unique "necessity" and "impossibility" of writing, the "forbidden vocation" that he sees as comparable only to that of Kafka (ibid., p. 242). Genette locates Flaubert at the source of the "déromanisation" of the novel.

13   I will return to this question later. Other examples of Flaubert's use of colored glass include the remarks of the painter in *L'Education sentimentale* ([Paris: Garnier, 1964], p. 47), and the "vitrail gothique" of *Bouvard and Pécuchet*: "Le clocher de Chavignolles se montrait dans le lointain, produisant un effet splendide [The Chavignolles spire appeared in the distance, producing a splendid effect]" (*Bouvard et Pécuchet, édition critique*, ed. Alberto Cento [Naples and Paris: Istituto Universitario Orientale and Nizet, 1964], p. 366). Here as in the draft of *Madame Bovary* Flaubert emphasizes the effect produced by looking through (rather than at) stained glass.

14   References to *Jean Santeuil* (abbreviated as JS, followed by page numbers) are taken from *Jean Santeuil précédé de Les Plaisirs et les jours*, eds. P. Clarac and Y. Sandre (Paris: Bibl. de la Pléiade, 1971).

15   In this context, Proust's understanding of Modernist aesthetics is corroborated by his studies of Mâle and Ruskin. See also Marcel Muller's interpretation of the magic lantern and Proust's understanding of Gothic windows in *Préfiguration et structure romanesque dans "A La Recherche du temps perdu"* (Lexington, Mass.: French Forum, 1979).

16   *Bouvard et Pécuchet*, p. 395.

17 I will return to this question and its textual markers in the following chapter.
18 Letter dated Aug. 14, 1846, to Colet, *Corr.* I, p. 302.
19 Ibid.
20 Letter of Jan. 16, 1852, to Colet, *Corr.* II, p. 31.
21 Letter of Jan. 31, 1852, to Colet, ibid., p. 40.
22 Letter of March 20, 1852, to Colet, ibid., p. 57.
23 Letter of Jan. 15, 1853, to Colet, ibid., p. 238.
24 See the letter of Dec. 3, 1853, to Bouilhet, ibid., p. 472, and the letter dated Dec. 8, 1877, to Turgenev, *Supp.* IV, p. 52.
25 Letter dated June 12, 1904, to Mme de Noailles in response to her novel, *Le Visage émerveillé*, in *Correspondance de Marcel Proust*, ed P. Kolb (Paris: Plon, 1971), vol. IV, p. 156.
26 Letter of Nov. 27, 1913, to Lucien Daudet, in response to Daudet's article, "Du Côté de chez Swann," published that morning in *Le Figaro*. Ibid., vol. XII, p. 343.
27 In *Figures I*, Genette discusses Proust's aesthetic terminology, although with conclusions that differ from those presented here, 42–44.
28 "Projets de Préface," CSB 211–15.
29 These moments speak to each other by *correspondance*: "Comme de longs échos qui de loin se confondent / Dans une ténébreuse et profonde unité [Like long echoes that melt from far away / into a shadowed and deep unity]."
30 Baudelaire, p. 11.
31 "de la convertir en un équivalent spirituel" (III, 879).
32 For a psychoanalytical interpretation of abjection as an effect of the blurring of boundaries between subject and object, see Julia Kristeva, *Les Pouvoirs de l'horreur* (Paris: Seuil, 1981). Like conversion, abjection is operative on religious, psychoanalytic, and artistic levels.
33 *La Première Education sentimentale* (Paris: Seuil, 1963), p. 236. The abbreviated title, 1ère ES, and page numbers in parentheses will refer to this edition of the novel written between 1843 and 1845. Neil Hertz discusses Sartre's reading of Jules's "conversion" in relation to the crisis of Pont-L'Evêque in "Flaubert's Conversion" (*The End of the Line* [New York: Columbia University Press, 1985], chapter 4). For Sartre, Flaubert's conversion is neither religious nor scriptural; it is a "conversion à l'optimisme."
34 1ère ES, 280.
35 In the same entry Flaubert wrote: "Le cygne de Mantoue c'est Virgile [Virgil is the swan of Mantua]" *Dictionnaire des idées reçues, éd. diplomatique*, by Léa Caminiti [Naples and Paris: Liguori and Nizet, 1966], p. 63).
36 Letter dated Jan. 15, 1852, to Colet, *Corr.* II, p. 31.
37 In his introduction to *Bouvard et Pécuchet* (pp. xiv, lxxii), Alberto Cento presents conclusive evidence that refutes countless interpretations of Flaubert's text based on the "comme autrefois." Cento offers no interpretation of why Flaubert's niece might have been impelled to insert

266   The Orient of Style

these words, however. The difference between "ils copient" and "ils copient comme autrefois" is the difference between writing and the copying of ledgers (the jobs both characters left to pursue their scientific projects together).

38 See Cento, ibid., p. xxxvii, and Caminiti, p. 12.
39 See Cento, p. xxxvii, and Caminiti, pp. 12–13.
40 Letter of March 20, 1852, to Colet, *Corr.* II, p. 57.
41 "A Une Passante," Baudelaire, p. 93.
42 Letter dated Aug. 6, 1846, to Colet, *Corr.* I, p. 275.
43 Baudelaire, p. 32.
44 *Confessions*, VII, xvii, 23.
45 Ibid.
46 Ibid.
47 Letter dated Aug. 30, 1846, to Colet, *Corr.* I, p. 321.
48 Ibid.

4 Necropolis and Carnival

1   See "La Vocation Artistique" below.
2   Letter of Jan. 16, 1852, to Colet, *Corr.* II, p. 31.
3   Letter dated July 6, 1852, to Colet, ibid., p. 127.
4   Letter dated Sept. 1, 1852, to Colet, ibid., p. 145.
5   These remarks are included in Flaubert's response to questions asked by Taine. For both questions and answers, see *Correspondance, Supplément 1864–1871* (Paris: Conard, 1954), p. 93.
6   Letter dated Jan. 15, 1853, to Colet, *Corr.* II, p. 238. The term of color occurs often in Flaubert's letters. In 1873, he writes to Mme Roger des Genettes: "On ne sait pas assez tout le mal que donne une phrase bien faite. Mais quelle joie quand tout y est! c'est-à-dire la couleur, le relief, et l'harmonie" (*Correspondance* 7 [Paris: Conard, 1930], p. 111).
7   Letter dated June 6, 1853, to Colet, *Corr.* II, p. 349.
8   Letter written in late December 1875 to George Sand, *Corr.* 7, p. 281.
9   Letter dated Jan. 3, 1853, to Colet, *Corr.* II, p. 229.
10 Ibid., p. 230.
11 Letter dated May 18, 1857, to Mlle Leroyer de Chantepie, *Corr.* II, p. 717.
12 Ibid.
13 Letter dated March 27, 1852, to Colet, ibid., pp. 61–62.
14 Giotto's images play a major role in Proust's aesthetic construction, according to Proust's conception of the artist's vision explicitly developed in his remarks about Flaubert. I will return later to the question of reality and its role in the aesthetics of Flaubert and Proust.
15 Flaubert's correspondence contains numerous examples. In a letter dated Dec. 23, 1853, he writes to Colet: "Le Fait se distille dans la Forme et monte en haut [Fact is distilled in Form and rises up high]"

(*Corr.* II, p. 485). Flaubert writes to George Sand in mid-March 1876: "Enfin, je crois la forme et le fond deux subtilités, deux entités qui n'existent jamais l'une sans l'autre [In the end, I believe that form and content are two subtleties, two entities that never exist without each other]" (*Corr.* 7, p. 290). At the end of his life, Flaubert repeated: "La réalité ne se plie point à l'idéal, mais le confirme [Reality does not give way before the ideal, but confirms it]." (See *Corr.* 8, particularly the letter of May 2, 1880, to Mme Roger des Genettes.)

16 In a letter dated April 18, 1854, Flaubert writes to Colet: "Il faut couper court avec la queue lamartinienne et faire de l'art *impersonnel* [It is necessary to get rid of the Lamartinian tail and create *impersonal* art]" (*Corr.* II, p. 555). In the same letter, Flaubert alludes to the style of *Madame Bovary* in these terms: "où ma personnalité est aussi absente que celle de l'empereur de Chine [my personality is as absent as that of the emperor of China]" (ibid., p. 551).

17 CSB 12–15. This pastiche was originally published in *Le Figaro* (*Supplément littéraire*) on March 14, 1908. In his article/letter on Flaubert, written twelve years later, Proust refers to this text as "un pastiche, détestable d'ailleurs, de Flaubert [a pastiche of Flaubert, and moreover a dreadful one]"(p. 594).

18 *Madame Bovary*, ed. C. Gothot-Mersch. (Paris: Garnier, 1971), p. 343.

19 Ibid., pp. 229–30.

20 *L'education sentimentale*, ed. Edouard Maynial (Paris: Garnier, 1964), p. 50.

21 Letter dated Jan. 3, 1853, *Corr.* II, p. 230.

5 The Sea of Ink

1 Letter of Aug. 14, 1853, *Corr.* II, p. 394.

2 For nineteenth-century Europe, the "Orient" included the Middle East and North Africa. See the chapters entitled "Les Romantiques français et l'Orient" and "L'Orient de Flaubert" in Jean Bruneau, *Le "Conte Oriental" de Flaubert* (Paris: Denoël, 1973), pp. 1–80.

3 Flaubert and Du Camp left Marseille for the Near East in 1849; they travelled through Greece and Italy as well, before Flaubert's return to Croisset in June. In July he resumed relations with Colet and in September he began *Madame Bovary*. Letters from the period through 1851 are quoted from *Corr.* I with extensive notes by Jean Bruneau. See the *Notes de voyages*, annotated by René Dumesnil (Paris: Belles-Lettres, 1948).

4 In his *Souvenirs littéraires* ([Paris: Hâchette, 1882–83], vol. 1), Maxime du Camp states that Flaubert discovered the name of his future character while contemplating the second cataract of the Nile at Djebel-Aboucir. According to Claudine Gothot-Mersch, this story is pure legend. See the excellent introduction to her edition of *Madame Bovary* (Paris: Garnier, 1971), p. viii. Page references to *Madame Bovary* refer

to this edition. The passage from Du Camp's *Souvenirs* may be found in Jean Bruneau's edition of Flaubert's *Oeuvres complètes* (Paris: Seuil, 1964), vol. 1, p. 28. Page references to the *Trois contes* refer to the edition by Edouard Maynial (Paris: Garnier, 1961) and page references to *Salammbô* refer to the edition of 1964 by the same editor and publisher.

5   See my remarks on Baudelaire in "Allegory and Conversion."
6   Letter dated Jan. 16, 1852, to Colet, *Corr.* II, p. 30, and letter of July 6, 1852, to Colet, ibid., p. 127.
7   See Maynial's "Introduction" to the *Trois Contes*, p. ii.
8   Jean Bruneau quotes it in his notes to the sketch "Une Nuit de Don Juan" (in *Oeuvres complètes* II, p. 721) in order to explain that Flaubert gave up the project because its theme resembled that of the first *Tentation* (condemned by Bouilhet and Du Camp prior to the departure for the Orient).
9   Letter dated June 25, 1876, to Turgenev, *Corr.* 7, 1930, p. 312.
10 Letter dated November 14, 1850, written in Constantinople, *Corr.* I, p. 708.
11 Ibid.
12 Ibid., p. 707.
13 Ibid., p. 710.
14 Letter dated Oct. 7, 1850, ibid., p. 695.
15 Ibid.
16 Ibid.
17 *Notes de voyage*, vol. II, p. 585, entry for June 12, 1858.
18 Letter of July 12, 1877, to Madame Roger des Genettes, *Supp.* 4, 1954, p. 6.
19 The first occurrences are in letters dated September and October 1875 to Flaubert's niece, Mme Roger des Genettes, and Turgenev. He also wrote to George Sand about the work. He seems to have completed *La Légende* in March 1876, and his correspondence shows him to have recovered somewhat from the black mood—perhaps the most depressed period of his life—that affected him in 1875.
20 Letter dated June 19, 1876, *Corr.* 7, p. 309.
21 These include the *Légende Dorée*, mentioned throughout the correspondence. See the study and documentation of Benjamin F. Bart and Robert Francis Cook, *The Legendary Sources of Flaubert's Saint Julien* (Toronto: University of Toronto Press, 1977).
22 See *Abbot Suger on the Abbey Church of Saint-Denis and Its Art Treasures* trans. Erwin Panofsky (Princeton: Princeton University Press, 1946).
23 Letter dated Nov. 14, 1850, to Bouilhet, *Corr.* I, p. 708. Further quotations of Flaubert's early sketch refer to this page.
24 Flaubert thought this inability essential to femininity: "Non! mon bon! je n'admets pas que les femmes se connaissent en sentiment. Elles ne le perçoivent jamais que d'une manière *personnelle* et relative [No! my good man! I do not admit that women understand sentiment.

They only perceive it in a *personal* and relative manner]" (Letter of January 11, 1859, to Feydeau, *Corr.* 4, 1927).

25 Pommier-Leleu, p. 457. See also *Madame Bovary, ébauches et fragments*, ed. G. Leleu (Paris: Corti, 1935), II, p. 294.

26 A reading of the correspondence brings to light to what extent Charles's pronouncement to Rodolphe ("C'est la faute de la fatalité! [It was the fault of fatality!]" [355]) resonates in Flaubert's own voice. Despite Rodolphe's cynical cue to the critics to read Charles's statement as his crowning stupidity, Flaubert's frequent evocations of fate impose a more subtle reading of the encounter between lover and husband in the final paragraphs of the novel.

27 Flaubert may have seen Italian paintings of Saint Anthony accompanied by a stag; the iconographic tradition of the Middle Ages and early Renaissance also includes paintings of Saint Eustachius, another hunter, who was converted by a stag wearing a cross between his antlers. For background on the extensive tradition of folklore concerned with saint and stag, see Maynial's introduction and notes to the *Trois Contes*.

28 See Bart and Cook.

29 It is to the irreducible and unpredictable allegory of conversion that results from Flaubert's "other" vision of the stained-glass window turned into writing that Flaubert refers in an otherwise incomprehensible statement (and one that has long mystified critics): "En comparant l'image au texte on se serait dit: 'Je n'y comprends rien. Comment a-t-il tiré ceci de cela?' [The reader comparing the image with the text will think: 'I can't understand a thing. How did he derive the one from the other?']." (Letter dated Feb. 16, 1879, to Charpentier, *Corr.* 8, p. 207.)

30 Maynial reads this as a reference to Flaubert's nervous attacks (n. 182, p. 440).

31 Letter of Feb. 7, 1874, *Corr.* 7, p. 117.

32 *La Tentation de Saint Antoine*, in *Oeuvres* (Paris: Bibl. de la Pléiade, 1951), vol. 1, p. 164.

33 See the letters of Sept. 25 and Oct. 3, 1875, *Corr.* 7 (1930), pp. 262–67, and the letters of Oct. 2 and 3, *Supp.* 3, (1954), pp. 210–13.

34 Letter dated October 3 to Madame Roger des Genettes, *Corr.* 7, p. 267. The same statements appears in other letters.

35 Letter to Bouilhet, May 23, 1855, in *Corr.* II, p. 575, and letter to Colet, Dec. 16, 1852, ibid., p. 208.

36 March 25, 1852, ibid., pp. 278–79.

37 A genetic study including commentary about the "undecidable" status of parody and symbolism in *La Légende* gives evidence of the ways Flaubert's text goes beyond the dimensions of medieval Romanticism. See Pierre-Marc de Biasi, "L'élaboration du problématique dans *La Légende de Saint Julien l'Hospitalier*," in *Flaubert à l'oeuvre* (Paris: Flammarion, 1980), pp. 69–82.

38 For Sartre, the object of Flaubertian conversion is optimism. Loss and suffering are assimilated into the rule of "Qui perd gagne [Loser take all]." In this sense, it is perhaps ironic testament to psychoanalysis that the fine grain of Sartre's fantasmatic obsession with Flaubert leads him to illustrate the limits of intelligent psychology. The conflict between the heights of fantasy and the depths of ideology marks every page of *L'Idiot de la famille* (Paris: Gallimard, 1971). For Sartre's discussion of the figure of Julien, see vol. 3, pp. 2106–36.
39 *La Cathédrale* (Paris: Livre de Poche, 1966), p. 282. See Dina Sherzer, "Narrative Figures in *La Légende de Saint Julien l'Hospitalier*," *Genre* VII, no. 1 (March 1974), pp. 54–70.
40 This formula recalls the begetting of Cain, interpreted in Daniel Sibony, *L'Autre incastrable* (Paris: Seuil, 1978).
41 For a reading of the intersection between glance and speech partly concerned with these prophecies, see Michael Issacharoff, *L'Espace et la nouvelle* (Paris: Corti, 1976), pp. 40–48.
42 Criticism of the story tends to emphasize this parallelism. See, for example, Frederic J. Shepler, "La Mort et la rédemption dans les *Trois contes* de Flaubert," *Neophilologus* 56 (Oct. 1972), pp. 407–16.
43 Letter dated April 24, 1852, to Colet, *Corr.* II, p. 75.
44 Letter of Dec. 14, 1853, to Colet, ibid., p. 478.
45 Letter of Aug. 6, 1846, to Colet, *Corr.* I, p. 276 and letter of April 24, 1852, to Colet, *Corr.* II, p. 75.
46 *Corr.* II, p. 75.
47 Letter of Aug. 6, 1846, *Corr.* I, p. 276.
48 Letter to Colet, Easter Sunday, 1853, *Corr.* II, p. 280.
49 Letter dated July 9, 1875, to Flaubert's niece, ibid., p. 245.
50 Letter dated Aug. 26, 1853, to Colet, ibid., p. 415.
51 See *La Violence et le sacré* (Paris: Grasset, 1972) and *Des Choses cachées depuis la fondation du monde* (Paris: Grasset, 1978).
52 One of the finest examples of Flamboyant Gothic is the Church of Saint-Maclou in Rouen, not far from the cathedral.
53 The femininity of sentiment recalls Flaubert's remark to Feydeau, in a letter dated Jan. 11, 1859, *Corr.* 4, 1927, quoted earlier.
54 Letter dated Aug. 26, 1853, to Colet, *Corr.* II, p. 415.
55 Letter of Dec. 23, 1853, to Colet, ibid., p. 483.
56 Letter dated Aug. 21, 1853, to Colet, ibid., p. 403.
57 Letter of Sept. 30, 1855, to Bouilhet, ibid., p. 599.
58 Letter of Sept. 17, 1847, to Colet, *Corr.* I, p. 471.
59 Letter of March 27, 1853, to Colet, *Corr.* II, pp. 282, 284.
60 Letter of July 11, 1858, to Mlle Leroyer de Chantepie, *Corr.* II, p. 822.
61 *Corr.* I, p. 709.
62 "En revenir à l'antiquité, c'est déjà fait. Au moyen âge, c'est déjà fait. —Reste le Présent [Return to antiquity, it has been done already. To the Middle Ages, done already.—The Present remains] (ibid.)."
63 Letter dated Dec. 27, 1852, to Colet, *Corr.* II, p. 218.

64 Ibid.
65 Ibid., p. 219.
66 Letter of October 1858 to Feydeau, ibid., p. 837.
67 Letter of Aug. 14, 1853, ibid., p. 395.
68 For a different interpretation of the final sentences (135), see Shoshana Felman, "Flaubert's Signature: *The Legend of St. Julian the Hospitable*," in *Flaubert and Postmodernism*, eds. Naomi Schor and Henry F. Majewski (Lincoln: University of Nebraska Press, 1984), pp. 46–75.
69 Letter of May 23, 1855, to Bouilhet, *Corr.* II, p. 575.
70 Letter of Feb. 16, 1879, *Corr.* 8, p. 207.
71 Letter dated Sept. 8, 1860, to Amédée Pommier. *Corr.* 4, 1927, p. 397.
72 See *Oeuvres complètes*, vol. 2, p. 460. Benjamin F. Bart discusses it in "Psyche into Myth: Humanity and Animality in Flaubert," *Kentucky Romance Quarterly* 20, no. 3 (1973), pp. 317–42. His interpretation of the dream and its role differs from my own.
73 *Oeuvres complètes*, vol. 2, p. 460.
74 Letter of June 27, 1855, *Corr.* II, p. 584.
75 Letter of Aug. 21, 1853, to Colet, ibid., p. 402.

6 Crimson and Diamonds

1 Letter from Flaubert to Sainte-Beuve, quoted in the dossier to *Salammbô*, p. 356.
2 Quotations from *Salammbô* in parentheses in the text will be taken from the edition by Edouard Maynial (Paris: Garnier, 1961), including Flaubert's replies to Sainte-Beuve and Froehner. Flaubert included these defenses of his novel, as well as a letter from Sainte-Beuve, in the editions following 1874, when Lévy's publication rights expired and Flaubert gave the novel to Charpentier. See René Dumesnil's introduction in *Oeuvres* (Paris: Bibl. de la Pléiade, 1951), p. 705.
3 In this context, the reception of Flaubert's novels can be read as a symptom of the effects created by different forms of allegory.
4 See Maynial's introduction, p. v.
5 Letter of July 11, 1858, to Mlle Leroyer de Chantepie, *Corr.* II, p 822.
6 See the discussion of these moments in "Autobiographies of Style."
7 This does not truly occur in *La Tentation* because Flaubert's Saint Antoine is represented as living in a world of fantasy and theology much more than in a historical context. The latter, as "world" versus "sainthood," is reduced, on the one hand, to abjection rendered through absorption and estrangement (the realm of fantasy), and on the other, to the stylite's point—the desolate fraction of earth that throughout the book only tenuously supports Saint Antoine's weight.
8 Ibid., pp. 355–56.
9 I will return to the relation of modernity and allegory in the discussion of Flaubert and Proust seen in light of Benjamin's categories in the last section of this study.

10 Jean Pommier, in "La Muse du département" (*L'Année Balzacienne*, [1961], vol. 3, pp. 192–220), notes an interesting parallel between Flaubert's subtitle, "Moeurs de province," and *La Comédie humaine* (ibid., p. 203).
11 See, for example, the letter dated November 1862 to Ernest Renan, *Supp.*, p. 302, and the letter dated January 1863 to Laure de Maupassant, *Corr.* 5, p. 73.
12 For evidence of the shifts in the title, see Flaubert's correspondence between 1857 and 1862 in the volumes cited earlier and in Maynial's edition of the novel, p. 377.
13 See the letter of July 15, 1861, to Feydeau in *Corr.* 4, p. 441, and the letter of Aug. 1, 1861, to Jules Duplan, *Supp.*, p. 269.
14 See the letter to Sainte-Beuve, pp. 355, 357.
15 Letter dated Nov. 29, 1859, to Feydeau, *Corr.* 4, p. 348.
16 See *Charles Baudelaire*.
17 Letter dated Sept. 19, 1852, to Colet, *Corr.* II, p. 159.
18 Ibid.
19 I will return to this question in the final chapter.
20 See Flaubert's comments to Sainte-Beuve, who directed his protest against Salammbô's embrace of the snake in "Le Serpent" (360). Flaubert may have been particularly cautious because of the trial concerning *Madame Bovary*.
21 See Sima Godfrey, "The Fabrication of *Salammbô*: The Surface of the Veil," *MLN* 95:4 (1980), pp. 1005–16.
22 "Le rôle des cités antiques dans Baudelaire et de la couleur écarlate qu'elle mettent çà et là dans son oeuvre [The role of ancient cities in Baudelaire and the touches of scarlet color that they leave here and there in his oeuvre]" ("A Propos de Baudelaire," CSB 633). See Flaubert's letter of Oct. 3, 1857, to Jules Duplan: "J'en suis arrivé, dans mon premier chapitre, à ma petite femme. J'astique son costume, ce qui m'amuse: . . . . Je me vautre comme un cochon sur les pierreries dont je l'entoure. Je crois que le mot pourpre ou diamant est à chaque phrase de mon livre. Quel galon! mais j'en retirerai. [I have reached, in my first chapter, my little woman. I'm fixing up her costume, it amuses me: . . . . I wallow like a pig in the gemstones that I am putting all around her. I suspect that the word crimson or diamond is in every sentence of my book. Such ornaments and trimmings! but I will take some of them off]."
23 Letter of Oct. 8, 1857, to Bouilhet, *Corr.* II, p. 769.
24 Letter of Sept. 8, 1860, to Amédée Pommier, *Corr.* II, p. 397, and letter dated the end of November 1857 to Feydeau, ibid., p. 782.
25 Letter of Nov. 4, 1857, to Mlle Leroyer de Chantepie, *Corr.* II, p. 773.
26 Letter to Mlle Leroyer de Chantepie, ibid.
27 Letter dated the end of February 1861 to Feydeau, *Corr.* 4, p. 425.
28 Letter of March 25, 1846, *Corr.* I, p. 258.
29 In the section on Proust I will examine this structure of allegory through

a reading of "'Les Vices et les Vertus' de Padoue et de Combray."
30 Letter of Sept. 13, 1852, to Colet, *Corr.* II, p. 157.
31 Letter of Nov. 4, 1857 to Mlle Leroyer de Chantepie, *Corr.* II, p. 773.
32 Letter of Dec. 27, 1852, to Colet, *Corr.* II, p. 218.
33 *Madame Bovary*, p. 352. According to Feydeau, Flaubert was called "le sire de Vaufrylard" in the salon of Madame Sabatier. See Serge Cigada, "Un nuovo documento su *Madame Bovary*: Il pittore Vaufrylard," *Rivista di letterature moderne e comparate* (March 1958), pp. 30–34.
34 *Schriften*, vol. 1, p. 482, *Zentralpark* 20.
35 Ibid., p. 489, *Zentralpark* 36.
36 For Benjamin's concept of "das Ausdruckslose," or "Ausdruckslosigkeit," see his interpretation of the death's head in *Gesammelte Schriften* IV.1, p. 112. He also discusses "the depth of the inexpressive in tragedies" in his essay on Molière's *Malade imaginaire*.
37 Letter of Aug. 14, 1853, to Colet, *Corr.* II, p. 392.
38 See the Garnier edition of *Madame Bovary* for a reproduction of this drawing that appeared in the issue of September 5–12, 1869. It shows the author holding a magnifying glass in his right hand and the uplifted heart impaled on a knife in the other; beneath the dripping heart is the inkwell. Lying on a table at the left can be seen a child-sized pair of exposed legs in petticoat and boots.
39 Letter dated July 3, 1852, to Colet, *Corr.* II, p. 124.
40 Letter of Sept. 7, 1853, to Colet, *Corr* II, p. 427.
41 Letter of Dec. 27, 1852, to Colet, *Corr.* II, p. 218.
42 "Flaubert et la phrase," in *Le degré zéro de l'écriture, suivi de Nouveaux essais critiques* (Paris: Seuil, 1972), pp. 135–44.
43 *Après Freud* (Paris: Gallimard, 1968), "La Maladie de Flaubert," pp. 293–329.
44 Letter dated Dec. 12, 1853, to Colet, *Corr.* II, p. 483.
45 Letter of Sept. 16, 1853, *Corr.* II, p. 431.

7 Passing Forms

1 My reading of "Le Cygne" in "The Allegory of Conversion" and the discussion of allegory in Baudelaire appear to confirm the extraordinary identification made by Flaubert between his oeuvre and that of his contemporary. Unlike Flaubert's other major attachments to contemporary writers—Colet, the young Du Camp, Bouilhet, Feydeau, the Goncourts, and so on—Flaubert's identification with Baudelaire was almost exclusively literary. They met and corresponded very little. I will return later to the relation between the aesthetics of Baudelaire and Flaubert.
2 See the epigraph of "The Image of Modernity."
3 For a discussion of Proust's new style, see especially the following chapter, "La Charité de Giotto," and the final chapter.
4 See "Necropolis and Carnival" above.

5   All quotations from *A la recherche du temps perdu* are taken from the edition by Pierre Clarac and André Ferré (Paris: Bibliothèque de la Pléiade, Gallimard, 1954) and indicated by volume and page in parentheses within the text.
6   See "The Allegory of Conversion" above.
7   Letter dated Jan. 21, 1847, to Colet, *Corr.* I, p. 431.
8   *Oeuvres complètes*, vol. 1, p. 47.
9   Ibid., vol. 1, p. 172.
10 Ibid., vol. 1, p. 139.
11 Marcel Muller analyzes what may be the central difficulty in interpreting Proust's novel in his book, *Les Voix narratives dans la "Recherche du temps perdu"* (Geneva: Librairie Droz, 1965). The author's original and subtle vocabulary of critical distinctions (organized around the key terms of "la dissimulation," "le flagrant délit," "l'aveu") points toward the dimension of confession spotlit by Augustine and darkened in Proustian shadows.
12 P. 100.
13 In *Proust and the Art of Love* (New York: Columbia University Press, 1980), J. E. Rivers offers a useful discussion of Proust's political contexts. See Jeffrey Mehlman's incisive remarks on "dejudaized Judaism" (an epithet coined by J. E. van Praag and repeated by Hannah Arendt) in "Literature and Collaboration: Benoist-Méchin's Return to Proust," *MLN* 98 (1983), pp. 968–82.
14 *Correspondance de Marcel Proust*, ed. Philip Kolb (Paris: Plon, 1976), vol. II, p. 66. For an interpretation of this letter, see Jean Recanati, *Profils Juifs de Marcel Proust* (Paris: Buchet/Caster, 1979), chapter 1.
15 Even a cursory reading of Proust's correspondence (to say nothing of his work on Ruskin or his fiction) reveals his close reading of the Bible. See Albert Mingelgrün, *Thèmes et structures bibliques dans l'oeuvre de Marcel Proust* (Lausanne: L'Age d'homme, 1978), for an illuminating study of biblical stylistics in the *Recherche*.
16 See Paul de Man, *Allegories of Reading* (New Haven: Yale University Press, 1979), chapter 3, and Richard A. Macksey, "Proust on the Margins of Ruskin," in *The Ruskin Polygon*, eds. J. D. Hunt and F. M. Holland (Manchester: University of Manchester Press, 1981), pp. 172–97.
17 Mehlman discusses the Proustian exodus in terms of French history. See "Literature and Collaboration."
18 Proust's meditation on idolatry is threaded throughout many of his writings on Ruskin. See *Pastiches et mélanges* in *Contre Sainte-Beuve*, eds. Pierre Clarac and Yves Sandre (Paris: Bibliothèque de la Pléiade, Gallimard, 1971). For an interpretation of Proust's apprenticeship to Ruskin, see Richard A. Macksey's "Proust on the Margins of Ruskin," and his "'Conclusions' et 'Incitations': Proust à la recherche de Ruskin," *MLN* 96 (1981), pp. 1113–19.
19 See Octave Mannoni, *Clefs pour l'imaginaire ou l'Autre Scène* (Paris: Seuil, 1969), pp. 100–114.

20 *Enarrationes in Psalmos*, CXLIV, 13. See also Jean-Marie Le Blond, *Les Conversions de Saint Augustin* (Paris: Aubier, 1950).
21 Architecture of Time Dialectics and Structure," in *Proust*, ed. René Girard (Englewood Cliffs, N.J.: Prentice-Hall, 1962), p. 109.
22 "Zum Bilde Prousts," in Walter Benjamin, *Schriften II* (Frankfurt am Main: Suhrkamp Verlag, 1955), p. 143.
23 Ibid., p. 143.
24 Ibid.
25 Ibid., p. 143.
26 Ibid. The two Ways ("Côtés") meet in the retrospective arrangement of a final evocation, a last look back: remembered childhood waves to the aging ruins of allegorizing memory. Under the influence of this vision of a now invisible geography, the landscape suddenly rises up to reveal its identity. Mirrored in the instant, the clasping of the Ways recalls the moments in *La Légende* when Julien sees the image of his father in the water. In a moment of "déchiffrage," "vérité" is unmasked by its "figure": both Julien and Proust's narrator renounce death, and turn to the sea of ink.
27 Ibid., p. 142.
28 Ibid., p. 143.
29 Ibid.
30 Letter to Jean-Louis Vaudoyer, May 2, 1921 (III, 1277). Proust saw the painting in 1902 and admired it once again in 1921, in the company of Vaudoyer; afterwards, Vaudoyer marked the occasion by taking pictures of Proust—the final photographs. On his deathbed, Proust asked for the pages concerning Bergotte's death. Representation moves in two directions at once: "art" may portray "life," but the effects of the oeuvre on life ("c'était lui qui parlait pour elle")—the effect of portrayal, representation, and the silence it leaves behind it—infiltrate life with the artifices of allegory and the ruses of fiction. The complicated spiral of "art" and "life" finds a more recent echo in Paul de Man's "Autobiography as De-facement," *MLN* 94 (1979), pp. 919–30, reprinted in *The Rhetoric of Romanticism*.
31 See Georges Bataille, *La littérature et le mal* in *Oeuvres complètes IX* (Paris: NRF, Gallimard, 1970), pp. 919–30.
32 J. E. Rivers, *Proust and the Art of Love*.
33 See Jean Recanati, *Profils Juifs de Marcel Proust* (Paris: Buchet-Castel, 1979); Jeffrey Mehlman, "Literature and Collaboration," *MLN* 98 (1983), pp. 968–82.
34 In his discussion of the influence of Gothic art on Proust's novel, Marcel Muller analyzes Swann's Mosaic identity. See *Préfiguration et structure romanesque dans "A La Recherche du temps perdu"* (Lexington, Mass.: French Forum, 1979).
35 At the matinée the narrator notes that Bloch has changed his name in an attempt to pass through aristocratic veto of his Jewish origin (III, 952).
36 See Recanati, chapter 2.

8 La Charité de Giotto

1. Bernard Brun, "Le *Temps retrouvé* dans les avant-textes de Combray," *Bulletin des Informations Proustiennes* 12 (1981), p. 20.
2. Ibid.
3. For a discussion of Proust's relationship to Ruskin, see Richard A. Macksey, "Proust on the Margins of Ruskin," in *The Ruskin Polygon*, eds. J. D. Hunt and F. M. Holland (Manchester: University of Manchester Press, 1981), and, by the same author, "'Conclusions' et 'Incitations': Proust à la Recherche de Ruskin," *MLN* 96 (1981), pp. 1113–19. For a discussion of Proust's correspondence with Emile Mâle, see Richard Bales, *Proust and the Middle Ages* (Geneva: Librairie Droz, 1975).
4. *En mémoire des églises assassinées*, III. *John Ruskin*, in *Contre Sainte-Beuve*, précédé de *Pastiches et mélanges* et suivi de *Essais et articles*, ed. P. Clarac with Y. Sandre (Paris: Gallimard, 1971), p. 115.
5. The reading of the cathedral as a visible representation of the biblical text is crucial for Proust, following Mâle and Ruskin. Spectacular examples and analyses according to this reading can be found in Mâle's *L'Art religieux du XIIIe siècle en France* (Paris: Livre de poche, 1961) and in Ruskin's works, e.g., *The Bible of Amiens*, translated by Proust. In the *Recherche*, Elstir's remarks about cathedrals (addressed to the young narrator) are the most explicit references to this aspect of the theories of Mâle and Ruskin, but this reading is a touchstone of Proust's general aesthetic.
6. Proust's letters to Marie Nordlinger indicate the important literary investment represented by Proust's "apprenticeship" to Ruskin. The work on Ruskin functions as a bridge leading to Proust's mature writing. See especially *Correspondance de Marcel Proust*, ed. Phillip Kolb (Paris: Plon, 1970), vol. 4. Kolb describes 1904 as "l'année Ruskin par excellence" for Proust (ibid., p. vi).
7. N.A.Fr. 16733, p. 117.
8. In the sacrament, as in Proust's interpretation of allegory, the presence of the Word is *real*. See my earlier discussion of Proust's terms of "conversion" and "transubstantiation." For a different interpretation of the latter term, see Genette's "Proust Palimpseste," in *Figures I* (Paris: Seuil, 1966).
9. See Jacques Lacan, *Séminaire XX, Encore* (Paris: Seuil, 1975), pp. 29–34, 131, and *R.S.I.* (supposedly forthcoming as Séminaire XXII) in *Ornicar?* (Paris: Seuil, n.d.). The Real eludes conceptualization and forms a "gap" in the Imaginary and Symbolic. Lacan's suggestions concerning sexuality as the link between life and death via reproduction, and the woman as "pas-toute" imply that insofar as femininity in psychoanalysis means maternity and maternity is the evidence that woman is "pas-toute" or is lacking something by virtue of possessing an absence that manifests itself as "folle, énigmatique" (131)—the description of feminine jouissance—the "trou" of jouissance is inde-

pendent of, and in some sense opposed to, the "trou" of sexual reproduction seen as bearer of the Real.
10 In the introduction to his translation of Ruskin's *La Bible d'Amiens*, Proust describes the statues of the West porch of Amiens Cathedral: "Au-dessous de la Foi est l'Idolâtrie adorant un monstre [Below Faith is Idolatry worshiping a monster]" (CSB 97).
11 See I, 124, for the disappearance of Charity, and III, 567–91, for the erasure of Swann's name and memory after his death.
12 N.A.Fr. 16733, p. 116.
13 The following paragraphs owe much to Brun, pp. 18–20.
14 See Kazuyoshi Yoshikawa, *Etudes sur la genèse de 'La Prisonnière' d'après des brouillons inédits* (Paris: Sorbonne, 1976), unpublished thesis.
15 Here as in the interpretation of the Giotto reproduction, an interpretive reading brings into view a level of textual complexity not available within the framework of genetic studies.
16 N.A.Fr. 16733 (116–22).
17 See Cahiers 47, 48, 50. Jo Yoshida, *Proust contre Ruskin: la genèse de deux voyages dans la 'Recherche' d'après des brouillons inédits* (Paris: Sorbonne, 1978), unpublished thesis.
18 Bernard Brun posits the existence of intermediary and preceding manuscripts that have not yet been found.
19 N.A.Fr. 16703 (16 ff.)
20 Bernard Brun, p. 20.
21 The disappearance and reappearance of this beautiful coat and its role in the aesthetics of allegory recall Salammbô and the cloak of Tanit. See "Crimson and Diamonds."
22 I am extending Lacan's "instance de la lettre" from the field of the unconscious to the domain of aesthetic allegory. This distinction may be less one of operation than of effect, since the productions of the unconscious do not necessarily include the element of violence implicit in the seductions of allegory.

9 La Vocation Artistique

1 This quotation from Proust's *Cahiers* is taken from J. M. Cocking, *Proust: Collected Essays on the Writer and His Art* (Cambridge: Cambridge University Press, 1982), pp. 127–28.
2 See Richard Macksey, "The Architecture of Time: Dialectics and Structure," in *Proust: A Collection of Critical Essays*, ed. René Girard, pp. 104–21.
3 See "Necropolis and Carnival" above, for an interpretation of Proust's reading of Flaubert.
4 In Proust's own time, another writer influenced by Flaubert was reducing the unit of construction even further. In *Finnegans Wake*, and on a more modest level in *Ulysses* before it, James Joyce transgressed the limits of the word itself and made it the minimal unit of prose con-

struction. See my book, *Joyce's Catholic Comedy of Language*.
5   This episode and especially its "allitération perpétuelle" have been extensively studied in the context of Proust's "contenant"/"contenu" opposition. (See Genette, *Figures III* (Paris: Seuil, 1972), pp. 53–54; Jean-Pierre Richard, *Proust et le monde sensible* (Paris: Seuil, 1974), p. 21; Joan Rosasco, "Aux sources de la Vivonne," in *Recherche de Proust*, pp. 142–62; Ph. Lejeune, "Les Carafes de la Vivonne," ibid., pp. 162–96.) For Genette and others, it would be impossible to connect this passage with Proust's statements on style and analogy, because the presence of metaphor would appear to be subsumed by the dominant figure of metonymy: Proust's manuscripts have been quoted to support this conclusion. Two questions have not been asked, however: what is the immediate context of the Vivonne episode, and what is the role of this passage within the aesthetic frame of the *Recherche*?
6   See Genette, p. 54.
7   This is confirmed by the manuscript passages. See Rosasco.
8   The image of the fishing rod or line enters into at least two metaphorical lines of Proustian thought: the discourse of desire (the lure of seduction and the catch) and the "lignes de fond" that will extend the water image into the interiority of the subject. Through an act of "translation," the "oeuvre d'art" will be drawn out of the self and its invisible world.
9   A classic example of this is the replacement of the tenor by the vehicle, or vice versa, in an articulated metaphor. Lacan borrows Jakobson's concept of the metaphorical function of language in order to posit metaphor as a model for the fall and rise (of language) that structures the relation between consciousness and the unconscious. See "Fonction et champ de la parole et du langage dans l'inconscient," in *Ecrits* (Paris: Seuil, 1966).
10 "Tu excitas, ut laudare te delectet, quia fecisti nos ad te" (*Confessions*, I, 1). The continuation of this passage anticipates the Flaubertian-Proustian heart that will be veiled by the modern "adieu au personnel" and its fictions: 'And our heart is unquiet as long as it does not rest in you."
11 See "Passing Forms" above.
12 Recent studies of Proust's style tend to be more specialized, partly because of the extensive body of Proust criticism since the time of Curtius and Spitzer, and partly because of the developments in linguistics and narratology. For example, Genette's work in *Figures II* and *Figures III* is based on the element of "Récit" in Proust's text, thus implying the exclusion of "prose poétique" in favor of a more restricted notion of style.
13 "Le Style de Marcel Proust," in Leo Spitzer, *Etudes de style* (Paris: Tel, 1980), p. 397. Further references to this work will be found in parentheses in the text.
14 Page numbers refer to Stephen Ullmann, *The Image in the Modern*

French Novel (New York: Barnes and Noble, 1963). Ullmann discusses Proust's image in an earlier work, *Style in the French Novel* (Cambridge: Cambridge University Press, 1957), pp. 189–209.
15 See *Proust* (Paris: Gallimard, 1943).
16 III, 871. See the final section of this chapter, entitled "Félicité, ravissement, beauté."
17 For this expression, see *Oeuvres complètes* (Paris: Seuil, 1964), vol. 2, p. 720.
18 See "La Charité de Giotto" above.
19 Letter of Oct. 25, 1853, to Colet, *Corr.* II, p. 456.
20 Letter of Jan. 16, 1852, to Colet, *Corr.* II, p. 31.
21 See Pichois's dossier in Baudelaire's *Oeuvres complètes*, pp. 1293–1305. Pichois writes that the elements of this new writing, including the aesthetic encounters between truth and beauty, poetry and realism, the eternal and the ordinary, and so on, were completely different from the writings of Chateaubriand and his generation (pp. 1303–4). He quotes Baudelaire: "J'associerai l'effrayant avec le bouffon, et même la tendresse avec la haine [I will associate the frightful with the comic, and even tenderness with hatred]."
22 Ibid., p. 1259.
23 See ibid., p. 1295.
24 Letter of April 24, 1852, to Colet, *Corr.* II, p. 75.
25 Letter of March 27, 1853, to Colet, *Corr.* II, p. 287.
26 *Oeuvres complètes*, vol. 1, pp. 275–76.
27 Ibid., p. 275.
28 Ibid., p. 276.
29 Proust describes some of Baudelaire's verse as "immense, déroulé" (CSB 252). The "anneaux" he mentions may include a reference to the preface of *Le Spleen de Paris*, where the author describes his work as the "tronçons" of a serpent. This final section of Proust's novel includes a pertinent remark about impersonality in Flaubert: "Ce n'est pas ... son goût pour la bourgeoisie ... qui a fait choisir à Flaubert comme sujets ceux de *Madame Bovary* et de *L'Education sentimentale* [It is not ... Flaubert's taste for the bourgeoisie ... that led him to choose the subjects of *Madame Bovary* and *L'Education sentimentale*]" (III, 888).
30 Genette quotes Proust's sentence in an attempt to argue against Proust's disregard of metonymy as "a very important slip [lapsus]" (*Figures III*, p. 31).
31 Milton Hindus's famous judgment of "too much of a muchness" was taken up in the Proust criticism of Ullmann and others.
32 See the epigraph to "Autobiographies of Style" above.
33 See "Passing Forms" above.
34 In "A Propos de Baudelaire," the Wagner allusion allows Proust to make an explicit identification with Baudelaire through the influence of opera on poetic style. The reference to Carpaccio operates a more

elusive identification with Ruskin, because he "rediscovered" the neglected Venetian allegorist. It is certainly not by chance that Venice (the site of Proust's own Ruskinian pilgrimage) is included in the allegorical folds of this sentence; it is not only an early hint of the Combray-Venice architecture discussed earlier, but it also evokes the lights and colors of style itself, inscribed by the painter of memory in a prefiguration of "le vernis des maîtres."

35 "Carnation," the mystical color of a flower that appears in an early version of the Petite Madeleine and its "acte magique" (CSB 212), recalls the incarnation—the theological mystery that will lead to resurrection through the Virgin. Like many theologians and mystics, Proust takes up these terms in an aesthetic sense.

36 ES, part III, chapter 6, p. 419.

37 Proust indirectly indicates the connection between the sublime speech in L'Education sentimentale and Flaubert's own vocabulary when he remarks of the exchange between the two characters, "c'est un peu *trop bien* pour une conversation entre Frédéric et Madame Arnoux. Mais, Flaubert, si au lieu de ses personnages c'était lui qui avait parlé, n'aurait pas trouvé beaucoup mieux [It is a little *too refined* for a conversation between Frédéric and Mme Arnoux. But Flaubert, if instead of his characters he himself had spoken, would not have found anything much better]" (CSB 587).

38 Letter of Oct. 8, 1846, to Colet, *Corr.* I, p. 380.

39 Letter of Dec. 23, 1853, to Colet, *Corr.* II, p. 483.

40 Gabrielle Leleu and Jean Pommier, *Madame Bovary, nouvelle version* (Paris: Corti, 1949), p. 383.

41 See "The Sea of Ink" above.

Bibliography

Primary Works

Baudelaire, Charles. *Oeuvres complètes*. Ed. Claude Pichois. Paris: Bibliothèque de la Pléiade, 1975 and 1976.
Flaubert, Gustave. *Oeuvres complètes*. 13 vols. Paris: Conard, 1910–1916.
———. *Correspondance. Supplément*. 4 vols. Paris: Conard, 1954.
———. *Oeuvres complètes*. Paris: Seuil, 1964.
———. *Oeuvres complètes*. Ed. Maurice Bardèche. 16 vols. Paris: Club de L'Honnête Homme, 1971–75.
———. *Correspondance*. Ed. Jean Bruneau. 2 vols. Paris: Bibliothèque de la Pléiade, 1973 and 1980.
———. *Oeuvres*. Eds. Albert Thibaudet and René Dumesnil. 2 vols. Paris: Bibliothèque de la Pléiade, 1951.
———. *La Première Education sentimentale*. Paris: Seuil, 1963.
———. *Madame Bovary*. Ed. Claudine Gothot-Mersch. Paris: Garnier, 1971.
———. *Salammbô*. Ed. Edouard Maynial. Paris: Garnier, 1961.
———. *L'Education sentimentale*. Ed. Edouard Maynial. Paris: Garnier, 1964.
———. *Les Trois Contes*. Ed. Edouard Maynial. Paris: Garnier, 1961.
———. *Bouvard et Pécuchet, édition critique*. Ed. Alberto Cento. Naples and Paris: Istituto Universitario Orientale and A.G. Nizet, 1964.
———. *Dictionnaire des idées reçues, édition diplomatique*. Ed. Léa Caminiti. Naples and Paris: Liguori and A.G. Nizet, 1966.
———. *Madame Bovary, nouvelle version*. Eds. Jean Pommier and Gabrielle Leleu. Paris: Corti, 1949.
———. *Notes de voyages*. Ed. René Dumesnil. Paris: Belles Lettres, 1948.
Huysmans, J. K. *La Cathédrale*. Paris: Livre de Poche, 1966.
Proust, Marcel. *A la recherche du temps perdu*. Eds. Pierre Clarac and André Ferré. Paris: Bibliothèque de la Pléiade, 1954.
———. *Jean Santeuil précédé de Les Plaisirs et les jours*. Ed. Pierre Clarac. Paris: Bibliothèque de la Pléiade, 1971.

———. *Contre Sainte-Beuve* précédé de *Pastiches et Mélanges* et suivi de *Essais et articles.* Ed. Pierre Clarac. Paris: Bibliothèque de la Pléïade, 1971.
———. *Correspondance générale de Marcel Proust.* 6 vols. Paris: Plon, 1930–36.
———. *Correspondance.* Ed. Philip Kolb. Paris: Plon, 1970.
———. *Lettres à André Gide.* Neuchâtel and Paris: Ides et Calendes, 1949.
———. *Correspondance avec sa mère.* Paris: Plon, 1953.
———. *Marcel Proust à Jacques Rivière.* Paris: Plon, 1955.
———. Ruskin, John. *La Bible d'Amiens. Traductions, notes, et préface par Marcel Proust.* Paris: Mercure de France, 1926.
———. *Sésame et les lys. Traductions, notes, et préface par Marcel Proust.* Paris: Mercure de France, 1935.
———. *Textes retrouvés, avec une Bibliographie des Publications de Proust.* Eds. Philip Kolb and Larkin B. Price. Urbana: University of Illinois Press, 1968.
———. *Matinée chez la Princesse de Guermantes. Cahiers du Temps Retrouvé.* Critical edition by Henri Bonnet and Bernard Brun. Paris: Gallimard, 1982.

Secondary Works

Abbot Suger on the Abbey Church of Saint Denis and its Art Treasures. Trans. Erwin Panofsky. Princeton: Princeton University Press, 1946.
Agulhon, M., ed. *Histoire et langage dans "L'Education Sentimentale."* Paris: Sedes, 1981.
Albaret, Céleste, and Belmont, Georges. *Monsieur Proust.* Paris: Laffont, 1973.
L'Arc, no. 79 (1980). *Flaubert.*
Auerbach, Erich. *Mimesis, The Representation of Reality in Western Literature.* Trans. by W. R. Trask. Princeton: Princeton University Press, 1973.
———. *Scenes from the Drama of European Literature.* Minneapolis: University of Minnesota Press, 1984.
Augustine, Saint. *Les Confessions.* Paris: Desclée de Brouwer, 1955.
———. *De Trinitate.* Paris: Desclée de Brouwer, 1955.
———. *Sermons pour la Pâque.* Ed. Suzanne Poque. Paris: Cerf, 1966.
Autret, Jean. *L'Influence de Ruskin sur la vie, les idées, et l'oeuvre de Marcel Proust.* Geneva: Droz, 1955.
Bales, Richard. *Proust and the Middle Ages.* Geneva: Droz, 1975.
Bart, Benjamin F., ed. *Madame Bovary and the Critics.* New York: New York University Press, 1966.
———. *Flaubert.* Syracuse: Syracuse University Press, 1967.
———. "Psyche into Myth: Humanity and Animality in Flaubert." *Kentucky Romance Quarterly* 20, no. 3 (1973), pp. 317–42.
——— and Cook, Robert Francis. *The Legendary Sources of Flaubert's Saint*

Julien. Toronto: University of Toronto Press, 1977.
Barthes, Roland. *Le Degré zéro de l'écriture and Nouveaux Essais critiques.* Paris: Seuil, 1953 and 1972.
———. *Fragments d'un discours amoureux.* Paris: Seuil, 1977.
———. *Le Bruissement de la langue.* Paris: Seuil, 1984.
Bataille, Georges. *La Littérature et le mal.* Vol. 9 of *Oeuvres complètes.* Paris: Gallimard, 1979.
Beaumont, E. M., J. M. Cocking, and J. Cruickshank, eds. *Order and Adventure in Post-Romantic French Poetry.* Oxford: Blackwell, 1982.
Beckett, Samuel. *Proust.* New York: Grove Press, 1970.
Bem, Jeanne. *Désir et savoir dans l'oeuvre de Flaubert: Etudes de la Tentation de Saint Antoine.* Neuchâtel: La Baconnière, 1979.
Benjamin, Walter. *Schriften.* 2 vols. Frankfurt am Main: Suhrkamp. 1955.
———. *Gesammelte Schriften.* Eds. Rolf Tiedemann and Hermann Schweppenhäuser. Frankfurt am Main: Suhrkamp, 1974.
Benveniste, Emile. *Problèmes de linguistique générale.* 2 vols. Paris: Gallimard, 1974.
Bersani, Jacques. *Les Critiques de notre temps et Proust.* Paris: Garnier, 1971.
Bersani, Leo. *Marcel Proust: The Fictions of Life and Art.* New York: Oxford University Press, 1965.
———. *A Future for Astyanax.* New York: Columbia University Press, 1969.
Blanchot, Maurice. *Le Livre à venir.* Paris: Gallimard, 1959.
Bouillard, Henri. *Conversion et grâce chez Saint Thomas d'Aquin.* Paris: Aubier, 1944.
Brée, Germaine. *Du Temps Perdu au temps retrouvé.* Paris: Belles Lettres, 1950.
———. *The World of Marcel Proust.* Boston: Houghton Mifflin, 1966.
Brombert, Victor. *The Novels of Flaubert.* Princeton: Princeton University Press, 1966.
———. "La Première Education sentimentale: Roman de L'Artiste." *Europe,* nos. 485–87 (1969), pp. 22–37.
———. "Le Cygne de Baudelaire: Douleur, Souvenir, Travail." *Etudes Baudelairiennes* 3 (1973), pp. 254–61.
Brun, Bernard. "Le Temps retrouvé dans les avant-textes de Combray." *Bulletin d'Informations Proustiennes* 12 (1981), pp. 16–25.
Bruneau, Jean. *Album Flaubert.* Paris: Gallimard, 1972.
———. *Le "Conte Oriental" de Flaubert.* Paris: Denoël, 1973.
Bruss, Elizabeth W. *Autobiography: The Changing Situation of a Literary Genre.* Baltimore: Johns Hopkins University Press, 1976.
Bucknall, Barbara J. *The Religion of Art in Proust.* Urbana: University of Illinois Press, 1969.
Bulletin d'Informations Proustiennes. Paris: Presses de l'Ecole Normale Supérieure, no. 1 (Spring 1975).
Butor, Michel. *Improvisations sur Flaubert.* Paris: Editions de la Différance, 1984.
Carlut, Charles, ed. *Essais sur Flaubert: En l'honneur du professeur Don Demorest.* Paris: A. G. Nizet, 1968.

Cattaui, Georges, and Philip Kolb, eds. *Entretiens sur Marcel Proust.* Paris: Mouton, 1966.
Cazelles, Henri. "Conversion et Pénitence selon la Bible." *Cahiers Confrontation* 9 (1983), pp. 123–34.
Chambers, Ross. "Simplicité de Coeur et Duplicité Textuelle: Etude d' 'Un Coeur Simple.'" *MLN* 96 (1981), pp. 771–91.
Chantal, René de. *Marcel Proust, critique littéraire.* Montréal: Presses de l'Université, 1967.
Cigada, Serge. "Un nuovo documento su *Madame Bovary*: Il pittore Vaufrylard." *Rivista di letterature moderne e comparate* (1958), pp. 30–34.
Cocking, J. M. *Proust. Collected Essays on the Writer and his Art.* Cambridge: Cambridge University Press, 1982.
Coleman, Elliott. *The Golden Angel.* New York: C. Taylor, 1954.
Compagnon, Antoine. *La Troisième République des lettres.* Paris: Seuil, 1983.
Courcelle, Pierre. "Antécédents autobiographiques des Confessions de Saint Augustin." *Revue de Philologie* 31 (1957), pp. 23–51.
Culler, Jonathan. *Flaubert: The Uses of Uncertainty.* Ithaca: Cornell University Press, 1974.
Danger, Pierre. *Sensations et objets dans le roman de Flaubert.* Paris: A. Colin, 1973.
De Biasi, Pierre-Marc. "L'Elaboration du problématique dans *La Légende de Saint Julien L'Hospitalier.*" In *Flaubert à l'oeuvre*, ed. Raymonde Debray-Genette, 69–102. Paris: Flammarion, 1980.
De Man, Paul. *Blindness and Insight.* Second Edition, revised. Minneapolis: University of Minnesota Press, 1983.
———. *Allegories of Reading.* New Haven: Yale University Press, 1979.
———. *The Rhetoric of Romanticism.* New York: Columbia University Press, 1984.
Debray-Genette, Raymonde, et al. *Travail de Flaubert.* Paris: Seuil, 1983.
Deleuze, Gilles. *Proust et les signes.* Third Edition. Paris: PUF, 1971.
Demorest, Don L. *L'Expression figurée et symbolique dans l'oeuvre de Gustave Flaubert.* Paris: University of Paris, 1931.
Descharmes, René. *Autour de Flaubert.* Paris: Mercure de France, 1912.
Diamond, Marie J. *Flaubert, The Problem of Aesthetic Discontinuity.* Port Washington, N.Y.: Kennikat Press, 1975.
Donato, Eugenio. "Divine Agonies: Of Representation and Narrative in Romantic Poetics." *Glyph* 6 (1979), pp. 90–122.
Doubrovsky, Serge. *La Place de la Madeleine.* Paris: Mercure de France, 1974.
Ellison, David R. *The Reading of Proust.* Baltimore: Johns Hopkins University Press, 1984.
Etudes Proustiennes. Under the direction of Jacques Bersani, Michel Raimond, Jean-Yves Tadié. Paris: Gallimard, 1973, 1975, 1979, 1982.
Europe 48, nos. 496–97 (1970). *Proust.*
——— 49, nos. 502–3 (1971). *Flaubert.*
Festa-McCormick, Diana. *Proustian Optics of Clothes.* Stanford: Stanford

University French and Italian Studies, 1984.
Fischer, C. E. W. *Etudes sur Flaubert inédit.* Leipzig: Julius Zeitler, 1908.
Fletcher, Angus. *Allegory: The Theory of a Symbolic Mode.* Baltimore: Johns Hopkins University Press, 1964.
Fowlie, Wallace. *Climate of Violence: The French Literary Tradition from Baudelaire to the Present.* New York: Macmillan, 1967.
Freud, Sigmund. *Gesammelte Werke.* 18 vols. Frankfurt am Main: S. Fischer, 1960–68.
———. *The Standard Edition of the Complete Psychological Works.* 24 vols. Ed. James Strachey. London: Hogarth Press and Institute of Psychoanalysis, 1953–74.
Gans, Eric L. *The Discovery of Illusion: Flaubert's Early Works 1835–1837.* Berkeley: University of California Press, 1971.
Genette, Gérard. *Figures I.* Paris: Seuil, 1966.
———. *Figures II.* Paris: Seuil, 1969.
———. *Figures III.* Paris: Seuil, 1972.
Gérard-Gailly, Emile. *Le Grand amour de Flaubert.* Paris: Aubier, 1944.
Girard, René. *Mensonge romantique et vérité romanesque.* Paris: Grasset, 1961.
———, ed. *Proust: Twentieth Century Views.* Englewood Cliffs: Prentice-Hall, 1962.
———. *La Violence et le sacré.* Paris: Grasset, 1972.
———. *Des Choses cachées depuis la fondation du monde.* Paris: Grasset, 1978.
Giraud, Raymond, ed. *Flaubert: Twentieth Century Views.* Englewood Cliffs, N.J.: Prentice-Hall, 1964.
Godfrey, Sima. "The Fabrication of *Salammbô*: The Surface of the Veil." MLN 95 (1980), pp. 1005–1016.
Gothot-Mersch, Claudine. "La Genèse de "Madame Bovary."" Paris: Corti, 1966.
Green, Anne. *Flaubert and the Historical Novel.* Cambridge: Cambridge University Press, 1982.
Harari, Josué V., et al. *Textual Strategies: Perspectives in Post-Structuralist Criticism.* Ithaca: Cornell University Press, 1979.
Hassine, Juliette, *Essai sur Proust et Baudelaire.* Paris A. G. Nizet, 1979.
Henry, Anne. *Marcel Proust, Théories pour une esthétique.* Paris: Klincksieck, 1981.
———. *Proust romancier: le tombeau égyptien.* Paris: Flammarion, 1983.
Hertz, Neil. *The End of the Line.* New York: Columbia University Press, 1985.
Hindus, Milton. *The Proustian Vision.* New York Columbia University Press, 1954.
———. *A Reader's Guide to Marcel Proust.* New York: Farrar, Straus and Cudahy, 1962.
Hommage à Marcel Proust. Paris: Gallimard, 1927.
Houston, John Porter. *The Shape and Style of Proust's Novel.* Detroit: Wayne State University Press, 1982.
Issacharoff, Michael, ed. *Langages de Flaubert. Actes du Colloque de London*

(Canada). Paris: Minard, 1976.
Kenner, Hugh. *The Stoic Comedians*. Berkeley: University of California Press, 1974.
Kristeva, Julia. *Les Pouvoirs de l'horreur*. Paris: Seuil, 1981.
La Capra, Dominick. *Madame Bovary on Trial*. Ithaca: Cornell University Press, 1982.
La Varende, Jean de. *Flaubert par lui-même*. Paris: Seuil, 1951.
Lacan, Jacques. *Ecrits*. Paris: Seuil, 1966.
———. *Séminaire I*. Paris: Seuil, 1975.
———. *Séminaire XX*. Paris: Seuil, 1975.
———. *Séminaire XI*. Paris: Seuil, 1978.
———. *Séminaire II*. Paris: Seuil, 1978.
———. *Séminaire III*. Paris: Seuil, 1981.
Lacoue-Labarthes, Philippe, and Jean-Luc Nancy. *L'Absolu littéraire*. Paris: Seuil, 1978.
Le Blond, Jean-Marie. *Les Conversions de Saint Augustin*. Paris: Aubier, 1950.
Lejeune, Philippe. *Le Pacte autobiographique*. Paris: Seuil, 1975.
Leleu, Gabrielle, *Madame Bovary: ébauches et fragments inédits*. 2 vols. Paris: Conard, 1936.
Louria, Yvette. *La convergence stylistique chez Proust*. Geneva: Droz, 1957.
Lukács, Georg. "Erzählen oder Beschreiben?" In *Begriffsbestimmung des Literarischen Realismus*. Ed. Richard Brinkmann. Darmstadt: Wissenschaftliche Buchgesellschaft, 1969, pp. 33–85.
———. *Writer and Critic and Other Essays*. Ed. Arthur D. Kahn. New York: Universal Library, 1971.
Macksey, Richard. "'Conclusions' et 'Incitations': Proust à la Recherche de Ruskin." *MLN* 96 (1981), pp. 1113–19.
———. "Proust on the Margins of Ruskin." *The Ruskin Polygon*. Eds. J. D. Hunt and F. M. Holland. Machester: Manchester University Press, 1981.
Mâle, Emile. *L'Art religieux du treizième siècle en France*. Paris: Livre de Poche, 1961.
Mallet, Jean-Claude, ed. *Flaubert à l'oeuvre*. Paris: Flammarion, 1980.
Mannoni, Octave. *Clefs pour l'imaginaire ou l'autre scène*. Paris: Seuil, 1969.
Mauriac, Claude. *Proust par lui-même*. Paris: Seuil, 1957.
Mauriac, François. *Du côté de chez Proust*. Paris: Table Ronde, 1947.
———. *A La Recherche de Marcel Proust*. Paris: Hachette, 1949.
Mehlman, Jeffrey. *A Structural Study of Autobiography*. Ithaca: Cornell University Press, 1974.
———. "Literature and Collaboration: Benoist-Méchin's Return to Proust." *MLN* 98 (1983), pp. 968–82.
Mendelson, David. *Le Verre et les objets de verre dans l'univers imaginaire de Marcel Proust*. Paris: Corti, 1968.
Milly, Jean. *Proust et le style*. Paris: Lettres modernes, 1970.
———. *La Phrase de Proust*. Paris: H. Champion, 1983.

———. *Proust dans le texte et l'avant-texte.* Paris: Flammarion, 1985.
Mingelgrün, Albert. *Thèmes et structures bibliques dans l'oeuvre de Marcel Proust.* Lausanne: L'Age d'Homme, 1978.
MLN 93, no. 4 (1978). French issue. *Autobiography and the Problem of the Subject.*
Monnin-Hornung, Juliette *Proust et la peinture.* Geneva: Droz, 1951.
Muller, Marcel. *Les Voix narratives dans la "Recherche du temps perdu."* Geneva: Droz, 1965.
———. *Préfiguration et structure romanesque dans "A La Recherche du temps perdu."* Lexington, Mass.: French Forum, 1979.
Nadeau, Maurice. *Gustave Flaubert, écrivain.* Paris: Lettres Nouvelles, 1969.
———, and Roland Barthes. *Ecrire . . . Pour quoi? Pour qui? Dialogues de France-Culture.* Grenoble: Presses Universitaires, 1973.
Nathan, Jacques. *Citations, références, et allusions de Marcel Proust.* Paris: A. G. Nizet, 1969.
O'Connor, John R. "Flaubert: *Trois Contes* and the Figure of the Double Cone." *PMLA* 95, no. 5 (1980), pp. 812–26.
Olney, James, ed. *Autobiography: Essays Theoretical and Critical.* Princeton: Princeton University Press, 1980.
Painter, George. *Marcel Proust.* 2 vols. Paris: Mercure de France, 1966.
Pierre-Quint, Léon. *Marcel Proust, sa vie, son oeuvre.* Paris: Sagittaire, 1946.
Pommier, Jean. *La Mystique de Marcel Proust.* Paris: Droz, 1939.
———. *Dialogues avec le Passé.* Paris: Nizet, 1967.
———. "La Muse du département." *L'Année Balzacienne* 3 (1961), pp. 192–220.
Pontalis, J. B. *Après Freud.* Paris: Gallimard, 1968.
Poulet, Georges. *Etudes sur le temps humain.* Edinburgh: University Press, 1949.
———. *Les Métamorphoses du cercle.* Paris: Plon, 1961.
———. *L'Espace proustien* Paris: Gallimard, 1963.
Réau, Louis. *Iconographie de l'art chrétien.* Vol. 3. Paris: PUF, 1959.
Recanati, Jean. *Profils Juifs de Marcel Proust.* Paris: Buchet-Castel, 1979.
Recherche de Proust. Paris: Seuil, 1980.
Rey, Pierre-Louis. *Marcel Proust: sa vie, son oeuvre.* Paris: F. Birr, 1984.
Richard, Jean-Pierre. *Littérature et sensation.* Paris: Seuil, 1954.
———. *Proust et le monde sensible.* Paris: Seuil, 1974.
Rivers, J. E. *Proust and the Art of Love.* New York: Columbia University Press, 1980.
Rousset, Jean. *Forme et signification.* Paris: Corti, 1962.
———. *Narcisse romancier.* Paris: Corti, 1971.
———. "Positions, distances, perspectives dans *Salammbô*." *Poétique* 2, no. 6 (1971), pp. 145–54.
———. "Le Statut narratif d'un personnage Swann." *Etudes Proustiennes* II (1975), pp. 135–70.
Ruskin, John. *The Works of John Ruskin.* Vol. 24, Eds. E. J. Cook and Alexander Wedderburn. London: George Allen, 1906.

Sartre, Jean-Paul. *L'Idiot de la famille.* 3 vols. Paris: Gallimard, 1971–72.
Schlossman, Beryl. *Joyce's Catholic Comedy of Language.* Madison: University of Wisconsin Press, 1985.
Scholem, Gershom C. "Le Nom de Dieu." *Diogène,* nos. 79–80 (1972), pp. 60–80.
———. "Mystique juive et monde moderne." *Cahiers Confrontation* 9 (1983), pp. 110–20.
Schor, Naomi. "Pour une thématique restreinte: Ecriture, parole, et différence dans *Madame Bovary.*" *Littérature,* no. 22 (1976), pp. 30–46.
———, and Henry F. Majewski, eds. *Flaubert and Postmodernism.* Lincoln: University of Nebraska Press, 1984.
Shattuck, Roger. *Proust's Binoculars.* New York: Alfred A. Knopf, 1963.
———. *Marcel Proust.* Princeton: Princeton University Press, 1982.
Shepler, Frederic J. "La Mort et le Rédemption dans les *Trois Contes* de Flaubert." *Neophilologus* 56, no. 4 (1972), pp. 407–16.
Sherzer, Dina. "Narrative Figures in *La Légende de Saint Julien L'Hospitalier.*" *Genre* 7, no. 1 (1974), pp. 54–70.
Sibony, Daniel. *L'Autre incastrable.* Paris: Seuil, 1978.
Singleton, Charles. *Dante's Commedia: Elements of Structure.* Baltimore: Johns Hopkins University Press, 1977.
Spitzer, Leo. *Etudes de style.* Paris: Gallimard, 1970.
Starkie, Enid. *Flaubert: The Making of a Master.* New York: Atheneum, 1967.
Starobinski, Jean. *La Relation critique.* Paris: Gallimard, 1971.
Steegmüller, Francis. *Flaubert and Madame Bovary.* New York: Farrar, Straus and Giroux, 1968.
Strauss, Walter A. *Proust and Literature.* Cambridge: Harvard University Press, 1957.
Tadié, Jean-Yves. *Proust et le roman.* Paris: Gallimard, 1971.
Thibaudet, Albert. *Gustave Flaubert.* Paris: Gallimard, 1935.
Thorlby, Anthony. *Gustave Flaubert and the Art of Realism.* London: Bowes and Bowes, 1956.
Todorov, Tzvetan. *Théories du symbole.* Paris: Seuil, 1977.
Toynbee, Paget, ed. *Dantis Alagherii Epistolae. The Letters of Dante.* Oxford: Clarendon Press, 1966.
Turmel, Jacques. *L'Histoire des dogmes.* Vol. 5. Paris: Rieder, 1936.
Ullmann, Stephen. *Style in the French Novel.* Cambridge: Cambridge University Press, 1957.
———. *The Image in the Modern French Novel.* Cambridge: Cambridge University Press, 1960.
Van Tieghem, Philippe. *Les Grandes doctrines littéraires en France.* Paris: PUF, 1965.
Vogely, Maxine Arnold. *A Proust Dictionary.* Troy, N.J.: Whitston, 1981.
Weiskel, Thomas. *The Romantic Sublime.* Baltimore: Johns Hopkins University Press, 1976.
Yoshida, Jo. "Proust contre Ruskin: la genèse de deux voyages dans la

'Recherche' d'après des brouillons inédits." Ph.D. diss., Paris: Sorbonne, 1978.

Yoshikawa, Kazuyoshi. "Etudes sur la genèse de 'La Prisonnière" d'après des brouillons inédits" Ph.D. diss., Paris: Sorbonne, 1976.

Zola, Emile. *Les Romanciers naturalistes.* Vol. II of *Oeuvres complètes.* Ed. Henri Mitterand. Paris: Cercle du livre précieux, 1966.

Index

Adieu au personnel, 91, 98, 126–27, 189, 213, 225, 267 n.16
Aesthetic principles: and authorial persona, 20; and psychoanalysis, 121
Allegory: and Charity (Giotto), 178, 163, 192; and concept of figural language, 2–3; defined in Modernism, 117; as a mode of representation, 36–37; and the Orient, 113; and reproduction, 194–222 passim; and stained glass, 76–106; and structure, 131, 180, 198, 214, 255
Allegory of conversion, 4, 16, 17–37, 73, 81, 86, 92, 119, 127–28, 135, 144–45, 155
Amour mystique, 74, 81–82, 88–106, 107, 118
Anthony, Saint, 271 n.7
Antiquity and modernity, 71–139, 270 n.62
Auerbach, Erich, 262 n.30
Augustine of Hippo: *The Confessions*, 35, 167–68, 227
Autobiography and fiction, 65, 167, 177, 178, 192, 204, 209–10, 233, 244

Bales, Richard, 276 n.3
Balzac, Honoré de, 10, 53, 213
Baptistery of Saint-Marc, 202–7, 211, 217

Baroque, 18, 95, 111, 133
Barthes, Roland, 136
Baudelaire, Charles: "Le Coucher de Soleil Romantique," 144; "Le Cygne," 3–5, 18, 31–32, 34, 76, 106, 111, 133–34, 247; *Les Fleurs du Mal*, 5, 12, 143, 150, 157, 244, 247; "Harmonie du Soir," 150; "L'Imprévu," 151, 230; "Le Mauvais Vitrier," 263 n.7; "La Mort des Artistes," 144; "Les Petites Vieilles," 150, 155; *Le Spleen de Paris*, 245–48; "Une Charogne," 34–35; "A Une Passante," 31, 34, 230
Benjamin, Walter, 5, 18, 118, 133–34, 169–77, 189, 229, 247, 263 nn.5–6, 273 n.36
Bersani, Leo, 8–9
Biasi, Pierre-Marc de, 269 n.37
Bible, 160, 163, 218, 274 n.15
Blanche, Jacques, 46
Blank space of style, 55–67 passim, 103–4, 127, 148, 157, 173, 175, 200, 244
Book about nothing, 24, 32, 34, 109, 244
Botticelli, Sandro, 193–95, 205
Bouilhet, Louis, 71; and Du Camp, 109
Brombert, Victor, 261 n.1, 262 n.23
Brun, Bernard, 197–99, 277

n.13, 277 n.18
Bruneau, Jean, 268 n.8

Carpaccio, Vittore, 203–22, 250–51; and Fortuny, 206–8, 260
Cathedral (style), 80, 84, 96, 99, 104, 131, 145, 148, 212
Cento, Alberto, 265 n.37
Cigada, Serge, 273 n.33
Color and style, 46–48, 84, 129, 183, 266 n.6
Correspondance and style, 15, 26–27, 30, 40, 46, 170, 228, 247, 251, 265 n.29
Conversion and "fondre," 27–28
Continuity and style, 40–41, 65, 129
Copying and style, 33, 139, 257 n.37

Dante, 2–3, 116, 209, 258
Daudet, Lucien, 265 n.26
De Man, Paul, 2–3, 274 n.16, 275 n.30
Dreyfus, Alfred, 158, 175

Easter and Passover, 163, 166, 204, 221
Ecstasy and style, 38–67 passim
Excess and style, 88–89, 96, 104, 121, 131

Fatality, 90, 93, 114, 117, 120, 125, 127, 269 n.26
Fernandez, Ramon, 240
Flaubert, Caroline, 75–76; and Du Camp, 130
Flaubert, Gustave: on Baudelaire, 8, 14, 24; and the "gueuloir," 63, 129, 133, 241, 256; and ideal of style, 24–25, 256; and identification with Madame Bovary, 134–37; and projects, 73–74, 99, 108; and the Sentence, 137
Flaubert, Mme, 75–76, 105
Freud, Sigmund, 64–66, 94–95, 263 n.4

Genette, Gérard: 9, 264 n.12, 276 n.8, 278 n.12, 279 n.30
Giotto and Charity, 40, 50, 62, 156–77 passim, 178–222, 235; and Ruskin, 181–92; and the Virgin, 208
Glass and style, 18; effect of colored glass, 19–26, 76–85, 93–106, 129–39, 258, 264 n.7, 269 n.29
Goethe, [J.W.], 5
Gothot-Mersch, Claudine, 267 n.4
Grimoire, 5, 151, 220, 243

Hertz, Neil, 265 n.33
Hindus, Milton, 279 n.31
History and allegory, 117
Hopkins, Gerard Manley, 7

Idolatry, 181, 187, 213
Imperfect, eternal, and style, 43–45, 53, 60, 69, 147

Joyce, James, 6–7, 277 n.4
Judaism, 158–64, 176, 202, 215–16; and Halévy, 218–20

Kolb, Phillip, 276 n.6
Kristeva, Julia, 265 n.32

Lacan, Jacques, 132, 192, 276 n.9, 277 n.22, 278 n.9
Leonardo da Vinci, 153
Levin, Harry, 14
Life story: and allegorical style, 38–67, 83, 110, 138, 225–26
Lukács, Georg, 10–14, 32, 42

Macksey, Richard, 169, 274 n.16, n.18, 276 n.3
Magic lantern. *See* Glass
Mâle, Emile, 180–92, 276 n.3, n.5
Mallarmé, Stéphane, 63, 99
Mehlman, Jeffrey, 274 n.13, n.17
Melancholy, 18, 22, 26, 29, 30, 44,

85, 91, 92, 100, 108, 110 117, 123, 137, 253
Memory, involuntary: and style, 17–18, 30, 39–67 passim, 75, 108, 132, 200, 241–60
Metaphor, 220–22, 227–33, 242–60
Modernism: and comparative approach, 66; in Flaubert and Baudelaire, 127, 143–45, and Proust, 63; and Romanticism, 32, 37, 237; and Ruskin, 190; and style, 1–7; and vocabulary, 12
Muller, Marcel, 264 n.15, 274 n.11, 275 n.34
Music and style, 29–30, 53–54, 149–50, 165, 225–45 passim, 246, 247–60 passim; and painting, 238; and Wagner, 225–35, 235, 237–60 passim
Mystery, 151; and art, 153; and Unknown, 165, 243–55

Nordlinger, Marie, 276 n.6
Novel of the unconscious, 17, 249, 252

Orient and style, 71–139 passim, 230–32, 267 n.2; and femininity, 103, 107, 118, 195

Painting and style: and color, 84, 130, 178–222, 260; and iconography, 269 n.27; and "le fondu," 25–31, 103, 148, 152–55, 255, 258, 259; and pleasure, 193
Perpetual alliteration and style, 147, 174, 218, 229–33, 247, 252, 277 n.5
Petite Madeleine, 23, 27, 66, 162, 165, 175, 236, 242, 253, 259, 280 n.35
Pichois, Claude, 279 n.21
Poetic prose (style), 145, 245–60
Polybius, 115

Pommier, Jean, 137
Pontalis, [J. B.], 136–37
Proust, Marcel: on Baudelaire, 13–16, 146, 272 n.22, 279 n.29, n.34; on Flaubert, 16, 17–67, 146, 280 n.37; and pastiche, 52, 56, 57, 186, 267 n.17; on poetic prose style, 248–60; on *Tendres Stocks*, 30, 148

Ravishment and style, 39, 54–55, 106, 123–24, 253–55, 257
Romanticism: and genetics, 198; and gothic, 78, 82; and modernity, 8–12, 18, 28, 55, 132, 143, 244; and Symbolism, 1–2, 33
Rousset, Jean, 15
Ruskin, John, 180–201 passim, 274 nn.15–16, n.18

Sade, Marquis de, 115
Sainte-Beuve, Charles-Augustin, 12, 111, 114, 272 n.20
Sartre, Jean-Paul, 31, 86, 121, 137, 265 n.33
Scott, Walter, 78–79
Silence and style, 20, 54–67 passim, 127, 234
Spitzer, Leo, 239–42
Stendhal, 13, 14
Style: allegory of conversion, 4
Sublime and style, 36–37, 55–59, 100, 102, 118, 121, 123, 138, 241, 246; and Baudelaire, 154; sexual, 114, 122–23

Theology and aesthetics, 6, 159, 166
Thibaudet, Albert, 263 n.35
Time and allegory, 59–67, 152, 169–77, 215, 225–60
Translation as style, 15–16, 38–39, 52–53, 133, 145, 256
Transubstantiation, 26, 100, 152, 220–22, 228, 232

Ullmann, Stephen, 239–40, 278 n.14

Vaudoyer, Jean-Louis, 275 n.30
Vermeer, Jan, and style, 24, 146, 172–73, 190, 193, 258
Vices and Virtues, 156–260 passim

Zaimph and style, 126–39
Zola, Emile, 9–10, 49

About the Author

Beryl Schlossman is an Assistant Professor in the Department of French and Italian at Emory University. She is the author of *Joyce's Catholic Comedy of Language.*

Library of Congress
Cataloging-in-Publication Data
Schlossman, Beryl
The Orient of style : modernist allegories of conversion / Beryl Schlossman.
Includes bibliographical references and index.
ISBN 0-8223-1076-7 (cloth). —ISBN 0-8223-1094-5 (pbk.)
1. French literature—19th century—History and criticism. 2. Baudelaire, Charles. 1821–1867—Style. 3. Flaubert, Gustave, 1821–1880 —Style. 4. Proust, Marcel, 1871–1922—Style.
5. Modernism (Literature)—France. 6. French language—Style. 7. Allegory. I. Title.
PQ295.M63S35 1991
840.9'007—dc20   90-38620 CIP

www.ingramcontent.com/pod-product-compliance
Lightning Source LLC
Chambersburg PA
CBHW070753230426
43665CB00017B/2346